HARVARD ECONOMIC STUDIES
Volume CIV

The studies in this series are published by the Department of Economics of Harvard University. The department does not assume responsibility for the views expressed.

WATER-RESOURCE DEVELOPMENT
The Economics of Project Evaluation

By

OTTO ECKSTEIN

HARVARD UNIVERSITY PRESS
Cambridge, Massachusetts

Library of Congress Catalog Card Number 58-7501
Printed in the United States of America

TO MY PARENTS

Foreword

THE federal water-resource program has been the subject of much controversy in recent years. Among the points of contention have been the methods by which federal agencies have evaluated and justified their proposed projects. In each case, a benefit-cost analysis is prepared which provides estimates of the value of outputs and of their costs. Projects are usually considered justified only if total benefits exceed total costs.

The present study analyzes the procedures for measuring benefits and costs employed by the two major agencies which are building federal water-resource projects today: the Bureau of Reclamation of the Department of the Interior and the Corps of Engineers, U.S. Army. The analysis is based on the theory of welfare economics; it treats benefit-cost analysis as a means of testing the quality of a project and of selecting the most desirable projects from the point of view of economic efficiency. It is assumed that judgments about changes in the distribution of income and about the political and social objectives must be left to Congress and to administrators, and that the national interest is best served by benefit-cost analyses which reveal each project's impact on the total real national income to be enjoyed by the country.

In Chapters II to IV the portions of the theory of welfare economics are outlined which pertain particularly to project evaluation, and the benefit-cost criterion is derived from the theory. Chapters V to VIII are devoted to the procedures in four major fields of water-resource development: flood control, irrigation, navigation, and electric power. The present extent of cost sharing by the beneficiaries is explored together with the amount of local charges that economic analysis suggests. Finally, as part of the study of the financial features of projects, the principles and techniques by which joint costs can be allocated are discussed.

Foreword

An earlier version of this study was submitted to Harvard University as a doctoral thesis in 1955. The description of federal procedures is based largely on agency practice in the period 1953 to 1955. The subsequent revision takes into account some of the recent changes; on the whole, however, federal practice has evolved very slowly, and so the description, at least in broad outline, can be considered typical for the years since World War II.

I am happy to acknowledge the aid I have received from many persons at different stages of this work. Professor Arthur Smithies, under whose direction the thesis was written, has given me much encouragement and friendly criticism. Several members of government agencies have taken the time to explain technical points and have introduced me to much material. I am particularly grateful to the late Mr. Henry Erlanger, formerly of the Bureau of the Budget and the TVA; also to Mr. Reed A. Elliot of the TVA and to Dr. John V. Krutilla, formerly with that agency, Dr. Fenton Shepard and Mr. Melvin Scheidt of the Bureau of the Budget, Mr. Mark Regan of the Department of Agriculture, Mr. A. R. Johnson of the Department of the Interior, and Mr. Robert Fraser of the New England Division of the Corps of Engineers. Mr. Henry Caulfield and Mr. Maynard Hufschmidt, formerly of the Department of the Interior, and Mr. Johnson and Dr. Krutilla have read the manuscript and have provided me with many valuable comments. Chapters II and III have benefited from comments by Professor Carl Kaysen. Chapter III has also been improved by discussions in the Harvard Water Resources Seminar. I also wish to thank my wife, who helped me in the research for the revision. Any errors and all opinions are entirely my responsibility, of course.

Much of this study was carried out during tenure of a Research Training Fellowship of the Social Science Research Council, which permitted me to travel and relieved me of all other duties.

Cambridge, Massachusetts   O. E.
January 1958

Contents

Contents

Tables

Tables

Tables

Water-Resource Development

CHAPTER I

Introduction

EVER since 1802, the federal government has carried on programs to develop America's water resources. In the nineteenth century, improvement of our navigable streams was the main objective; in the twentieth, many other objectives have claimed the government's attention, such as irrigation of land in the dry areas of the West, control of floods, generation of hydroelectric power, supply of water for domestic and industrial uses, provision of recreational facilities, reduction of stream pollution, and so on. As the economy has expanded, the need for these activities has also grown. The value of property vulnerable to floods has increased, the demand for power has doubled and redoubled, the traffic on our rivers has risen sharply, the need for water is becoming more acute in many regions, and even the recreational use of our rivers and lakes has mushroomed in recent years.

The expenditures of the federal government have become correspondingly large, and in the fiscal year 1955, over $800 million were spent. This sum represents much the largest share of all the civil public works activities carried on at the federal level of government; it is important, therefore, that these activities are carried on with efficiency, that the needs of the country are met, and that the money is well spent.

The present study is concerned with the economics of the four largest water-resource programs: flood control, navigation, irrigation, and electric power. In particular, we shall analyze the procedures by means of which the merit of projects in these fields is evaluated. These procedures have been the subject of considerable controversy; there is no agreement on common standards among all agencies and Congress has only limited confidence in the evaluations which are submitted. It is hoped that this volume

1

will make some contribution toward improving the evaluation standards which are employed.

1. *The Nature of the Decision Process*

To show the tenuous trail that a project plan travels before it results in construction, we shall outline the procedure which is applied to the navigation and flood-control projects of the Corps of Engineers. Typically, a group of people in a locality will express a desire for a certain project, perhaps for a flood-control project or for a deepening of a navigational channel, and will contact their congressman to request a federal survey.[1] The congressman will try to have an item authorizing the survey included in the annual omnibus bill for rivers and harbors or in the bill for flood control. If duly authorized, the Corps of Engineers will undertake, first, a preliminary survey, and if its results are promising, it will follow it up with a more complete survey. Public hearings will be held in the affected localities, and if the district engineer of the area finds that the project is feasible, he will prepare a recommended plan of improvement. Feasibility is interpreted to mean that "the benefits, to whomsoever they may accrue, are in excess of the estimated costs," following a requirement specified in the Flood Control Act of 1936.[2]

The district engineer will prepare a project report, which will contain his recommendations. This report will be reviewed by the Board of Engineers for Rivers and Harbors, a permanent board sitting in Washington, which may hold public hearings if requested by some of the interested parties. The Chief of Engineers will add his own recommendations, and the project report will then be submitted to other agencies that have an interest in the water resources of the area and to the governments of states that will be affected, who will append their comments and recommendations. The report and all comments will be sent to the U.S. Bureau of the Budget, which will review the report to determine whether it is "in accord with the program of the President" and will state whether it has objection to transmission to the

---

[1] House of Representatives, Committee on Public Works, *Hearings of the Subcommittee to Study Civil Works*, 82 Cong., 2 sess., p. 72: Reply of the Corps of Engineers to questions of the Subcommittee.

[2] Flood Control Act of 1936, Section I.

Congress. The Budget Bureau has a Division of Resources and Civil Works containing about forty employees, including engineers and economists who are specialists in project evaluation in the resource field; they will go over the project report and the suggested plan of improvement to see whether all provisions are consistent with the general policies set down for the program and to verify the various estimates of the report. Their review is limited by the small size of both the staff and their appropriation, which almost precludes any kind of field investigation in the area of the project.

All project reports and comments, regardless of the recommendation of the Bureau of the Budget or of other agencies, are submitted to the Congress, specifically to the Committee on Public Works of the House of Representatives. The law requires this transmission of all reports, since the survey is essentially undertaken on behalf of the Congress.[3] The House Committee on Public Works will consider the report, publish it as a House Document, and hold hearings. If it sees fit, it may include authorization of the project in the annual omnibus flood-control or navigation bills. If the project is authorized, it will become part of a large backlog of projects which have not yet been started. In 1951, for example, some nine hundred projects for navigation and flood control, estimated to cost $8 billion, were in this category, a number greater than the number that had been constructed up to that time.

While most project investigations are undertaken in response to local initiative, Congress has also ordered the Engineers to undertake comprehensive surveys of the water-resource potential of river basins. The reports which have resulted, known as the "308" Reports, have provided the fundamental planning for some of the largest programs that have been undertaken. The survey for the Tennessee River first revealed the potential of that basin; similarly, the programs on the Columbia and Missouri rivers were outlined, at least in part, in the "308" Reports. Congress has also provided funds for bringing some of these reports up to date. Each year the Corps of Engineers prepares its budget requests

[3] For some of the administrative and political implications of this direct link between an executive agency and the Congress, see A. Maass, *Muddy Waters: the Army Engineers and the Nation's Rivers* (1951).

on the basis of general principles outlined by the President. For instance, during the Korean War, no projects were started that did not assist the military program; when the Republicans took office in 1953, a policy of "no new starts" was in effect for quite some time. The Bureau of the Budget notifies the Corps of Engineers how much money will be available within the President's budget for its programs. (The fundamental decisions about the absolute size of the budget and the main division by function are of course reached at the highest policy levels.) The Corps of Engineers allots part of the total for projects that are under construction and applies the remainder to the projects that they feel to be most urgent in the various river basins, that fit into their general development program, and that "create the maximum additional benefits."[4]

The budget requests are reviewed by the Bureau of the Budget, which often disagrees about particular projects. The differences between the two agencies are resolved by negotiations,[5] and a final list of projects is drawn up which becomes part of the President's budget.

The Appropriations Committee of the House holds hearings on the budget and is free to make any changes in the list of projects to be constructed. Members of Congress endeavor to add projects in which they are especially interested. According to Representative Dondero, Chairman of the House Public Works Committee in the 83rd Congress, "When a project is not on the list that the Bureau of the Budget publishes, any effort on the part of a member of Congress to have another one added to that list has a rough road to travel in order to have it included, regardless of its merits."[6] But Representative Cannon, Chairman of the House Appropriations Committee in the 84th Congress, takes a less sanguine view. "A Senator can walk into the Senate Appropriations Committee and put anything into a bill he wants. When we get to [Senate–House] conference, they say we can't knock that out; that's Senator so-and-so's project....You'd be

[4] *Hearings...Civil Works*, testimony of General L. A. Pick, Chief of Engineers, p. 30. These three criteria may be contradictory; there is no evidence to indicate their priority in case they conflict.

[5] *Hearings...Civil Works*, p. 31.

[6] *Hearings...Civil Works*, p. 33.

Introduction

astounded at what some Senators get away with."[7]   Nor did he feel that "logrolling" was any less prevalent in the House.

In 1955, after a period of five years during which very few projects were started because of the Korean emergency and the reëxamination of policy by the incoming Republican administration, Congress rebelled at the lack of "new starts" and added 107 projects to the President's appropriations requests for the fiscal year 1956. President Eisenhower commented strongly:

> The second matter which concerns me is the large increase in the number of new construction starts for the Corps of Engineers and the Bureau of Reclamation. Many of these projects which have been added by the Congress have not had detailed engineering studies completed. As a result, we have no basis for determining their financial soundness and their ultimate cost to the federal government.
>
> In all, 107 unbudgeted projects were added by the Congress. We can only guess what their total cost...will ultimately be because of this lack of detailed engineering studies on many of them.   The best guess that can be made at the present time is upwards of $1,500,000,000, but when planning is completed, this guess, in the light of past experience, may well prove far too low.   While the first-year appropriations made in this bill amount to only $47,000,000, the appropriations and expenditures in future years will increase sharply and quickly reach a half-billion-dollar level.[8]

The experience of 1955 is in part attributable to the difference in policy between the Republican administration and a Congress under Democratic control.   But even in 1954, under a Republican Congress, there was considerable divergence between the new starts which were requested in the President's budget and those for which the Congress decided to vote money, as Table 1 shows. In the long run, however, Congress influences the choice of

[7] Testimony before the Committee on Government Operations, House of Representatives, June 28, 1955, reported in the New York *Times*, June 29, 1955, p. 20.

[8] Statement issued by President Eisenhower in connection with the signing of an appropriations bill, July 15, 1955, reported in the New York *Times*, July 16, 1955.

5

projects more subtly, through the anticipation of Congressional wishes on the part of the agencies in drawing up their budget requests.

Once the appropriations bill has passed through Congress and has been signed by the President, the funds are available for construction. Final plans and construction cost estimates are prepared by the district engineer, and invitations to private construction firms to submit contract bids are issued. The low bidder is awarded the contract unless there is an excessive difference between the low bid and the district engineer's own cost estimate. The contractor can then commence the work and the project is begun.

Table 1. Budget requests and actual appropriations for new starts, fiscal year 1955

	Number of projects	
	Corps of Engineers	Bureau of Reclamation
Budget requests	17	3
Appropriations for requested projects	14	3
Projects appropriated but not requested	9	8

Source: *The Budget of the United States Government for the Fiscal Year, 1955, 1956, 1957.*

The number of authorized projects that have not been started destroys much of the value of the authorization process. While failure to receive authorization is a very severe setback to a project, there is no assurance that even if the project passes this hurdle it will actually be undertaken. Projects may have been authorized ten or more years ago at the time they are finally submitted for construction funds.[9] In the interim, many changes take place in the country's economy and in the area of the project. When the requests for funds are drawn up on the basis of plans that have been brought up to date, they often are a multiple of the figures in the original authorization. The Corps of Engineers

[9] *Hearings...Civil Works,* p. 32, testimony of General Pick.

is free to change the engineering features of projects and even the size and location. Only if a project changes its scope entirely and has new purposes added, need the Engineers resubmit it for a new authorization. Part of each project report is an economic analysis. The district engineer will apply certain criteria which are applied to all project studies of the Corps; all the contributions to national output and welfare that the Corps recognizes will be estimated and valued to derive an estimate of national benefit. All the costs are also estimated and a benefit-cost ratio will be computed. Unless the benefit-cost ratio is greater than one, the project does not possess economic feasibility.

The economic analysis will be revised on occasion, either as part of a general program review, or at the time a project is considered for inclusion in the list of appropriation requests. Costs are recomputed by applying construction cost indices to the various components, while benefits are revalued at the prices which are assumed to represent long-term average prices at that time.

Some of the benefits, such as protection of human life and provisions for national defense, cannot be expressed in monetary terms. Such benefits are considered intangible and are described briefly as part of the economic analysis.

Each project report will also contain a financial analysis. As part of the policy of each program, the federal government requires that local interests make certain contributions of money or property. The local contribution is estimated and indication is given whether the local interests are willing to meet this obligation. Generally, projects are not submitted for construction unless the local contribution has definitely been assured.

There is much more in every project report. Usually there is a description of the local economy, a general discussion of the need for the project, a description of some of the possible plans of improvement, various maps, and a fairly detailed account of the physical aspects of the plan. Unfortunately, the presentation of the physical features of a project is much more detailed than the supporting figures of the economic and financial analysis.

The procedures are very similar for the Bureau of Reclamation, which is the other important builder of public works projects in the water resource field, but whose activities are confined to the seventeen Western states.[10] Only in the earlier stages, up to authorization, are there significant differences. Surveys can be initiated by the Secretary of the Interior,[11] though it may be at the request of local groups provided they offer to pay half the survey cost. Congress can also order a survey, of course. Authorization can come in two ways; Congress can give it to specific projects, or the Secretary of the Interior can authorize a project through a secretarial finding of feasibility. The latter requires that the project be possible from the engineering point of view and that revenues can be collected from the reimbursable purposes which will equal their total cost. This requirement is laid down in the Reclamation Act of 1939.[12] Congressional authorization needs to be used only if a project lacks financial feasibility, if the Secretary desires some departure from usual reclamation policy, or if any of the affected states or the Secretary of the Army object to the project. But in recent years, Congressional authorization has been used for all projects as a matter of departmental policy.

In addition to the required tests of engineering and financial feasibility, each project report contains an economic analysis in terms of benefits and costs,[13] which is similar to the analysis of the Corps of Engineers in form, but which differs significantly in concept.

Before a project reaches construction, it must be reviewed by other agencies, by the affected states, and by the Budget Bureau. A request for funds must become part of the President's budget and must be met by Congressional appropriation.

[10] The TVA has been a third major construction and operation agency in this field, though its recent appropriations have been small. Since it is organized as a public corporation, with unique autonomy from Washington, its decision process for new projects is quite different, even though it applies to Congress for construction funds. The early planning stages are an internal matter and are handled much more like the planning and investment decisions of a private corporation. We do not discuss the planning techniques of the TVA in the present study, though many lessons may be drawn from its experience.

[11] *Hearings...Civil Works*, p. 514.

[12] Reclamation Act of 1939, section 9a.

[13] *Hearing...Civil Works*, p. 548, testimony of Commissioner of Reclamation M. W. Straus.

2. *Too Many Agencies?*

In addition to the Corps of Engineers and the Bureau of Reclamation, numerous other agencies participate in water-resource development. The Bonneville Power Administration, the Southeastern Power Administration, and the Southwestern Power Administration of the Department of the Interior are marketing agencies for the electricity generated at multipurpose systems in three areas. The Tennessee Valley Authority has almost sole jurisdiction over all phases of water-resource development in its region. The Soil Conservation Service of the Department of Agriculture runs a program of flood control on small upstream tributaries and on rivers that are off the main stream. The Indian Service is in charge of all developments on land set aside as Indian reservations. The Federal Power Commission has general regulatory authority over hydroelectric power development, and supplies the basic market studies which determine the need for the power output of all Corps of Engineer projects. And many other agencies enter the picture in various incidental ways.[14]

With the exception of the TVA, each of these agencies has a traditional function which was entrusted to it by the Congress. Perhaps because of historical accident, the administrative organization of federal water-resource activities is defined in terms of functions rather than of areas such as river basins. Since the development of most rivers is of a multipurpose nature, involving several functions, a number of agencies often carry on programs in the same basin. The studies of the first Hoover Commission revealed that there was much overlapping of jurisdiction, leading to serious disagreements and delays,[15] and to a lack of coördination in planning development programs. Uneasy compromises among agencies, achieved through negotiation and based on ambitions of bureaucratic empire builders rather than on the maximization of the nation's welfare, are the result of the unsound administrative structure.[16]

[14] For a survey of federal agencies and their water-resource activities in one region, see C. McKinley, *Uncle Sam in the Pacific Northwest* (1952).

[15] The Commission on Organization of the Executive Branch of the Government, *Report on Department of the Interior*, March 1949, pp. 27–31.

[16] For an important example, see Commission on Organization of the Executive Branch of the Government, 1949, *Task Force Report on*

Numerous proposals for administrative reform have been advanced in recent years. The President's Water Resources Policy Commission[17] recommended that the present agencies be replaced by river-basin development agencies so that one organization would be in charge of all activities in each river basin, the natural unit of water-resource development. No action has been taken on this proposal, though there was considerable support for a Missouri Valley Authority and a Columbia Valley Authority during the Truman administration. Needless to say, such proposals run into the stiffest opposition from existing agencies and from local interests who fear so powerful a federal agency and who find their bargaining position enhanced by interagency competition. There is also serious question whether the new problems that would be created by the conflicts among river-basin agencies and by the new political pressures that such explicitly regional organization would produce would be any more desirable than the present difficulties.

The first Hoover Commission favored a reorganization of the Department of the Interior, letting the Department absorb the civil functions of the Corps of Engineers and of other federal construction activity, while moving some of its present bureaus to other departments.[18] With all project-building agencies under one roof, the Secretary of the Interior would be able to establish common standards and to adjudicate interagency disputes. The Commission also recommended a Board of Impartial Analysis to be directly attached to the White House, which would have the staff to provide independent evaluations of all projects before they were sent to Congress. The President did not choose to submit a reorganization plan embodying these recommendations to Congress, nor would such a plan have had much chance of enactment into law. The Army Engineers serve the Congress well and have accumulated so many friends over the years that

---

Natural Resources, Appendix L–6, "Development of Missouri River Basin Resources—A Case Study in the Organization of Federal Activities," by E. A. Ackerman, pp. 106–148. Also see A. Maass, "In Accord with the Program of the President", C. J. Friedrich and J. K. Galbraith, eds., *Public Policy* (1952), III, 77–93.

[17] Report of President's Water Resources Policy Commission, *A Water Policy for the American People* (1950), vol. I, pp. 43–53.

[18] Commission on...Executive Branch, *Report on Department of the Interior*, pp. 7–16.

any attempt to reduce their autonomy or the scope of their activities is likely to fail. At the same time, supporters of the Bureau of Reclamation are not anxious to have it lose its regional character as a development agency of the seventeen Western states through consolidation into a nationwide agency. It is also an open question whether the Secretary of the Interior would have the power to make the agencies adhere to policies set by him. Past experience has shown that the agencies develop such strong political support among the groups who are subsidized through their activities that the Secretary finds it difficult to impose his policies; consolidation of several agencies into one department is likely to accentuate this condition rather than to weaken it.

The second Hoover Commission, appointed by President Eisenhower, recommended the appointment of a Water Resources Board, to be composed of five full-time public members plus the secretaries of the Army, of the Interior, and of Agriculture, as well as the chairman of the Federal Power Commission. This board was to recommend policies to the President and to the Congress and was to devise methods for coördinating programs of the agencies at the Washington and the field levels. If the public members of the board enjoyed the confidence of the President and the Congress, they could become a significant constructive influence, though their effectiveness is likely to be circumscribed by the political power which the agencies derive from their client relationships.

3. *Some Internal Reforms*

There has also been much concern within the government about the lack of coördination in planning and the jurisdictional disputes among agencies. Before World War II, the National Resources Planning Board was to act as a clearing house for all activities in the field, but it never received the administrative power to assure full coöperation by the agencies, nor did it have any political support in Congress that would have bestowed authority on its voice; in 1943 it was abolished altogether.

In 1946, the Federal Inter-Agency River Basin Committee (FIARBC), composed of representatives of the agencies concerned with water-resource problems, was formed at the initiative of the agencies. Interagency committees were formed in several

11

of the major river basins to improve coördination at the planning and operating levels. The Arkansas–White–Red River Inter-Agency Committee or AWR was appointed to coördinate planning in that area; the New York–New England Inter-Agency Committee, or NYNEIAC, was formed to survey the possibilities of further water-resource development in the Northeastern United States. Committees have also been formed in the Columbia and Missouri basins and in the Pacific Southwest, but their meetings are relatively infrequent and controversial issues are generally avoided. What coördination does occur at the field level is through more informal arrangements among agencies and through contacts among their personnel. In the Columbia basin, for example, the Engineers have invited the formation of an advisory committee of representatives of other agencies, an arrangement which has been found more workable for the interchange of views and the settling of differences before they become major issues. But the planning of projects remains uncoördinated, preventing the most logical development of the water resources in each area. Even in the case of the AWR, where coördination was carried to the highest degree yet achieved among agencies, the Inter-Agency Committee was confined to the splicing of the different plans previously prepared by the agencies individually.

FIARBC also appointed a Subcommittee on Benefits and Costs, instructed to formulate principles of project evaluation which would be acceptable to all agencies. This committee has issued a number of reports on various aspects of benefit-cost analysis, and in May 1950 set forth a complete set of principles for project evaluation.[19] Since the FIARBC or its subcommittee have no power of their own but merely represent an opportunity for negotiation and research, the subcommittee had the choice of making its principles so broad that all existing practices could be interpreted to be consistent with them, or of taking a more independent stand and proposing tighter standards with no assurance that they would be accepted. The principles proposed are a compromise between these two alternatives—leaning toward independence. The subcommittee does endorse a clear

[19] Federal Inter-Agency River Basin Committee, Subcommittee on Benefits and Costs, *Proposed Practices for Economic Analysis of River Basin Projects* (May 1950). This report is usually called the "Green Book."

12

framework of analysis and makes many specific recommendations which go counter to much existing agency practice. On some other issues, it leaves sufficient ambiguity to permit certain practices which are contrary to its general point of view, but which are particularly close to the hearts of specific agencies. Compliance with their recommendations has been very uneven; some agencies were able to abide by their recommendations at little cost, while for others it would have meant serious upsets to their programs. The practices of agencies remain inconsistent. The subcommittee continues its work, but progress is slow.

Steps have also been taken to reform the reviewing process within the executive branch of government. In the spring of 1952, the Estimates Division of the Bureau of the Budget was split into a number of divisions, organized along functional lines. One of the offshoots is the Division of Resources and Civil Works, which reviews all projects of all agencies and checks whether they are in accord with the program of the President. In order to promote greater uniformity of evaluation standards and of financial practice, this division has prepared a circular[20] that contains a summary of the basic policies of water-resource programs, that notifies the agencies of the considerations which will guide the Bureau of the Budget in its evaluations of projects, and that requires them to submit certain data on a uniform basis which will permit comparisons within the entire water-resource program. While the circular could not order the agencies to adopt a specific set of evaluation principles, it does state what kind of benefits and costs would be considered most heavily by the Budget Bureau in its reviews. In 1955 the Budget Bureau prepared a much expanded circular which called on the agencies to insist on more local contributions toward the cost of projects. While a preliminary draft was being circulated, the Public Works' Committee of the House made an investigation, including public hearings,[21] thereby clearly conveying that it felt that the Bureau of the Budget was making policies of a scope greater than the committee felt proper. The revision of Circular A–47 has never been promulgated officially.

[20] Bureau of the Budget, *Circular No. A–47*, December 31, 1952.

[21] U.S. Congress, House Committee on Interior and Insular Affairs, *Discussion of Budget Bureau Circular A–47 and the Related Power Partnership Principle*, 84 Cong., 1 sess., 1955.

To accelerate the process of coördination, the Republican administration replaced the FIARBC with the Inter-Agency Committee on Water Resources in May 1954. The new committee was to consist of representatives at a higher policy level; the level of the officials attending the meetings of the old committee had fallen to a degree that made it clear that nothing very important was likely to transpire. The new committee was to consist of officials at the assistant secretary level, but in fact it has turned out to be little different from its predecessor.

At the same time President Eisenhower appointed an Advisory Committee on Water Resources Policy, composed of the secretaries of Agriculture, Defense, and Interior. This committee, which used the findings of the Second Hoover Commission as its point of departure, submitted its report after twenty months of staff work and study in December 1955.[22] It recommended three new organizations. In the center of the administrative structure of federal water-resources activity is to be a coördinator of water resources in the executive office of the President, who is to take the lead in setting down principles and standards and in coördinating agency activities and is to assist in making water-resource policy consistent with other federal policies. He is also to be permanent chairman of the second administrative structure, the already existing Inter-Agency Water Resources Committee in Washington, and will have the chairmen of the regional Water Resources Committees reporting to him. The regional committees are to keep up-to-date, comprehensive plans including work schedules for their areas and are to provide annual reports which will provide much of the material for the coördinator's comprehensive annual report on the entire water-resources program. Finally, there is to be yet another organization, a Board of Review for Water Resources, consisting of three full-time members appointed by the President to serve at his pleasure, who are to be individuals of high professional qualification and independent of any agency. The board is to evaluate all project reports in terms of policy and criteria laid down by Congress and by the coördinator of water resources, to recommend changes in plans and in criteria, and to be available for consultation by the

[22] The President's Advisory Committee on Water Resources Policy, *Water Resources Policy*, December 22, 1955.

President, the coördinator, and the agencies. Whether this cumbersome administrative arrangement, with its apparently powerful coördinator and its advisory board grafted onto the present interagency structure, will actually be established, and, if so, whether it will lead to the use of consistent criteria and to successful integration of the various programs, remains to be seen. On paper, it may seem like an administrator's nightmare. But with proper staffing it may prove effective, with the coördinator prodding the agencies into coöperation and the Board of Review acting in a quasijudicial capacity and offering an obstacle to the worst of pork-barrel projects. A similar structure has served the Corps of Engineers well, with the chief of Engineers both the chief administrator and policy-maker of the agency, but with the Board of Engineers for Rivers and Harbors providing an independent review of projects.

These internal attempts to improve the organization of federal water-resource activities have been predicated on the assumption that existing agency structure can be made more workable. Since the strong political position of the agencies precludes a more drastic reorganization, it may be only realistic to try to promote increased coördination and adoption of common standards and no more. Yet it must be recognized that there will be severe limits to the reform which can be accomplished within such a framework. Any change which could endanger the over-all expenditure level of an agency or which would disturb the regional disbursement patterns is likely to be foredoomed. And coördination of programs is circumscribed by the necessity of keeping each agency's jurisdictional preserve intact.

4. *The Need for Evaluation Standards*

The number of projects which local interests and the agencies might desire to build in any period will always exceed the number for which funds can actually be made available. Competing claims for money within the federal budget and the difficulty of increasing the general level of taxation impose a limit on the total funds available for water-resource development. Thus, choices among projects are unavoidable. To some extent, politics will determine what projects will be undertaken, but there must also be general standards by which projects can be appraised and compared, for political bargaining is no more than one facet of the decision process. At every stage, from the beginning of project formulation to the voting of the appropriations for construction, choices must be made among politically attractive propositions. The determination of the scope and the nature of projects at the planning stage requires that the agency have rules which can be applied. At subsequent stages, while it may be necessary to preserve some balance in expenditures among fields and regions, the problem still remains of selecting projects within these categories.

Evaluation standards also serve to express the national interest in the decision process. Congress and administrative officials have found it desirable to set up certain minimum standards which a project must meet before it can be authorized, regardless of its political attractiveness. The higher the criteria are set, the smaller will be the national cost of the pork-barrel aspects of the programs, which gives the general public a considerable stake in the quality of these standards.   It is equally important that the evaluation of various project plans be well publicized, because it is only in this way that legislators are free to judge whether a particular project is in the national interest, and, in the event of a conflict between local and national interest, whether the local advantage is worth the national sacrifice.   The public should also be informed about the merit of projects, for only an informed public opinion can assure that the challenge of water-resource development will be met in a way that promotes the welfare of the country as a whole.[23]

For these reasons it seemed worth while to review the criteria which are used by the agencies for project evaluation.   In the present study, agency practices are examined in some detail from the point of view of the principles which economic theory suggests. The theory of welfare economics, which gives us rules for decision making on the basis of specific assumptions about the nature and

[23] Similar views can be found in M. M. Regan and E. L. Greenshields, "Benefit-Cost Analysis of Resource Development Programs," *Journal of Farm Economics* (November 1951), pp. 866–878; and in S. V. Ciriacy-Wantrup, "Benefit-Cost Analysis and Public Resource Development," *Journal of Farm Economics* (November 1955), pp. 676–689. A more pessimistic view of benefit-cost analysis can be found in A. Smithies, *The Budgetary Process in the United States* (1955), pp. 335–346.

the objectives of the economy, is particularly well suited for this purpose.

5. *The Plan of This Study*

Our study of investment criteria for the water-resource field will include, first, the general theoretical framework of benefit-cost analysis outlined from the point of view of the theory of welfare economics. Assumptions will be discussed and some rationale for the program will be found in the theory. Then we shall discuss some general issues of benefit-cost practice, such as the form of the benefit-cost criterion, interest rates, and adjustments for risk which are encountered in all fields to which the analysis is applied. With concepts stated, we shall examine the specific evaluation practices of the major agencies for some of the major programs, indicating the differences between actual practices and the criteria that welfare economics suggests, and shall propose certain changes which would make the practices consistent with the theory, and thus also consistent with each other.

Finally, we shall raise some questions about the financial analyses of various programs. Although project evaluation and reimbursability are separate problems, and our concern is primarily with the former, we cannot avoid some discussion of the financial policies. First, for purposes which are reimbursable, financial analysis can act as an independent check on benefit-cost analysis, since projects that score high on the latter criterion should be able to meet their financial obligations relatively easily. In later years, the financial analysis can easily be verified from actual revenue data, while some of the benefit-cost estimates can never be subjected to *ex post* testing. Second, one of the criteria on which a project must be judged, and which benefit-cost analysis disregards altogether, is the redistribution of income which a project brings about. Since our notions of equity about the division of the national income are based on ethical value judgments which are clearly outside the realm of economics, project evaluation cannot include a judgment on this score. But it ought to provide the means with which the Congress and the public can exercise their own judgment. Some of the present financial policies obscure the nature of the redistribution, and the data which are presented are misleading. Estimates of the actual division of costs and benefits among the beneficiaries of the various programs and the taxpayers should be part of each project report and can be a ready by-product of the financial analysis. Third, the new "partnership approach" to resource development of the Republican administration calls for an increase of user charges. The economic analysis of the present study throws some light on the feasibility of raising more revenues and indicates some limits beyond which user charges cannot be raised.

CHAPTER II

The Theoretical Basis of Benefit-Cost Calculations

THE theory of welfare economics is a useful point of departure in developing some amount of theoretical foundations, for it can tell us how a purely private competitive economy will solve the problem of resource allocation, in what sense this solution can be considered to represent a social optimum, and what assumptions must hold in order for this solution to be achieved. Where actual conditions violate the assumptions, some form of government intervention may be justified. Examination will also reveal the limits of economic objectivity, indicating what value judgments a policymaker must accept before he can abide by the rules which the economic analysis suggests.

Initially, it should prove valuable to sketch the theory of the competitive economy and then discuss its assumptions in some detail. The implications for evaluation of public projects will then be explored and the limits of applicability of benefit-cost analysis be indicated.

1. *The Market Mechanism in the Private Economy*

A private-enterprise economy relies on the market place to work out its allocation of resources. Prices established in competitive markets provide the owners or managers of productive enterprises with guideposts established by the wishes of consumers, who in turn face prices which reflect the costs of production.[1]

Let us first look at competitive theory from the point of view of the household sector. Each consumer is assumed to have a set

---

[1] For a detailed exposition of the working of the market mechanism, see T. Scitovsky, *Welfare and Competition* (1951), pp. 29–188. Also see A. P. Lerner, *The Economics of Control* (1944).

of preferences, based on physical need, aesthetic desires, social influences, or other motives. If we assume, though only for the sake of simplicity in exposition, that the consumer can choose among only two commodities, we can express his set of preferences in an indifference map such as is shown in Figure 1. Each curve on this diagram indicates all the combinations of goods X and Y among which he is indifferent; he is just as satisfied with combination 1 consisting of very little X and a great deal of Y

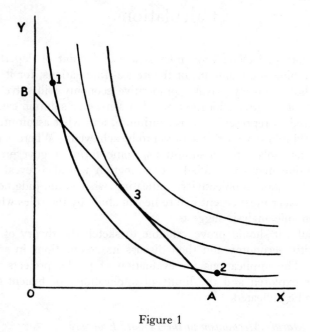

Figure 1

as he is with combination 2 where he has more of X but less of Y. Any combination on an indifference curve further to the right is preferable to a combination on a lower indifference curve, since, for every point on the lower curve, there exists a point on the higher curve at which the consumer has more of both commodities. The consumer seeks to maximize the satisfaction which he can achieve with a given limited income and with a given set of market prices. His income and the prices determine what combinations of X and Y he is actually able to purchase.

The Theoretical Basis

Let us suppose that his income is sufficient to purchase OA units of X if he devotes all of it to this one purpose. He can also obtain any of the combinations on the line AB, where the slope of the line shows at what rate he can increase his purchase of one commodity if he curtails his purchases of the other while staying within his income, and thus is equal to the ratio of the prices of X and Y. We call AB the consumer's expenditure line. The highest indifference curve that the consumer can reach is the indifference curve which is just tangent to his expenditure line. The combination of X and Y at the point of tangency is his preferred position, given his income: all higher points are unattainable, and so are all other points which are as desirable. The important property of this optimum point is that the rate at which he is willing to give up X for Y, as shown by the indifference curve, is exactly equal to their price ratio as shown by the slope of the expenditure line.

Indifference curves are usually assumed to have the shape shown in the diagram because the consumer is less willing to substitute X for Y as he gets more of Y and less of X. Should the price of one commodity, say X, fall relative to the price of the other, he would substitute X for Y up to the point where his willingness to substitute X for Y is at a rate equal to the new relative prices.

The business sector has an analogous choice: what combination of goods should be produced and, in addition, what methods of production should be employed? Each firm is faced with a set of prices of products and of factors of production. It is assumed that it will arrange its activities in such a way that its profits will be maximized. Certain technical possibilities of production will be open to it; if the firm wishes to produce a specific quantity of a good, it is free to do so by combining different combinations of factors. There will be one combination which will be the least-cost combination; it will have the property that the factors will be hired in such proportion that the contribution to output of the last unit of the factors hired will stand in the same proportion as their prices. For example, the contribution to output at the margin of a factor costing \$2 must be twice as great as the contribution of a factor costing \$1. If the firm does not follow this rule it is not minimizing its costs and will earn less than its

21

maximum profits. But the prices of factors reflect their scarcity. Should a factor become more scarce, its price will rise and firms will substitute other factors for it in production.

The quantity which a firm will produce depends on product and factor prices as well as on the technical conditions of production. It will increase its output until the cost of producing the last unit, or marginal cost, is just equal to the price it brings in the market. Should it produce more it would suffer a loss on the extra units. Output short of this point would mean that the firm missed an opportunity to produce some units which would bring it additional profit.

Households, besides consuming output, also supply factors of production, thus closing the circular flow of the economy. For each consumer we can draw indifference curves between different quantities of factors offered and different amounts of consumption. For example, a consumer will be indifferent between a high level of consumption combined with many hours of work and a lower level of consumption and less work. The consumer is faced with a certain rate of factor remuneration, such as a wage rate, showing how much of consumer goods he can purchase with the income derived from an extra unit of factor service he supplies. At the optimum point, this rate of remuneration will be exactly equal to the rate at which the consumer is willing to supply additional factors for the sake of additional consumption.

It is through prices that the market mechanism brings the tastes of consumers and the technical conditions of production in the economy together and produces an allocation of resources. The techniques of production depend on the relative prices of factors, which in turn depend on the ease and willingness with which households supply them. The choice of outputs is determined by prices and marginal costs, the former influenced by the tastes of consumers, the latter by the technical possibilities and the factor prices. Where factors are supplied by households, prices again reflect tastes; factors supplied by business are allocated into those uses that can afford to offer the highest price, which will be in the production of those commodities which are favored by consumers' tastes.

If the assumptions of the model are met, including particularly the assumptions of profit maximization and rationality of consumers, the allocation of resources which will be produced will be what we call "efficient." By this we mean that the entire productive arrangements of the economy are operated in such a way that the welfare of consumers is maximized, that is, that they reach the highest indifference curves which the technical possibilities and the resources of the economy permit. This result is achieved for three reasons. First, all outputs are produced with

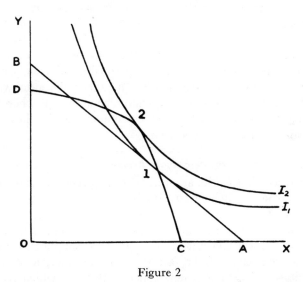

Figure 2

the least use of resources, that is, at least cost. Second, households supply their services in such quantity that the rewards just compensate for the service. Finally, with marginal costs equal to prices, the rate at which the production of one commodity can be expanded at the expense of another is exactly equal to the rate at which consumers are willing to substitute the two commodities for each other. If these two rates were not equal it would be possible to bring consumers to higher indifference curves by changing the composition of output. Figure 2 illustrates this point. Let us suppose that consumers are at point 1 on indifference curve I_1, having selected this point after being faced with the expenditure line AB. I_1 and I_2 are community indifference curves, derived by adding up the indifference maps of

23

individuals. If marginal costs are not equal to prices, then the line *CD*, which shows the ratio at which output of *X* can be increased by contracting *Y*, would not have the same slope as the expenditure line. With consumers demanding combination 1, firms will produce the same combination. If prices were brought to equality with marginal costs, the slope of the expenditure line would shift and consumers could reach point 2, which is on a higher indifference curve.[2] This is not to say that any one consumer could not reach a point which is preferable to point 2, but that the only way he could do so would be by transferring income from other consumers. Once the distribution of income is specified, each consumer reaches his optimal position only if the allocation of resources is efficient. Any other allocation would leave at least some consumers worse off, to an extent wherein it would not be possible for them to be compensated by those who would gain from the misallocation.

2. *Benefits and Costs in the Private Economy*

We can easily recast the arguments of the previous section into the terminology of benefit-cost analysis. On the cost side the meaning can be carried over completely; costs are determined by factor prices and by the technical conditions of production, where factor prices reflect consumers' willingness to supply the factors as well as the value of the factors in the production of other commodities. Benefit is a new concept, but one which readily fits into the model. The benefit of a commodity is simply its value to the consumer. But in equilibrium the consumer will spend his income in such a way that the marginal rates of substitution are equal to relative prices, that is, the relative values of commodities at the margin are equal to the relative prices, and if we pick one commodity as a common denominator for the relative prices and benefits, we can say that the resultant absolute benefit of a commodity is equal to the price which the consumer pays. Thus benefit is a measure of value and reflects consumers' willingness to allocate income to the purchase of the commodity.

[2] This assumes that the change in prices and in outputs does not affect the position of our consumer in the distribution of income. There are other difficulties in using community indifference curves, some of which are brought out below. I use them only as an expositional device.

We can also express the basic rule of profit maximization in terms of benefit and cost. We stated above that a firm must produce up to that point where price equals marginal cost. With benefit equal to price we can use the two terms interchangeably and say that the firm produces up to the point where marginal cost equals benefit, that is, the cost of producing the last unit must be equal to its benefit.

In the usage above, the term "benefit" has been applied on a per unit basis, corresponding to price. More commonly, it is used for a specific quantity of a commodity, analogous to the concept of total revenue. Thus we speak of the benefit of, say, 10 units of X; if the price of X is \$3, the benefit of the 10 units is \$30. In project evaluation, the latter concept is more useful because decisions will not typically be made in terms of adding or subtracting one unit of output, but rather in terms of blocks of units. Thus a certain change in design of a dam may add 10,000 units of output which may be worth \$3 each. The benefit of the change will be \$30,000. According to the fundamental rule of profit and welfare maximization, the change should be undertaken if its cost is less than or equal to \$30,000. Let us call all the extra costs of the change the marginal costs, and the extra benefits its marginal benefits. We can then rewrite our rule to say that marginal benefits must equal or exceed marginal costs and apply it to whatever may be the smallest possible quanta of decision making.

This rule must be applied to all marginal production decisions in the economy, whether they are made by private or by public enterprises. In the former case, profit maximization will drive firms to abide by the rule; for public undertakings, attainment of an efficient allocation of resources requires that the government agencies devise their project plans and make their project choices on the basis of criteria which produce the same result.

3. *The Assumptions of the Competitive Model*

Before we accept this rule as a blanket guide to policy, let us look at the assumptions which must hold for the model to be valid. We shall start with an examination of the assumptions that have to be made with regard to the consumers in the economy. First, consumers must be rational, in the sense that they have preferences on which they act with consistency. Second, their preferences must be such that their willingness to substitute one commodity for another in response to price changes diminishes as more and more is substituted. Finally, these preferences must be independent of the purchases of others, for otherwise the consumption of one household may lead to a loss of satisfaction in another which will not be reflected in the prices of goods.

Analogous assumptions are made about the producers of the economy. They must pursue the principle of profit maximization rationally, and production must be carried on under conditions of decreasing returns. If returns were increasing, the largest firm in an industry could undersell others till competition was destroyed. There must also be no physical interdependence among the production processes of different firms, for if the output of one firm influenced the productivity of another, the firm would be creating or destroying benefits for the country's consumers in ways that do not enter into its profit-maximizing calculations. Water pollution which reduces the usefulness of a river downstream without imposing costs on the polluter is a classic example of this kind of phenomenon.

The competitive model also makes assumptions about the structure of the economy's factor and product markets. The markets must be "perfect", which means that all participants have complete information about prices and commodities, and that all of them, on both sides of the market, are so small that they can exert no influence on the prevailing prices. In any literal sense, this assumption is violated in the typical industry of the American economy. But the possibilities of substitution in production and consumption are usually very large,[3] and the concentrations of market power on the selling side are sometimes offset by "countervailing" power on the buying side,[4] so that departure from the competitive result is sufficiently small to permit use of the model for the limited purposes of the present study. Our interest is confined, after all, to the evaluation of certain investment projects, the output of which consists of goods and services to which prices

[3] See J. A. Schumpeter, *Capitalism, Socialism and Democracy* (2 ed.; 1947), pp. 81–106.
[4] See J. K. Galbraith, *American Capitalism, the Concept of Countervailing Power* (1952), pp. 115–140.

or price equivalents can readily be applied. And while market imperfections are the rule rather than the exception in our economy, I assume in this study that the quantitative significance of the resultant distortions in the price structure of the relevant markets are not so large as to introduce errors of overriding magnitude.

In order for markets to be possible, commodities must be of a form which is marketable, that is, the sellers must be in a position to withhold the product from individual buyers, thus forcing the buyers to pay the market price to obtain the goods or service. Air, for example, is nonmarketable; even if it were scarce enough to have an economic value there would be no physical way of depriving individuals from using it. National defense is nonmarketable, since it is impossible to provide protection for only those people who voluntarily pay the requisite price. Goods and services of this latter kind are called collective goods and services and their provision has been the traditional duty of government.

The optimality of the competitive regime also presupposes that the resultant distribution of income is appropriate. If the distribution is bad as judged by some ethical standard, there may be other arrangements of the productive sector which may not be ideal from the point of view of the efficiency of the system in production and resource allocation, but which produce a better income distribution. Such an alternative system could not be said to be inferior, regardless of its lower efficiency. But it may be possible to create yet a third situation, in which the efficiency of the competitive system is combined with redistributive measures by government which produce a satisfactory division of the national income. It is this combination of the best productive arrangement coupled with governmental intervention to secure a proper income distribution that would represent the economic optimum.

The competitive system in its ideal form also assumes that the resources in the economy are relatively mobile. If there are differentials in the productivity of some resource in various uses, it must move to the use in which its productivity is highest. In the case of material resources, such mobility is a consequence of profit maximization; owners will sell to the highest bidder, and the producers who can create the most value with a resource will be willing to pay the highest price. The cost of transportation will enter the profit-maximizing calculations of buyers and sellers, producing an optimal spatial flow of resources.

But for the resource, labor, the case is much more complicated. For one thing, the labor market operates with very incomplete information; workers are unaware of opportunities elsewhere and are very hesitant to take the gamble of pulling up stakes and moving to a new town. People with families pay a substantial real cost when they move, one which is surely in excess of the money cost of moving themselves and their belongings, since it involves severe dislocations in their personal lives and the cutting of old ties and loyalties.

To some extent, these costs should be reflected in the wage structure. Surplus-labor areas, where the productivity of labor is not so high as in sections which are expanding, are likely to have lower money wages. But the existence of persistent regional unemployment is prima-facie evidence that the wages do not reflect the locational preference adequately. If wages fail to reflect these preferences of workers fully, then they do not provide perfect measures of real costs, and if productive enterprises base their calculations on them, they will not achieve an efficient allocation of resources.

Finally, the competitive model assumes that all resources and labor are employed. Even with perfect mobility, there may be a general lack of effective demand which leaves many kinds of resources idle throughout the different sectors of the economy. Under this condition prices do not reflect real costs or real benefits from the point of view of the country as a whole, and tampering with the market mechanism is justified, though the kinds of intervention may need to be circumscribed to assure the survival of the essential attributes of the market economy.

We have sketched the assumptions of the competitive model. Though reality meets none of them perfectly, we shall use the model as our theoretical framework. We shall take the position that under conditions of high employment prices are valid indicators of social benefits and of costs, as the model suggests, unless there are specific circumstances in the situation which require some modification of the analysis. Our reasons for this view are several. First, rejection of the fundamental assumption of

28

independent consumer sovereignty would be at odds with the philosophic position of this study; we postulate that individuals can best evaluate their own welfare and that economic analysis by public agencies must accept the evidence which consumers give of their desires through their behavior in the market place. Second, while there is certainly much room for improving the competitive structure of many industries in our economy, antimonopoly policies are not our concern in the present study. Insofar as there are monopoly elements, prices will exceed marginal costs, but from a quantitative point of view, these deviations are both widely—also perhaps evenly—diffused and relatively small, particularly in the range of markets most relevant to water-resource development. Projects in these fields produce outputs which in largest part are producer goods, such as raw materials, electric energy, and transportation services. In these areas advertising, consumer loyalty, and asymmetric market power concentrated on the side of the seller are less prevalent than in the markets for consumer goods.[5] Thus, while prices do not serve their function perfectly, we hold that they are generally adequate for the range of policy decisions with which we are concerned. At the same time, in any application of the methods of this study we must keep in mind the assumptions which validate the use of prices, and we must not hesitate, in certain situations, to reject them in favor of other measures of social benefit and cost.

To make clear some of the situations in which the competitive model requires amendment in the water-resource field, we shall examine in the following sections those assumptions which are violated particularly. We shall indicate how these violations justify some form of government intervention and we shall show how the principles of benefit-cost analysis must be adapted. It should be stressed that intervention need not take the form of public operation and ownership; government regulation, subsidies, or taxation may suffice to achieve a result of satisfactory efficiency. Nor do we argue that violation of efficiency conditions need automatically justify government intervention, for there are offsetting costs to drawing the government into a field of activity.

[5] This point is developed by I. M. D. Little in *The Price of Fuel* (1953), pp. xii–xiv.

29

Our study merely seeks to show on what grounds of efficiency government intervention could be explained, and how investment criteria for government projects should take account of these departures from the competitive model.

4. *Increasing Returns*

The existence of conditions of increasing returns raises a host of problems for the competitive model. Oligopoly with all its attendant issues of antitrust policy is one outcome. The acceptance of a state of natural monopoly with public regulation by commissions is another result. But there are instances where neither of these developments is possible. In the field under study, inland waterways are an important example. Since most of the costs of providing the system do not vary with the amount of use, average costs fall as volume rises until a point is reached where the capacity of the system is fully utilized. Under private enterprise, prices would have to be set in such a way that total revenues exceed total costs. With marginal costs below average costs, this condition precludes pricing of the use of the waterway at marginal cost. Discriminatory pricing, such as is used widely in the rates of public utilities, could conceivably be employed to assure that marginal users face prices equal to marginal costs while other users pay rates high enough to assure fulfillment of the total revenue requirement. But there is a related complication that rules out this private-enterprise solution. It takes many years before the demand for use of the service develops to a point where even a discriminatory pricing system would produce revenues sufficient to meet annual charges.[6] Development of waterways has therefore become a public undertaking.

Benefit-cost analysis can be adapted to deal with this problem, though the use of one price as an indicator of social value is ruled out. To ascertain whether a navigation system should be constructed, it must be shown that total benefit exceeds total cost. In order to approximate the total revenue that a perfect system of price discrimination could produce, the benefit accruing to different categories of shippers can be measured by the savings

---

[6] In the case of the TVA, 15 years passed before the navigation potential of the river began to be realized.

in transportation charges that would be realized through the waterway.[7] If there are possible choices about the scale of development of a waterway in terms of either depth of channel or upstream extension, the benefit and cost of these marginal changes can be measured similarly and all those which are justified on this basis should be undertaken.

5. *Physical Interdependence*

The interdependence of productive processes, often called non-pecuniary external economies or diseconomies of production, also can result in making prices invalid indicators of national benefits and costs. Since all the uses of the water in a river basin are interdependent, private management of the associated productive enterprises requires an elaborate system of charges and subsidies to make each firm pay for all the opportunities which are lost elsewhere through its activities or to reward it for services which it renders to other enterprises for which it cannot charge a price. A system of dams designed to produce the maximum amount of economic hydropower on a river would include some dams upstream that primarily act as storage reservoirs, while others downstream would generate power with little provision for storage. If the dams are under separate managements, each will be designed and operated to maximize its own output and revenue, unless there are agreements among the firms to run the river system as a unit, maximizing total output and sharing the revenue. But the agreements have to involve infinite details, spelling out operating procedures for every contingency of stream-flow patterns. It remains to be seen whether it is possible to write contracts which will provide reasonable, effective substitutes for centralized operation.

Where government constructs and manages a complex of inter-dependent economic activities, the rules of the market mechanism must be adapted. Decisions cannot be made as if the units in the system were independent, for to do so would be to contradict the rationale for government intervention. A benefit-cost investment criterion must measure all the effects on the other units of

[7] It will be seen in Chapter V that the transportation savings realized by shippers must be further modified because the rail charges exceed marginal costs.

the system. Where a unit is added to an existing system, the additional benefits and costs can be measured by comparing the differences of both sides of the criterion with and without the marginal unit. But if the system as a whole is being planned, criteria cannot be constructed for individual projects unless a specific set of assumptions is made about the order of construction. Typically, the first project in a system will reap very large benefits, while later additions, usually at less favorable sites, will run into diminishing returns. It would certainly be a mistake to assume that every project is the first to be built. Correct planning requires that all possible sequences of development be evaluated, and that only the best alternative plans be submitted for review. Benefit-cost ratios can be submitted for each project for each of the plans of development, making it clear that the interdependence cannot be ignored at any stage of the decision process, not even at the Congressional level.

Physical interdependence may also exist between a public project and private enterprises in the area. Small flood-control installations in agricultural areas, for example, will reduce flood damage and erosion from uncontrolled runoff. A benefit measure must include the increased income accruing to farmers. Similarly large flood-control projects protecting cities can be interpreted as a form of physical interdependence between private economic units and a public project.

6. *Mobility of Labor*

A smoothly functioning market economy requires considerable fluidity in the labor market. Since we are not concerned with the merits of the economic system as a whole and since we assume throughout our analysis that the present market economy will continue, there is no need to pass judgment on the general adequacy of labor mobility in the United States. But in evaluating public works, there often arises the issue whether labor which was idle, and which is employed by the project, would have continued idle or would have moved to a more favorable labor market. Certainly in periods of serious depression, when the main purpose of public works is the creation of employment opportunities, market-price criteria must be supplemented by employment criteria.[8] Market prices also cease to reflect real costs, since there are no lost opportunities where previously unemployed labor is hired.

But in ordinary times, there is a very strong case against rejecting the premise of labor mobility.[9] If projects are evaluated on the assumption that local idleness would not have been wiped out by migration of labor, the benefits of projects in such areas become larger than comparable projects elsewhere and are more likely to be done. But our economy requires that there be adaptation to changing demands, and selection of projects on this basis will slow down the process of change. Labor will not become available where it is needed but will be able to remain where its productivity is low. To help the market economy, government should promote mobility rather than retard it, and so public-works planning must make no categorical allowances for local pockets of unemployment.

There may be specific instances where government policy calls for special aid to a depressed area. In that event, sound policy formation is best promoted by making the cost explicit, which can only be accomplished if public works are evaluated on the usual criteria. Special assistance can take the form of undertaking projects which have relatively low benefit-cost ratios, too low to make them worth while under ordinary circumstances. By showing how much the project benefits fall short of ordinary justification standards for projects, the cost of aid is demonstrated.

There may also be cases where mobility must be rejected because the idleness is clearly of a very short-run character. If it is known that the labor will be back at work after a brief interval, it certainly cannot be expected to move for the interim. In the water-resources field, much of the benefit of flood control is of this sort. Floods lead to enforced idleness and to loss of production. Often mobility to other opportunities is impossible, leading to a genuine loss of national output and benefit. If flood control averts such losses, it creates a positive benefit.

[8] For a detailed discussion of the experience with such criteria in the 1930's, see National Resources Planning Board, *The Economic Effects of the Federal Public Works Expenditures, 1933–1938* (1940), a study directed by J. K. Galbraith, pp. 8–12, 74–92.

[9] This view is expounded at length in A. G. B. Fisher, *Economic Progress and Social Security* (1945), especially pp. 48–92.

7. *Full Employment*

The historical records show that our economy has operated at less than full employment a good part of the time. The market mechanism fails to provide an optimum when unemployment pervades most regions and industries, and an assumption about high mobility of resources does not restore the validity of prices as welfare guides to production if there are no alternative employments to which idle resources could be transferred.[10]

In times of depression, opportunity costs are less than money costs, and benefit-cost analyses must reflect this divergence. A perfect criterion would reflect at all moments in time the over-all state of economic activity. But investment criteria must never be ideal in the sense that they require an omniscient government to administer them. They must be of a form that reflects the empirical nature of the decision process of which they are a part. As we saw in Chapter I, the investment criterion for which we are looking must be of a sort which can be evaluated during the survey stage of project planning, but which will remain relevant till the money is appropriated. The only changes that can be made are the application of new sets of input and output prices, computations which can readily be carried out in Washington. Since a decade often passes between the survey and the construction, a general assumption must be made about the level of employment, and for the sake of comparability among projects, the same assumption must be made for all of them.

The assumption of high employment and steady growth at stable prices is the most appropriate choice. The nature of the water-resource development programs presupposes that the country will continue to expand, generating new needs for resources. A more pessimistic assumption would be inconsistent with the inherent premise of the program—that there is a strong need for the development of our water resources. It would also be at odds with the official policies of the government, which call for federal responsibility for the maintenance of high employment. On the other hand, an assumption of steady inflation is unacceptable because it would mean that government investments would

[10] This problem is examined in more detail in P. A. Samuelson, "Principles and Rules in Modern Fiscal Policy: A Neo-classical Reformulation," *Money, Trade and Economic Growth*, pp. 157–176.

be justified by price increases which, at least in part, would be caused by the program itself; it would be politically immoral for the federal government to operate any expenditure program on the assumption that it will finally be justified by the government's failure to maintain the value of the currency. In addition, the chosen assumption has the great practical advantage of permitting the use of actual prices and of prices which would be expected if the price level remained constant.

The over-all magnitude of the programs in any one year must be influenced by the general level of employment. Such variation can easily be introduced by asking Congress for appropriations for as many new starts for construction as the fiscal stabilization policy makes appropriate. If, in times of depression, a sufficient number of potential projects with benefit-cost ratios high enough to justify their construction exists, then it is only necessary to lower the cutoff point for justification. Should the ratios produced under the full-employment assumption be too low to justify the number of new starts required by countercyclical fiscal policy, then it may become necessary to make across-the-board adjustments for all projects. A reduction in the interest rate would be appropriate, indicating the lower opportunity cost of capital. Prices of factors can also be cut to reflect the degree of unemployment, with the reductions possibly differing among factors and among regions, depending on the circumstances at the time. These procedures preserve the long-term perspective of the benefit-cost analysis, yet make it clear that the social cost of undertaking projects at such times is particularly low and that the undertakings therefore are particularly attractive.

8. *The Distribution of Income*

The income distribution which results from the market mechanism is in no sense an absolutely ideal distribution. Under our system of private property, a certain distribution will result; under some other system of property, the market mechanism would produce a different division of the national income. The distribution which a country considers fair and equitable is a matter of judgment, which can only be made on a foundation of ethical values. The process by which differences about this conception of fairness are settled is a political one; the economist has no right to make this judgment for society. He has the duty, however, to make clear the economic implications of policies designed to determine or alter the income distribution in terms of growth, stability, efficiency, or other economic dimensions; and in certain situations, where the distributive effects are obscured by the technical complexities of the policies, he may be the only person who can inform the decision maker about the nature of the distributive results. But, because matters of distribution involve value judgments, there must be separate criteria for evaluating distributive effects. There is no logical way of incorporating distributive effects into the benefit-cost analysis, which must confine itself to the one dimension of benefit for the country as a whole.

In recent years, theoretical studies in welfare economics have shown that there are serious conceptual problems in the separation of the efficiency aspects of the economic system from the distributive question.[11] The difficulty lies in the fact that the change in income distribution associated with an economic act of government will result in changes of demand because of differences in tastes between the recipients and the source of the redistribution. If market prices change, they cease to be unambiguous measuring rods of benefits and costs, because a project may appear worth while at the prices prevailing before the undertaking, but not at the new set of prices. Under these conditions, the benefit-cost criterion ceases to be a single number and becomes a range, the end points of which are set by valuing benefits and costs at both sets of prices.

Fortunately there is good reason to believe that this complication ordinarily does not arise in connection with projects. The typical project, while often large in a physical sense, is very small in comparison to the economy as a whole. The redistribution of income that it accomplishes will lead to some shifts in demand if the tastes of the beneficiaries are different from that of the national average; but the share of the national income and of the total

---

[11] See N. Kaldor, "Welfare Propositions in Economics," *Economic Journal* (September 1939), pp. 549–552; T. Scitovsky, "A Note on Welfare Propositions in Economics," *Review of Economic Studies* (November 1941), pp. 77–88; P. A. Samuelson, "Evaluation of Real National Income," *Oxford Economic Papers* (January 1950), pp. 1–21; and I. M. D. Little, *A Critique of Welfare Economics* (1950).

national demand that has been redirected is a tiny portion of the total. Thus the prices of all commodities which have a national price pattern can be assumed to remain the same with and without the project. Prices which are set in local or regional markets will be affected by a project, of course, but the primary cause for such price changes is not the change in the distribution of income among persons with different tastes but rather the increase in supply of the commodity. We shall assume that changes in prices caused by a project are due to the increase in supply and not to differences in tastes.

9. *Price Variation Due to Large Changes in Inputs and Outputs*

A somewhat related problem is created by the fact that large projects will directly influence the prices of the factors which are purchased for them as well as the prices of their outputs. Typically, certain construction materials and certain kinds of labor will receive higher prices and wages when a large project is built in a region than at other times, and the price of outputs which must be sold within the region, such as electric power, will be driven down by a substantial increase in supply. In this situation, crude measures for the limits of benefits can be found by using both sets of prices, with and without the project. In the case of outputs, the "without" price represents an upper limit to benefit, since consumers purchased a smaller amount at that price, while the "with" price is a lower limit, since consumers are willing to buy the new, larger total for it. The actual benefit is somewhere between the limits; if the change is not extreme, national benefit can be approximated by applying a price which is an average of the two to the increase in output.[12] If the change is very large, such as the construction of vast new power facilities in a region, better approximations can be derived by dividing the demand into segments, and seeing at what price the different segments can be sold. This does not necessarily require that discriminatory pricing be applied, but it does suppose that market studies can determine what purchasers could be made to pay if discrimination were used.

The same arguments apply to supply. If the prices of factors

[12] This approximation assumes that the demand curves of the products are linear.

are bid up, the lower limit to real cost is measured by the "without" price, since the smaller amount was supplied at that price. The upper limit is the "with" price, since it draws the actual, larger supply. The actual social cost per unit lies between these limits and can be approximated by an average of "with" and "without" price.[13] The problem is less great with supply since most of the factors which are used in construction either are not specific to the area and are thus nationally priced, or are of a kind the price of which will be driven up in similar situations elsewhere, so that construction cost indices already reflect a compromise between the two limits.

10. *Nonmarketability, Collective Goods, and Social Choice*[14]

If a product is nonmarketable and if the individuals in a community desire to obtain it, they can act through governments to provide it for all. Some system of voting or of representation must exist to produce decisions for collective action to obtain collective goods. Unanimity is obviously too severe a criterion; majority rule is the standard method used in our country for reaching a decision, though there are many modifications in the direction of requiring unanimity on various issues, and the rule of one equal vote for every eligible voter is only vaguely approximated in most of our political processes which involve decisions.[15] In the present study, we make no attempt to evaluate the voting procedures; the political process which is the most important part of the decision-making machinery for public investments is accepted as one of the empirical data. This is not to say that we draw no inferences about the rationality of the process and its impact on the quality of the resultant programs, nor that we can suggest no improvements; but the principles of economic evaluation that emerge from our study do not presuppose any changes in the political processes of the Congress or the administration.

[13] This assumes linear supply curves.

[14] A detailed examination of this problem from a somewhat different conceptual view can be found in W. J. Baumol, *Welfare Economics and the Theory of the State* (1952), especially chap. 12. Also see A. De Viti De Marco, *First Principles of Public Finance*, (1936), chap. 1; and P. A. Samuelson, "The Pure Theory of Public Expenditures," *Review of Economics and Statistics* (November 1954), pp. 387–389.

[15] The severe theoretical difficulties which are encountered in deriving an ideal voting system are discussed in K. J. Arrow, *Social Choice and Individual Values* (1951).

The Theoretical Basis

We assume that there is an acceptable process by means of which the community decides whether or not to consume a collective good, and that economic criteria which show the benefits and costs to the country are a desirable aid to the decision process. Since decisions about public works are a relatively unimportant part of the political picture, the electoral process is not likely to offer a responsive choice mechanism for these collective goods. Few except those immediately affected will cast their votes on the basis of a candidate's stand on a public-works issue.

Benefit-cost analysis offers a more sensitive substitute; it is a method of approximating the results of consumer voting in the market place by means of computations which use the prices that consumers establish when they choose marketable commodities. The value or benefit of a collective good is established by estimating how much consumers would be willing to pay if the good were marketable. The benefit-cost criterion, under ideal procedures, provides the same answer that the market mechanism would provide if it were free to function for collective goods. The results under this criterion then become a part of the actual political decision process and influence the final outcome to a degree which is dependent on the principles which motivate the decision makers. If it were the desire of all participants in the political process to maximize the total national real income, they would simply abide by the results of the benefit-cost criterion. Since there are other ideals which they consider, such as changes in the income distribution, creation of noneconomic benefits, national defense, regional development, equitable distribution of government projects among areas, and many more ideals both noble and otherwise, the benefit-cost analysis is not the only criterion. The amount of influence exercised by the analysis will also be circumscribed by the degree of confidence that decision makers are willing to place in the quality of the figures that are actually produced. Thus strengthening of the criteria is likely to promote the weight given to the objective of maximizing national economic welfare as opposed to the other objectives.

11. *Collective Goods and the Limits of Benefit-Cost Analysis*

The benefit-cost analysis presupposes that it is possible to determine how much consumers would be willing to pay for the goods or services in question. For some kinds of public works it is fairly easy to estimate this amount. For example, the amount which an individual property owner would be willing to pay for flood control can be assumed to be equal, at least, to the damages which will be averted. In the case of irrigation the change in personal income is a good indication of the amount which beneficiaries would be willing to pay if they were rational farm entrepreneurs, though there are good reasons[16] why actual charges must be less. Navigation benefits can be measured by savings in the total transportation bill of the country. And, of course, there are some projects, the output of which is actually marketable, such as electric power, where the benefit can be derived from potential revenues.[17]

But there are other collective goods for which the problem of benefit estimation is much more difficult. All of the mentioned goods and services have one common denominator: benefits can be measured with actual prices which are established in regular markets. For example, benefits of flood control, in the form of averted damage, can be estimated from repair costs of property and from the market values of the goods which have been destroyed. The estimation of benefits therefore merely requires the determination of a set of clearly defined physical effects and of some expected market prices. But in the case of national defense —the most important collective good as judged by total expenditure—there is no price at all. Nor is there any empirical, operational procedure with which a price could be derived which would be suitable for a benefit measure. To determine the price that consumers would be willing to pay if they could purchase national defense, they would have to be interviewed. Since they know perfectly well that the defense budget will not be influenced by their response, and in view of the unpleasant tax possibilities of giving a high answer, they would have no reason to give truthful replies. And even if they were perfectly guileless, or if they could be convinced that no more than a measure of benefit was sought, their lack of experience in purchasing this "commodity" would result in answers which might be far different from the answers they would give if actual purchases were involved. This

---

[16] See Chapter VI.
[17] Though actual rates may be set below willingness to pay.

is not to say that people's desires with regard to national defense have no influence on the total national effort; the political process does reflect their willingness to be taxed. It merely means that it is impossible to construct an equivalent to the market mechanism to aid the collective political judgments; there is no way of constructing an investment criterion like the benefit-cost ratio.

There are other collective goods and services which pose equally insurmountable obstacles to benefit-cost measurement, perhaps foremost among which is education. But there are some which fall between the extremes. These pose the great temptation; benefit-cost ratios of sorts can be produced and sometimes the results sound rather plausible. Yet the figures are not based on appropriate market prices and the benefit-cost ratios are invalid and misleading. In Chapter V we shall examine one such instance, but here I shall cite only one example. There have been many attempts to measure the benefits of recreation. Since people actually hire the use of recreational facilities, one might expect that one could find prices that would measure willingness to pay. When a dam creates a lake, agencies look to the total expenditures which people make on fishing and swimming. But these expenditures are for travel, equipment, lodging, and so forth, and are not expenditures for the lake. A proper measure of benefit would be to indicate how much managers of the lake could collect in the form of user charges; since there are no charges for use of reservoirs or comparable bodies of water elsewhere, appropriate prices cannot be found. Such purposes as recreation must therefore be judged on other criteria, for the use of benefit-cost analysis for them not only is invalid, but casts general doubt and suspicion on procedures which can effectively serve a high purpose where they are appropriate.

In the case of water-resource development projects, the benefits which defy valuation at market prices are usually in the nature of by-products; they are never the primary justification. To assure proper consideration of such immeasurable outputs, an analysis of intangibles should be a part of every project report. Verbal discussion of the intangible benefits and costs will communicate the facts to Congress more clearly than invalid benefit estimates. Relevant figures may be submitted without forcing them into the benefit-cost framework; for example, recreation benefits of a project can be described in terms of estimates of expected use. The extra costs which must be incurred to make the intangible benefits available can be stated, and can be compared with the average costs on other projects of the same type, or even with the costs on comparable private facilities. Congress will thus be put in the position of deciding about the value of the intangible benefits, which is their proper responsibility as long as they do not delegate the decision through specification of operational criteria.

12. *The Market Mechanism and the Allocation of Resources Over Time*

So far our discussion has not explicitly considered the time dimension. The market mechanism results in an intertemporal distribution of resource use, production, and consumption which is optimal in an analogous sense to the timeless optimum. The present desires of consumers about future consumption interact with the production plans of producers to create a pattern of production over time which results in the maximum national real income as valued by the preferences of consumers in the present.

For the consumer, preference patterns include desired distributions of expenditure over time. If the consumer is free to borrow or to lend at the market rate of interest, he will arrange his expenditures in such a way that the total satisfaction during the entire period over which his plans extend be at a maximum, as judged by present preferences. If the consumer is free to borrow or to lend at the market rate of interest, this maximization requires that the satisfaction derived from the marginal expenditures in each period, discounted to the present, be the same; for example, if the interest rate is 5 percent, his present valuation of the satisfaction derived from the marginal expenditure in the second period must be 1.05 times as great as the value for the first period. Any other arrangement of expenditure could be improved by the consumer by switching expenditures from one period to another. Each consumer also has an expectation about the future pattern of his income receipts. If discounted at the interest rate, the present value of the income stream can be calculated and can then be transformed into an expenditure pattern of equivalent value, but one which maximizes total satisfaction. A rise in the interest rate would make a consumer shift his expenditures toward more remote periods as the amount of interest he can collect by waiting increases and as the satisfaction which results from the increased expenditure later on becomes larger. In other words, the opportunity cost of present consumption rises as the foregone interest payment rises due to a higher interest rate. As more future consumption can be gained by reducing present consumption, the transfer of expenditure into the future, which is really saving, becomes more attractive.

Profit-maximizing producers will make their investment plans in such a way that the present value of their future profits is at a maximum.[18] This requires that they invest up to that point at which the present value of the net-revenue stream made possible by the marginal dollar of investment is just equal to the dollar of cost, where net revenue of a period is defined as the difference between gross revenue and current costs. This principle can also be expressed on an annual basis: the firm invests up to that point at which the annual rate of return on the marginal dollar of investment (the marginal efficiency of investment) is just equal to the interest rate.

In equilibrium, the interest rate brings the capital market into balance. Consumers' plans to save are brought to equality with producers' plans to invest. The interest rate reflects both the time preference of consumption of consumers and the returns which can be earned on investments. At the margin, consumers are indifferent between a dollar of present consumption and a future income stream equal to the interest rate, while producers can invest these marginal dollars to yield a rate of return equal to the interest rate. Thus the economy can produce a future flow of goods that is just sufficient to compensate consumers for their sacrifice of present consumption. In this manner an optimal rate of saving (and investment) is achieved for the economy.

Under this condition, public investment must be made in accordance with the same principles. Investment must be pushed to that point at which the benefit stream of the marginal dollar

---

[18] For a discussion of this assumption and its implications, see F. A. and V. Lutz, *The Theory of Investment of the Firm* (1951), especially chap. 2.

of investment is equal to the interest rate. In the event that investment can only be varied in larger discrete amounts, the present value of the future net-benefit stream must at least be equal to the cost of the marginal investment. Or expressed in annual terms, the annual marginal benefit must at least be equal to the annual marginal cost where the latter includes the interest and amortization costs as well as the current costs of the marginal investment undertaking.[19]

It should be noted that the resultant optimum reflects only the preferences of those who have control over consumers' expenditures, presumably the heads of households. Future generations, born and unborn, have no say about this allocation over time; their desires are only represented by the consideration which the present generation of consumers shows to their interests. One might expect that this would lead to inadequate provision for the nation's future, but the high rate of capital accumulation and of economic growth is evidence to the contrary.[20]

The optimum presupposes that the capital market is perfectly competitive, that all consumers and producers can borrow or lend an unlimited amount at the prevailing interest rate. The facts are very different, of course. The amount of credit available to a firm is limited, and typically the borrowing rate is higher than the rate on government bonds. Since each firm must use its own borrowing rate in its internal calculations, its plans will not be optimal from the point of view of national welfare.

The causes of this market imperfection are not far to seek. The model assumes perfect foresight, which either eliminates

[19] This treatment of the problem of intertemporal allocation is extremely compact. A fuller version of the intertemporal equilibrium of producers and consumers can be found in J. R. Hicks, *Value and Capital* (1939), pp. 191–227, 325–328; and in Lutz and Lutz, *The Theory of Investment of the Firm*. The implications for intertemporal welfare economics are discussed in M. Reder, *Studies in the Theory of Welfare Economics* (1947), pp. 33–35.

[20] A more extensive theoretical discussion of this problem from a different point of view can be found in E. O. Heady, "Some Fundamentals of Conservation Economics and Policy," *Journal of Farm Economics* (November 1950), pp. 1182–1195; and in S. V. Ciriacy-Wantrup, *Resource Conservation Economics and Policies* (1952), pp. 97–110. Also see O. Eckstein, "Investment Criteria for Economic Development and the Theory of Intertemporal Welfare Economics," *Quarterly Journal of Economics* (February 1957).

risks or reduces them to an insurable basis. In the real world, every loan is a gamble, and the interest charge must reflect not only the pure rate of interest but also a compensation for risk taking. Since not all loans are equally risky, it cannot be expected that they will be made on uniform terms. Consequently, the expected rates of return on marginal projects in different sectors will also differ, which is a violation of the marginal efficiency conditions of competitive equilibrium.[21]

In addition, the general level of the interest-rate structure is influenced by the monetary policy of the Federal Reserve system. If the nation's economy were stabilized by monetary policy alone, one might suppose that the resultant rate was closely related to the pure rate of interest. But since the interest-rate policy is a part of a more complex stabilization program which includes fiscal policy and debt management as well, no such significance can be attached to the rates set by the monetary authorities.

There are two important consequences of these imperfections in the capital market. First, it cannot be assumed that any existing interest rate measures the time preference of the people of present consumption over future. In planning public works, a government must find a rate that reflects the people's desires with regard to making provision for the future. Since it cannot look to the market place, it must devise other means of selecting appropriate interest rates. This is a thorny problem to which we shall return at some length in a subsequent chapter. Absence of a unique optimal interest rate leads to the further difficulty that the actual rate of saving and investment need not be optimal, and so the level of public investment cannot be determined by pushing

---

[21] It can be argued that risk premiums are a part of efficient prices, leading to an optimal distribution of risk bearing. But actual risk premiums cannot be considered optimal in view of the failure of the system to exhaust the possibilities of reducing risk through pooling and the reduction of ignorance. There remains the open question, however, whether a socially optimal interest-rate structure does or does not reflect risk premiums. The answer to this question hinges on the assumption that is made about the relation of risk to the real national income. If the expected value of national income, regardless of the dispersion of risk of its components, is taken as the indicator of welfare, there is no place for risk premiums in the structure. If risk is considered a subtraction from real income, there will be an optimal set of risk premiums, but the optimum presupposes the existence of optimal insurance and of gambling possibilities which do not exist in the economy.

it to a point at which the annual benefits on marginal investments are just equal to their annual marginal cost as computed at the market rate of interest.

The final consequence of imperfection in the capital market is the divergence between the private and the social valuations of privately owned assets.[22] The value which a private individual places on an asset depends on the income or satisfaction he will receive from it and on the rate at which he capitalizes the annual return. With perfect access to the capital market, an individual would capitalize an asset at the market rate of interest, that is, would sell it only if he could get an equally large annual return by lending the proceeds of the sale at the market rate of interest as he would get from the asset itself. But if his access to the capital market is limited, he will capitalize at the borrowing rate if he needs money, or at the lending rate if he wants to continue to hold an income-producing asset. The resultant capitalization rate may be two or three times as high as the government bond rate, which will make his valuation of the asset much lower than it would be at public rates. In the markets for some types of assets, particularly agricultural land, all the buyers and sellers have high capitalization rates, which produces market values that are very low, and which do not reflect fully the social value of the asset. This divergence is important in public-works evaluation because it means that the market values of such assets do not fully reflect the social costs. Particularly if benefits are valued at very low rates of interest, it is conceivable that there will be a loss of national income through the transference of ownership of assets from individuals with high capitalization rates to the government with its low rates.[23]

---

[22] See Ciriacy-Wantrup, *Resource Conservation Economics and Policies*, pp. 100–102.

[23] This point is further considered in Chapter IV.

CHAPTER III

The Benefit-Cost Criterion

FOR at least twenty years, water-resource projects have been evaluated through benefit-cost analyses. Benefit-cost ratios have been computed to show that projects are justified and to aid in the selection of projects to be included in authorization and budget requests.

The evaluation of benefits and costs in each field offers its own set of difficulties, and in later chapters we shall take up some of them. There are other problems which cut across programs: prices, interest rates, and periods of analysis must be specified and must be applied uniformly in all fields in order to assure at least a minimum degree of comparability. The criterion can take several different forms; should projects with the highest benefit-cost ratios be selected; should the difference between benefits and costs be maximized; or should there be some other objective? The present chapter will discuss some of these common issues of project evaluation.

1. Economic Justification or Evaluation?

The Flood Control Act of 1936 requires that benefits must exceed cost, "to whomsoever they may accrue," for projects to be authorized. This legal requirement has molded the development of the benefit-cost analysis. Project reports present the results in such a way that they stress the legal economic justification, that the benefits do exceed the costs. Once this test is passed, all projects are on the same footing, and only the agency's judgment, based on political circumstances internal and external to the agency, need determine the choice of projects to be submitted for inclusion in the budget. Similarly, the Budget Bureau and the Congress, while perhaps considering this hurdle of economic

47

justification to be a necessary preliminary step, are free to place their stamp of approval on any "justified" project, and will be free to make the actual choice on political grounds.

In practice, the rate at which benefits exceed costs, as expressed by the ratio, also has an important influence on the choice of projects. As a matter of professional ethics and of service to the national welfare, all participants in the long decision process will tend to favor "good" projects over dubious ones, and will weigh the economic merit along with the other determinants. Thus the benefit-cost analysis serves both for justification and for relative evaluation of projects. But the two purposes conflict with each other, the former requiring loose standards which will boost poor projects past the shibboleth of a ratio of 1.0, the latter requiring consistency of standards so that the relative economic merit will be indicated.

As for justification, it should be recognized that the legal requirement which the Act of 1936 imposes on the agencies is, in fact, impossible to meet. Measuring all benefits and costs "to whomsoever they may accrue" is not only beyond the present ability of economic science, but presents conceptual difficulties which by their very nature can never be overcome except by making very specific assumptions on matters about which the Act does not prescribe.

First, "benefit" requires definition. In this study, in the Report of the Subcommittee on Benefits and Costs, and more or less in agency practice, the benefit of a project to an individual has been defined to correspond to that amount of money which he would be willing to pay if he were given the market choice of purchase. This concept can be derived from the classical economic theory of consumption, and has been presented in basic textbooks of economics for many years. It is likely that the persons who wrote and passed the Act of 1936 had this concept in mind, although it is not the kind of point which can be settled by judicial interpretation. Second, a method of comparing and aggregating the benefits that accrue to different people must be defined. Again, the simplest assumption, of adding the benefits of all people, weighted equally, probably adheres to the intention of the Congress and is consistent with the welfare economics of classical economists whose writings were dominant when the legislators acquired their economic ideas. But a profound value judgment about interpersonal comparisons underlies this assumption.

The same problems exist with regard to costs. For the sake of consistency they can be treated quite symmetrically with benefits weighted equally "to whomsoever they may accrue"; in fact, they can be considered negative benefits. The Subcommittee on Benefits and Costs recommends symmetry, and with some exceptions which we will note later, it is also a rule of agency practice.

Beyond the conceptual difficulties, there are some problems of measurement that are so acute that even with perfect forecasting of all the relevant data about the projects themselves, other information, particularly about costs, is necessary which is not available in quantitative form. If we want to measure all the costs of a project "to whomsoever they may accrue," we must include the social costs of taxation. The money costs of the project reflect the value of the resources which are used. But in addition, the total of the national income over the years is influenced by the distortions and misallocations of resources and of human effort which are the result of the high level of taxation. If we assume that federal government runs a successful business-cycle stabilization policy, then it follows that if a project were not done, some taxes would be cut and some of the disincentive effects of taxation would be ameliorated. Conversely, adding a project adds to the tax load and means further distortions and disincentives. If the government does not make the effort to keep the budget consistent with the needs of fiscal policy so that there will be no matching taxes, and if there is full employment, then projects will contribute to inflation, which involves its own peculiar sets of distortions and misallocations. Finally, if the government runs its policy in such a way that a cut in the resources program would mean an expansion of some other program, say national defense, the sum of all programs being prescribed by the people's tolerance level of taxation, then the real cost is the value of the program which is foregone because of the project. Should there be much unemployment, the effects will not occur, of course.

To some extent there will be offsets on the benefit side. If a project is completely self-financing, so that the government merely loans the funds for a period of time at interest, the extra taxes which must be raised at the time of construction will be offset by revenues to be collected later, which will permit corresponding tax cuts. If the social costs of financing remain the same over time, there will be complete cancellation, except for the financing of interest, as the project is paid off. Thus, the larger the share of a project that is reimbursable, the smaller will be the costs of this category.

These costs may be beyond measurement; but they are significant all the same. As long as they cannot be quantified, the total cost of a project cannot be measured and the test of economic justification cannot be performed with assurance, except where the margin of benefits over costs is very large.

Yet the emphasis on justification has meant that the most important fruits of the benefit-cost analysis are not reaped to the extent to which they could be. Relative economic evaluation is not being stressed, though this can be done more reliably. The costs in the above categories will be the same for all projects except for differences in reimbursability, and the latter are considered in the financial analysis. Also, major errors in forecasting over-all levels of economic activity, which will throw the absolute benefit-cost ratios far off, will not reshuffle the relative rankings of projects very drastically. And even specific errors of forecasting demands for one or more commodities will tend to cancel out in the comparisons of similar projects, though the evaluation of projects with different outputs will be incorrect.

The absolute measurement of benefits and costs, as required for the justification of projects, is an impossibility because of the arbitrariness of definitions, the complexity of some of the costs and benefits, and the requirements of forecasting. The relative measurement of benefits and costs, which is all that is needed to use the analysis as an instrument of choice among projects, can be done with much more confidence. The absolutes, which are still needed to determine the over-all level of the program in the resources field, must be determined in a more political way. In this connection it should be pointed out that in the other fields of government expenditure no comparable effort at measurement is made, so that even if the absolute measure did exist in the resources field, it still would not be able to serve as a guide for weighing the benefits of the marginal expenditures in this field against those of other fields.

2. Some Definitions

As far as possible, we shall adhere to the terminology which is used by the federal agencies. Let us set down a few definitions:

a *project* is a set of river-development measures, carried out alone or in part by the federal government;

a *program* is a set of projects, usually in one general area;

a *purpose* is one of the major objectives of governmental activity in the field of water-resource development, such as flood control, irrigation, navigation, power generation, conservation, water supply, and recreation;

project cost is the value of goods and services used to establish, maintain, and operate a project;

associated cost is the value of goods and services needed, beyond project cost, to make the output of the project available;

direct benefit is the value of the immediate products or services resulting from the measures for which project and associated costs were incurred;

indirect benefit is all other benefit attributable to the project that can be expressed in monetary terms;

intangible benefit is all the benefit that cannot be expressed in monetary terms.[1]

3. The " With and Without" Principle

In evaluating the benefits and costs of a project, two situations must be compared: the development of the economy with the project and the development that would occur without it.[2] The change in the path of the economic system because of the project involves certain costs and certain benefits, and it must be the objective of benefit-cost analysis to identify these changes. The

[1] These definitions follow the usage of the Subcommittee on Benefits and Costs, *Proposed Practices...*, especially p. 8, though we use "indirect" for the Subcommittee's "secondary," following recent agency nomenclature.

[2] For a detailed account of the "with and without" principle, see M. M. Regan and E. G. Weitzell, "Economic Evaluation of Soil and Water Conservation Measures and Programs," *Journal of Farm Economics* (November 1947), pp. 1275–1294.

"with and without" principle requires that the economic analysis contrast these two hypothetical situations.

These remarks may seem perfectly self-evident, but the principle forestalls application of the fallacious basis of comparison, "before and after." It prevents attributing to a project effects which are not caused by it, but which occur because of the passage of time or for other irrelevant reasons. The "with and without" principle is no more than a restatement of the fundamental analytic idea that any action be evaluated in terms of the difference it makes, that is, in terms of the effects which it specifically causes. It will be seen in subsequent chapters that it is a convenient and useful concept for organizing benefit-cost analyses.

4. *Two Concepts of Benefit: Market Value and Alternative Cost*

In our discussion in Chapter II, benefit was defined as being derived from individual tastes, as evidenced by the willingness to purchase at a price. In the case of marketable commodities for which the assumptions of the competitive model could be held to apply, benefit was equal to revenue, or to market value. For some purposes, including irrigation and flood control, benefit-cost analysis imputes an equivalent to market value. But for others, such as power and navigation, benefit is taken to be equal to alternative cost, the cost of providing comparable output by the cheapest alternative means. In the event that the alternative is not justified, benefit is again limited by willingness to pay.

Are these two concepts of benefit sufficiently similar to produce benefit-cost analyses which can be compared? In the range of situations in which the alternative cost concept is now applied, comparable results are produced. Power, municipal water supply, and navigation are the major purposes evaluated in this manner, and for each of them it can be assumed that the objective of the purpose will be met with and without the project. The benefit of the project is the stream of resources which is released from the alternative and which becomes available to produce other outputs. The value of these released resources will generally be equal to the reduction in the alternative cost, and the future stream of national income will be augmented by an equal amount. If we assume the alternative to be in private hands, the willingness to pay will never exceed the alternative cost, for the purchasers are free to turn to the alternative source of supply.

Where the alternative is not certain to be undertaken, its cost ceases to be a valid measure of benefit. Two types of situations can be envisaged in which the alternative might not be done. First, if its costs exceed its benefits, it is not justified. For example, if power capacity is expanded more than the demand at the going rate structure could absorb, the benefit is going to be less than the cost of alternative capacity, since the alternative would not be constructed; the extra power could only be marketed at a lower price and benefit would be circumscribed by the potential revenue. Second, the alternative, though justified, may not, in fact, be undertaken by any public or private body. For example, the benefit of a recreation facility need not be limited by the cost of an alternative facility if no one is going to develop the alternative. It can be seen from these cases that alternative-cost computations are not valid substitutes for estimates of market value unless there is a clearly defined objective which is going to be met in one way or another.

5. *Forms of Investment Criteria and Their Limitations*

In order to compare projects, the data on benefits and costs must be organized into some specific form which can serve as a criterion. The Subcommittee on Benefits and Costs mentions at least three possibilities: (1) compare the differences between benefits and costs, a criterion which is rejected because it obviously favors large projects over small; (2) compare the rates of return on investment, and (3) compare the ratio of benefits to costs, which is "the recommended basis for comparison of projects."[3] In order to determine the scale of development, separable segments of projects should be added as long as their benefits exceed their costs; this rule would produce project plans which maximize the difference between benefits and costs.[4]

At first glance it might appear that the ranking of projects according to their benefit-cost ratios would be the same as if they were ranked according to their rate of return; it would be expected that projects which yield more benefit per dollar of costs would

[3] Subcommittee on Benefits and Costs, *Proposed Practices...*, p. 14.
[4] Subcommittee on Benefits and Costs, *Proposed Practices...*, p. 37.

yield more return of benefits per dollar of investment; and if all projects had current costs in the same ratio to investment costs, the rankings would actually be the same. But a simple example will show that usually this will not be true.

Suppose that a chain of supermarkets has an investment in stores and fixtures of $10,000,000; suppose that its sales are $100,000,000 a year and that the operating profit on these sales is $5,000,000; and suppose that the interest rate is 3 percent. A benefit-cost ratio will show this investment to be rather poor. Annual benefits will be $100,000,000; annual costs will be $95,000,000 for current expenses including cost of goods sold, plus $300,000 annual interest charge on the investment. The ratio will be $100,000,000 to $95,300,000, or 1.05.

A calculation of crude rate of return will make this investment appear extremely profitable: an income of $5,000,000 a year is realized on an investment of $10,000,000 or a rate of 50 percent a year. This calculation, however, overlooks some of the most important costs of this kind of enterprise—the cost of carrying very large inventories. If we suppose that the stock of goods is turned over ten times a year, so that an average of $10,000,000 is tied up in inventories, and if the short-term rate of interest for this kind of loan is also 3 percent, then there is an additional cost of $300,000, so that the rate of return on fixed investment is 47 percent a year. The rate of return on all capital, fixed and circulating, is 25 percent, that is, an operating profit of $5,000,000 on a total investment of $20,000,000.

Suppose another investment opportunity is a hydroelectric project, which also requires an investment of $20,000,000, has annual revenues of $1,500,000, and annual expenses of $300,000. Suppose most of the operating expenses are weekly wages so that the amount of working capital needed is negligible. Let the interest rate again be 3 percent. Then the benefits will be $1,500,000 annually, the cost will be $300,000 operating expenses plus $600,000 interest on investment, and the ratio will be 1.60. The average rate of return will be 1,200,000/20,000,000, or 6 percent.

The hydroelectric project is preferable on the basis of a benefit-cost ratio, with a ratio of 1.60 versus 1.05, while the supermarket is much better on the basis of relative rates of return, with 25 percent versus 6 percent. Not only do we have two different and contradictory criteria, but neither one is really able to convey much about the relative merits of the two projects. The character of the two investments is so different that no numerical measure will suffice to evaluate them. A supermarket, in simplest terms, is a gamble that a certain location will do a sufficient volume of business at a markup which will cover all overhead, including store rent and labor. A criterion for supermarkets must express the expected volume and the likelihood that it will be adequate to cover costs. A hydroelectric project is a large fixed investment for a long period, with relatively assured demand and with small risks. The rate of return is a good indication of whether the project is a sound one.

Investment criteria must be adapted to the kind of projects among which the choice lies. In private industry, ordinarily the range of choice will encompass projects which will be similar. Even the largest multiproduct firms are usually based on some common element of technology, defined broadly. And in those rare cases where a firm's operations fall into very diverse groups, numerical criteria will be used primarily to choose among the opportunities within a group. The choice among groups, say among the divisions of a diversified company, will be done by committees of top management on the basis of discussion, weighing of intangibles, potential rates of return, long-run market position, and so on.

The benefit-cost ratio, like any investment criterion, is suited only for certain kinds of investment decisions. The economic nature of the costs must be reasonably uniform; there must be no extreme variations of capital intensity. The benefits must be uniform at least at the conceptual level and must have roughly equal degrees of uncertainty. And the life spans of the projects among which choices are to be made must be of the same order of magnitude.

6. *The Benefit-Cost Ratio Versus the Average Rate of Return*

The previous example showed that benefit-cost ratios yield a different ranking of projects than rates of return. Let us now examine the formal differences between the two criteria. To contrast the two criteria we need a minimum of definitions. Let

B = benefits received annually, as defined by agency practice; C = costs per year, including the charge on capital; K = fixed investment; O = operating, maintenance, and routine replacement costs incurred annually; i = interest rate; r = rate of return, and T = amortization period. With these definitions we can see that the present value of total cost is

$$\sum_{t=1}^{T} \frac{O}{(1+i)^t} + K,$$

the present value of total benefit is

$$\sum_{t=1}^{T} \frac{B}{(1+i)^t},$$

and the benefit-cost ratio is

$$\sum_{t=1}^{T} \frac{B}{(1+i)^t} \left[\sum_{t=1}^{T} \frac{O}{(1+i)^t} + K \right]^{-1}. \tag{1}$$

Putting the ratio on an annual basis by dividing numerator and denominator by

$$\sum_{t=1}^{T} \frac{1}{(1+i)^t},$$

we get

$$\frac{B}{C} = \frac{B}{O + K \left[\sum\limits_{t=1}^{T} \frac{1}{(1+i)^t} \right]^{-1}},$$

and letting

$$\left[\sum_{t=1}^{T} \frac{1}{(1+i)^t} \right]^{-1} = a_{iT},$$

we can write

$$\frac{B}{C} = \frac{B}{O + a_{iT}K}. \tag{2}$$

The annual capital charge per dollar of fixed investments is a_{iT}, representing both interest and amortization. Given i and T, numerical values for a_{iT} can be obtained from a table, "Annuity Whose Present Value is 1."[5] Equation (2) is the form in which the benefit-cost ratio is usually presented.

[5] This table is conveniently presented in *Mathematical Tables from Handbook of Physics and Chemistry* (Cleveland, Ohio: Chemical Rubber Publishing Company, 1948), pp. 306–313, and in other collections of mathematical tables.

The Criterion

The rate of return, r, is defined by the equation

$$K = \sum_{t=1}^{T} \frac{B-O}{(1+r)^t} \quad \text{or} \quad K = \frac{B-O}{a_{rT}}, \tag{3}$$

where

$$a_{rT} = \left[\sum_{t=1}^{T} \frac{1}{(1+r)^t} \right]^{-1},$$

and can be derived from the same table as a_{iT}. From (3) we get

$$B = a_{rT}K + O,$$

and so

$$\frac{B}{C} = \frac{a_{rT}K+O}{a_{iT}K+O}.$$

Solving for a_{rT} we get

$$a_{rT} = \frac{(B/C)(a_{iT}K+O)-O}{K} = \frac{B}{C}\left(a_{iT} + \frac{O}{K}\right) - \frac{O}{K}$$

or

$$a_{rT} = a_{iT}\left(\frac{B}{C}\right) + \frac{O}{K}\left(\frac{B}{C} - 1\right). \tag{4}$$

Given a_{rT}, r can readily be discovered by consulting the table. If there are no current costs, that is, if $O/K = 0$, the two criteria coincide. Then (4) becomes

$$a_{rT} = a_{iT}\left(\frac{B}{C}\right), \tag{5}$$

and whatever the interest rate, a higher benefit-cost ratio will result in a higher value for a_{rT} and hence for r. If the benefit-cost ratio is equal to 1, the two criteria will again correspond as the second term in (4) drops out of the equation.

The degree to which the use of benefit-cost ratios reshuffles the rankings of projects as compared to the rankings of rate of return depends on the range of values which O/K assumes for different projects. Projects of a similar type such as different hydroelectric projects, different irrigations projects, or different watershed projects, will have very similar values for O/K. But there will be much larger differences when we compare projects of different purposes. Without systematic search for the most extreme values, we find examples such as: an upstream flood

Table 2. Comparison of two investment criteria

Name of project	Type	O/K	B/C	r (percent)	Rank based on B/C	r
Rice Creek, Fla.*	River navigation	0.017	3.58	15.3	1	4
Bellhaven Harbor, N.C.*	Harbor improvement	0.034	2.42	12.4	2	5
Brazos River watershed*	Watershed improvement and flood control	0.088	2.42	19.7	2	3
Dauphin Island Bay, Fla.*	Harbor improvement	0.111	2.34	22.0	4	2
Collbran Project, Colorado*	Multipurposes especially irrigation and power	0.009	2.34	7.4	4	7
Sakonnet Harbor, R.I.*	Harbor improvement	0.012	2.12	7.8	6	6
Green River watershed, Ky. and Tenn.†	River and harbor improvement	0.075	1.71	22.9	7	1
Red River, Ark.‡	Flood control	0.014	1.23	5.5	8	8
Hackensack River, N.J.*	River and harbor improvement	0.016	1.19	5.1	9	9

* Basic data for these projects, including annual benefits, investment costs, current costs, and the benefit-cost ratio, are from case studies from Committee on Public Works, *Report of the Subcommittee to Study Civil Works*, 82 Congress, 1 sess., House Committee Print 24, *Economic Evaluation of Federal Water Resources Development Projects*, pp. 20–41.

† *Report on Green River Watershed*, House Doc. 568, App. D, table D-19 and D-27.

‡ *Report on Red River*, House Doc. 489, 83 Cong., 2 sess.

control project for the Green River Watershed has an O/K value of \$6,532,820/86,601,169 or 0.0754,[6] while a multi-purpose project of the Bureau of Reclamation has an O/K value of 0.009.

To show the range of values of O/K and to indicate the divergence between the two criteria, Table 2 gives values for O/K,

[6] *Report on Green River Watershed, Kentucky and Tennessee*, House Doc. 261, 82 Cong. 1 sess., App. D., table D–19, p. 121.

for *B/C*, and for the rate of return for a number of projects. The projects have also been ranked by both criteria.

It is quite obvious that the rankings differ markedly. The Green River Watershed project, which ranks highest judged by its rate of return, ranks seventh of the eight projects on a benefit-cost basis, while the Rice Creek project, with a benefit-cost ratio much higher than any other, only ranks fourth on its rate of return. Four projects with benefit-cost ratios of 2.34 and 2.42 have rates of return ranging from 7.6 percent to 22.0 percent.

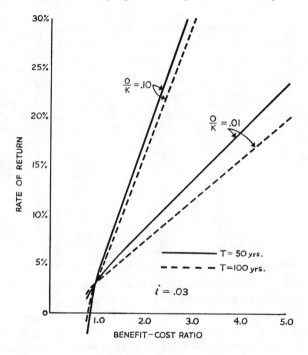

Figure 3

In order to permit easy comparison of the two criteria for a project, Table 3 has been calculated and charted. Each line represents a series of benefit-cost ratios and shows the corresponding rates of return, given a specific value for *O/K*.

It can be seen from Table 3 that the benefit-cost ratio is particularly favorable to projects with low values of *O/K*, that is, where most of the cost is an initial investment, and the year-by-year expenses are minimal. The irrigation and hydroelectric power project had the lowest O/K value; most of the river and harbor projects were low with one exception, but the two watershed improvement projects were very high. These results will generally be repeated for other projects, and may help to explain why the Bureau of Reclamation and the Corps of Engineers are quite enthusiastic about benefit-cost ratios, while the Department of Agriculture has been very reluctant to have its projects judged

Table 3. Benefit-cost ratios and rates of return for selected capital intensities and periods of analysis

Benefit-cost ratio	Rates of return			
	Period of 50 years		Period of 100 years	
	$O/K=0.01$	$O/K=0.10$	$O/K=0.01$	$O/K=0.10$
0.8	0.015	−0.02	0.020	−0.01
1.0	0.030	0.030	0.030	0.030
1.2	0.044	0.064	0.039	0.058
1.4	0.054	0.092	0.047	0.088
1.6	0.065	0.121	0.057	0.111
1.8	0.076	0.149	0.065	0.137
2.0	0.086	0.177	0.073	0.163
2.5	0.111	0.247	0.094	0.229
3.0	0.136	0.317	0.115	0.295
4.0	0.185	0.456	0.157	0.427
5.0	0.234	0.594	0.198	0.558

in that way.[7] Calculations of rates of return would make their projects appear in a much more favorable light.

But the rate of return would also be fallacious for agricultural projects, since the decision whether or not to make a certain commitment of resources for this kind of program is not primarily a decision about a fixed investment, but is a commitment for a large flow of resources, consisting of certain initial installations, large annual expenses for conservation payments, educational programs, and technical assistance, plus large private costs of both an investment and an operating kind. It is analogous to the supermarket in our earlier example.

[7] See A. Maass, "Protecting Nature's Reservoir," C. J. Friedrich and J. K. Galbraith, eds., *Public Policy* (1954), III, 71–106.

The Criterion

From a more abstract point of view, let us see under what circumstances each of the criteria leads to an optimal result. If all resources including capital are available in unlimited amount, though at increasing cost, optimal investment decisions would call for all projects which yield a rate of return greater than the interest rate, with the marginal project having a rate of return just equal to the interest rate. Use of benefit-cost ratios under these circumstances would require that all projects with ratios greater than 1.0 be done. A project which is marginal under the criterion of the rate of return will also be marginal under the benefit-cost ratio, since the two correspond when the benefit-cost ratio is unity. Any project with a rate of return less than the interest rate will have a lower benefit-cost ratio; it is only the ranking of projects above or below the margin that is affected when there is no rationed factor.

If capital is rationed but all other resources are available in sufficient quantity at their market prices, then the selection of those projects which have the highest rate of return on capital will lead to the production of the greatest future economic value stream. Similarly, if any one factor of production is rationed while all others are available, the optimum result is obtained if the highest rate of return is obtained on that factor. If those projects are done which have the highest benefit-cost ratios, then the implicit assumption is that it is the resource bundle "cost" which is rationed.

What does the bundle "cost" contain? In real terms, it is the set of present and future resources which go into the program of the natural resources field, that is, into all those projects that are subjected to benefit-cost analysis. These resources will not be a cross section of national product, but will contain a myriad group of factors with particularly significant representation of construction materials, machinery, labor, and electrical equipment. In ordinary times there is no particular shortage of these commodities, so they certainly cannot be considered to be rationed. And in times of emergency, when they are truly in short supply, the benefit-cost ratio could not serve as a rationing device because it does not discriminate finely enough among commodities and does not discriminate at all among the different periods in which they will be used.

But in money terms, "cost" has a very specific meaning here. The acceptance of a project means that the government is committed to incur a set of expenses over a fairly long period of time. These expenses are paid out of taxation, out of borrowing, and to a very small extent out of the revenue of the project.[8] At any one time, there are fairly clearly defined, politically determined limits to the amount of money which the government can expend on all its purposes, and these limits will depend on the acceptable levels of taxation, on the needs of debt management, monetary policy, and fiscal policy, and on the degree of urgency of the times. With the total expenditure roughly determined, the government must then allocate these funds to the various fields of activity, such as national defense, social welfare, and natural resources. Through evaluation of political sentiment and through the budgeting process, the total is divided among the fields, and the limits of expenditure on natural resources are set. Thus it is "expenditure" of federal money which is the rationed element. The tightness of this ration varies from time to time, but it is certain that it will never disappear altogether. If the rationing only applied to the current year, national welfare would be maximized if a criterion were used which maximizes the return on expenditure of the current year. But since, in fact, the rationing is perpetual, and since fluctuations of its severity cannot be foreseen, it is not unreasonable to assume that the rationing of federal money will remain equally tight over time. Benefit-cost ratios are based on this assumption; if, in each year, those projects are started which have the highest benefit-cost ratios, and if the marginal increment of each project has a benefit-cost ratio equal to the cutoff ratio of the program in the period, then the total return on federal expenditure will be maximized. Federal expenditure is considered the rationed commodity, and given this condition the present value of the future income stream that can be created is maximized.

It can thus be seen that the choice of expenditure criterion is

---

[8] While revenues constitute a substantial percentage of cost on some projects, typically they are not applied to the water-resource budget but are considered general Treasury revenues. For a different treatment of the problem of the choice of constraint, see the study by R. N. McKean, *Cost-Benefit Analysis and Efficiency in Government*, The RAND Corporation, RM–1445–RC (to be published), where a constraint on capital is viewed more sympathetically.

determined by the choice of the budgetary constraint which is assumed to limit the program. In the case of the typical private enterprise, it is capital which plays this role, and usually fixed capital, since funds for working capital can usually be obtained fairly readily at moderate cost. With capital limiting activity and growth, it must be allocated optimally, which can be accomplished by capital budgeting and by the use of a rate-of-return criterion.[9]

In the case of water-resource agencies, no one constraint really can be considered to apply with perfect precision; and yet some constraint must be applied, for otherwise projects will be developed to excessive scale, at the expense of other projects of economic quality greater than the worst segments of projects being built. The assumption employed in this study, that it is total federal expenditure which is the budget constraint, is believed to be the most reasonable that can be made. But here again American budgetary practice is peculiar; our unitary budget assigns project revenues to the general funds of the Treasury, and they have no effect on the available budget for the programs. Thus there is a strong argument in favor of ignoring the future revenues in defining the constraint.

From a broader point of view, the revenues that are produced do represent future additions to the fiscal resources of the federal government in the future. Even if the funds do not automatically flow back into the water-resource field, they will fall within some budget ration, and if we make the rather strong assumption that the value of marginal federal expenditure in all fields is the same and is equal to the cost of marginal taxes, it would not matter

---

[9] These statements are gross over-simplifications on at least two scores: first, it is not at all clear that it is lack of capital which limits the rate of growth of the modern corporation, in terms of both sales and profits. Initiative of management, the availability of managerial personnel, and the capacity of the organization to manage a limited number of new activities are, in many cases, the real bottlenecks to expansion. Where this is so, the expenditure criteria should show the return on these scarce factors rather than to capital. Second, even if capital is the limiting factor, the rate of return that can be earned by funds in the company must stay constant; otherwise the criterion must reflect differing opportunities for reinvestment at different points of time. The latter point has been explored in detail by J. Hirshleifer in "An Isoquant Approach to Investment Decisions," the RAND Corporation, P–1158, 23 Aug., 1957.

whether the funds go into the water-resource budget or into some other constraint. On this reasoning, the constraint should be applied to a concept of present value of net federal outlay. This modification would favor projects with high reimbursability.

While project revenues can be defended as modifying the constraint, the reasoning does not carry over to the taxes that are stimulated by the project through its repercussion effects. All economic activity stimulates taxes to some extent; to credit projects with contributing to the future tax base and hence to the future pool of budget money, it would need to be shown that projects are likely to generate particularly large amounts of taxes. Given the income distribution of project benefits, and given particularly the agricultural nature of the benefits in many cases, the reverse is much more likely to be true. Thus taxes which are generated should best be ignored.

There may be instances where the crucial rationing is the supply of capital to the associated private enterprises, such as the farms in the region. Under those circumstances, a better result may be achieved by either alleviating the private rationing or by maximizing the return on the private capital.[10]

On the basis of all those considerations, the total federal cost seems to me the most appropriate form of the constraint for those types of decisions for which a constraint is a proper part of the analysis, and hence the benefit-cost ratio the preferable criterion.

---

[10] In the case of navigation and flood control, the associated investments are modest and can hardly be considered subject to rationing—though political opposition may block local participation. Power projects under recent partnership arrangements require large associated investments, but scarcity of private capital has not been a significant reason for the slow progress of the projects of this kind.

Capital scarcity is a real problem for the farmers on irrigation projects (see Chapter VII, Section 8). But it would be incorrect to assume that there is some private stock of capital which limits development of the irrigation program and which would supersede federal funds as the dominant constraint. The quantities of private capital that are needed are large for one farmer, but are insignificant in relation to total private investment. It is the riskiness and the slow payoff which limit the availability of private funds. Solution of this problem can be considered one of the necessary preconditions to the realization of the benefits in the benefit-cost ratio.

It should be added that maximization of the benefit-cost ratio is not the best criterion, of course, but rather the insistence that the benefit-cost ratio exceed a certain level. See Section 8 below.

It would be defensible, however, to treat reimbursable costs as falling outside the constraint, treating them as negative benefits. There is considerable variation among agencies in the definition of cost in the benefit-cost ratio, and hence in the constraint which is implicitly assumed. All agencies include the entire federal cost on the cost side, but there are divergences in the treatment of private costs, which in some instances are considered among costs, in others as negative benefits.

The Bureau of Reclamation comes closest to being consistent with our criterion.[11] It places all project costs on the cost side of the ledger, and all associated costs which are incurred on the project's farms on the benefit side. Since the project costs are entirely federal and the associated costs private, their separation places the costs which fall under the federal budget constraint in the denominator of the ratio. The Corps of Engineers also places all project costs on the cost side and the associated costs on the benefit side, but the local contributions of cash, land, and easements are part of project costs, and, from our point of view, are therefore on the wrong side of the ledger. Since these costs are rarely as much as 20 percent of all project costs, and are usually much less, the error is relatively small. The practice understates their ratios, since subtraction of a negative constant from the numerator plus its addition to the denominator of a ratio greater than one always acts to reduce the result. Thus if benefits are 12, federal costs 7, and private costs 2, the benefit-cost ratio under our standards would be 10/7, or 1.43, while under the Engineer's standard it would be 12/9, or 1.33. The Department of Agriculture departs furthest from our standard. It includes all private costs on the cost side, and since these costs are large, sometimes twice as large as federal cost, their ratios are significantly lower than they would be by our standards.

7. *B/C or B–C?*

The procedure recommended by the Subcommittee on Benefits and Costs calls for the determination of the scale of a project on the basis of maximizing the difference between benefits and costs, which means, in practical terms, that all separable segments of a project be added to the project plan as long as the extra benefits

---

[11] Subcommittee on Benefits and Costs, *Proposed Practices...*, p. 68.

exceed the extra cost.[12]   The relative economic ranking of projects is to be based on the benefit-cost ratio.

These two steps will sometimes be at odds with each other. If a project plan is drawn up to include all separable segments for which benefits exceed costs, then the resultant ratio will be less than the maximum which could be derived if only the best segments were done.   Obviously the ratio is highest if only the best segment is included; as segments with lower ratios are added, the average ratio for the entire project is lowered step by step. To give a simple example, if a project consists of two equally large segments which can be done separately, and if the benefit-cost ratio of part *A* is 2.0 while that of part *B* is 1.2, the ratio for a project consisting of *A* and *B* will be only 1.6.   If the actual conditions of budgeting only permit projects with ratios above 1.7, the entire project will be rejected.

When will the *B–C* criterion be applicable?   It will lead to an optimal result if all prices reflect real costs, including the interest rate used in the computations, *and if all projects for which B exceeds C are actually constructed.*   If there is always a supply of project opportunities with benefit-cost ratios well above 1.0, so that the marginal return on expenditures at any time can be well above 1, the margin in any one project should not be pushed to unity.   It might be that in some years the total funds available are such that they just suffice to do all the separable segments of all the projects to be built which yield benefits at a rate greater than 1.6 per dollar of cost.   Ideally, from the economic point of view, at such a time each project should be planned in such a way that only those separable segments will be included which have a benefit-cost ratio in excess of 1.6.

Figure 4 illustrates this point for the case where expenditure on projects can be varied continuously.   Suppose that choice is confined to projects *A* and *B* and that budget conditions prevent complete development of the potential of both projects.   If project *A* is developed to point *a*, where the benefit of the marginal expenditure dollar is just equal to 1.0, project *B* cannot be developed because of the budgetary constraint.   The actual opportunity cost of marginal expenditures on *A* is not measured by the expenditure itself but by the opportunity which is foregone

[12] *Proposed Practices...*, pp. 12–13.

on project B; the total difference between benefit and cost can be increased by shifting funds from A to B. This can be seen from the gain in the shaded area for B which exceeds the loss suffered on project A. At the optimum the following condition must hold: *the benefit produced by the marginal dollar of expenditure must be the same on all projects (and on all purposes).* In our diagram this is at points c and d, given a specific budgetary constraint.

It has been argued that it would be wrong to use a limit well above 1.0 because the opportunity for doing the additional segments later may be lost forever. Often the scale of developing

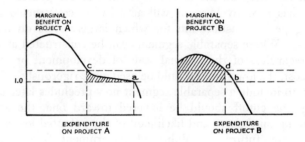

Figure 4

a project cannot be altered once the main installations have been built, so that the original choice of scale will fix the scope of the project forever, thereby precluding development of a potential which might be well worth realizing after some years of population growth and economic expansion, and after better projects elsewhere have been completed.

This argument has only limited validity. As far as the future potential of the project is concerned, reasonable forecasts of the future demands of the project's outputs would make allowances for the higher benefits in later years and would incorporate future values in the benefit estimate. Also, it can safely be presumed that government funds will not become so freely available in the next decades that such marginal segments of projects can be done except at the sacrifice of more worth while projects. As for the lost opportunities of the very remote future, they need not be weighed heavily since their loss is probably more than offset by the acceleration in the undertaking of the alternative projects.

But there is enough in the argument to preclude a mechanical application of a fixed cutoff point for marginal separable segments, a cutoff point which would presumably be roughly equal to the benefit-cost ratio of the poorest project which is actually constructed in the period. As a practical matter the following policy appears most reasonable:

1. On the basis of recent experience with and examination of the shelf of potential projects, each agency (or ideally the Bureau of the Budget) should recommend to its district offices the cutoff point of benefit-cost ratios of separable segments. The cutoff should be based on the benefit-cost ratio of the poorest project which has recently been or will actually be constructed in the coming period, justification for which largely rests on its economics. Where separable segments can be constructed at a later time regardless of the original scale of development or at little extra cost, the lower limit should be used quite rigorously. Where failure to include a separable segment now precludes later undertaking, the cutoff should be lowered toward one, the amount depending on the size and likelihood of the potential loss and the outlook for future availability of government funds for the resources field. For example, if the agency cutoff is at 1.8, but if a separable segment which can only be built as part of the project has a ratio of 1.1, with the potential benefits of a rather problematical nature and with a tight budget outlook for resource projects, the separable segment should be excluded. If another separable segment has a well-predicated ratio of 1.4 and if there is an easing of the budget situation in prospect, it might be well to include it in the project plan. The second of the two segments we have considered would stand a good chance of being included on its own merit in the near future if it could be done independently after the rest of the project has been built; the chances of the first segment being accepted on its own merit alone are rather small.

2. With the scale of development so determined, the benefit-cost ratios of different projects can be used to rank the economic worth of different projects. If the economic evaluation were the only criterion, the projects with the highest ratios should be chosen.

3. Serious consideration should be given to designing construction plans in a more flexible manner, which would permit partial development now without surrendering the remaining potential permanently. In some instances, "stage construction" does not increase costs inordinately and may provide an economical escape from the dilemma of overbuilding a few projects now or of surrendering good future opportunities.

It must be reiterated in this connection that, although our discussion has been carried on as if the benefit-cost analysis were the only criterion for projects, the other criteria may result in different rankings and may call for a different set of projects. The intangible analysis may lead to the exclusion of justified separable segments or it may lead to the inclusion of segments which have benefit-cost ratios of much less than unity. Similarly, the analysis of local financial participation may shed more light on the relative merits of projects. It certainly cannot be assumed that a procedure, such as the one outlined above, will ever be allowed to hold complete sway.

Yet, if the benefit-cost analysis is to be of assistance in determining the relative economic worth of projects, it must be done as if it were the determining criterion. If two criteria collide, and intangible or other considerations lead to the exclusion or inclusion of segments in a project plan contrary to the benefit-cost analysis, then the benefit-cost ratio must be based on the set of segments which are actually proposed. Only in this way will all the reviewing groups in the agencies, in the Budget Bureau, and in Congress be able to weigh the economics of a proposal.

8. *The Relevance of Alternative Cost and the Form of the Constraint*

A problem which is closely tied to the choice of constraint is the definition of benefit in terms of alternative cost. Earlier, it was stressed that the alternative must be more than hypothetical, but there are further limitations on its relevance. After all, every project has an alternative which is almost identical but costs $1 more, and so its benefit would always be limited to its cost plus a dollar. On the other hand, where some purpose would be accomplished in some other way in the absence of the project, the benefit presumably is limited by the cost of some alternatives. But where is the line to be drawn?

Our preceding discussion about constraints has implicit in it the solution to this question. We seek to maximize the change in national economic welfare that can be accomplished with a limited budget constraint, and in our analysis we assume that if the incentive to undertake some task is present, private funds can be raised at some borrowing cost. Economic welfare, in the present context, is defined as the difference between the money value of output and the costs incurred to produce it, that is, the change in real national income. The limited-budget money must be put into those uses where it increases economic welfare most. If a project has a private (or local) alternative, then the change in economic welfare attributable to federal development is equal only to the cost of the alternative, not to the money value of output. Where there is no alternative to federal development, benefit is measured by the value of output, of course.

What about the cost of alternative federal plans of development; is the benefit of a dam limited by the cost of the federal dikes it makes unnecessary? Alternative federal costs are not a limit to benefit, for if the constraint is effective, the value of the federal funds will be greater than the dollar figure. Thus the alternative cost which is foregone exceeds the dollar figure. An alternative federal development does not release the federal funds for some other undertaking; the drain on the pool of money within the constraint remains. Clearly economic efficiency requires that the least-cost method of federal development be selected; but the second best federal plan bears no relation to benefits. Thus the rule is as follows: alternative cost limits benefit if the alternative cost is met out of funds that lie outside the constraint. Following this rule assures that the change in economic welfare (or real national income) is maximized for the given budget constraint.

TECHNICAL NOTES TO CHAPTERS II AND III

The following notes state in mathematical form the models which are implicit to our analysis of the preceding two chapters.

I

We shall state briefly the derivation of benefit-cost analysis from the classical theory of welfare economics.

Assume that there are n individuals composing our economy. An individual i has preferences which can be described by a utility surface

$$U_i = U_i(x_{i1}, ..., x_{im}) \tag{1}$$

where x_{ij} is a quantity of the economic good j enjoyed by i, of a product if it has a positive sign, of a factor if it is negative. If i has an income y_i he will maximize his economic welfare by maximizing

$$\Phi = U_i(x_{i1}, ..., x_{im}) - \lambda_i(p_1 x_{i1} + \cdots + p_m x_{im} - y_i), \tag{2}$$

where p_j is the price of j ($j = 1, ..., m$).

If the utility surface is convex, the maximum conditions are

$$\lambda_i = \frac{\partial U_i}{\partial x_{i1}} \cdot \frac{1}{p_1} = \cdots = \frac{\partial U_i}{\partial x_{im}} \cdot \frac{1}{p_m}; \tag{3}$$

λ_i is the marginal utility of income and is assumed to be constant in the relevant range.

Suppose i receives an increment of income Δy_i which he uses to purchase—or to cease to supply—$\Delta x_{i1}, ..., \Delta x_{im}$. His change in welfare will be*

$$\Delta U_i = \frac{\partial U_i}{\partial x_{i1}} \Delta x_{i1} + \cdots + \frac{\partial U_i}{\partial x_{im}} \Delta x_{im}. \tag{4}$$

But since

$$\lambda_i = \frac{\partial U_i}{\partial x_{ij}} \cdot \frac{1}{p_j},$$

we can write

$$\Delta U_i = \lambda_i p_1 \Delta X_{i1} + \cdots + \lambda_i p_m \Delta x_{im},$$

or

$$\Delta U_i = \lambda_i \sum_{j=1}^{m} p_j \Delta x_{ij}, \tag{5}$$

which only says that the change in the welfare of i is equal to his marginal utility of income times the change in his income.

We define a change in the social welfare to be

$$\Delta W = \sum_{i=1}^{n} \Delta U_i,$$

* The higher-order terms of the Taylor expansion are zero because the $\partial U_i / \partial x_{ij}$ are constant. There are some applications in which a constant marginal utility of income is not a reasonable assumption. See below, Chapter IV, Section 9.

so

$$\Delta W = \sum_{i=1}^{n} \sum_{j=1}^{m} \lambda_i p_j \Delta x_{ij}. \tag{6}$$

To abstract from welfare effects of changes in the income distribution we assume that the marginal utility of income is the same for all individuals, or

$$\lambda_1 = \cdots = \lambda_i = \cdots = \lambda_n = \lambda. \tag{7}$$

Also let

$$\sum_{i=1}^{n} \Delta x_{ij} = \Delta X_j. \tag{8}$$

Then

$$\Delta W = \lambda \sum_{j=1}^{m} p_j \Delta X_j. \tag{9}$$

Since the utility function is uniquely determined only up to a monotonic transformation, and since our social welfare function is of the same degree of arbitrariness, we can write

$$\Delta W = \sum_{j=1}^{m} p_j \Delta X_j. \tag{10}$$

If a change in economic welfare involves no change in the amount of factors supplied by individuals, or if national income is defined to include the negative values of factor services, ΔW is equal to the change in national income.

II

A public project transforms economic goods, converting factors into products. Let $X_1, \ldots, X_k$ be quantities of products and $X_l, \ldots, X_m$ be quantities of factors. Let the production function of the project be represented by

$$K(X_1, \ldots, X_k, X_l, \ldots, X_m) = 0. \tag{11}$$

The increase in social welfare is maximized by maximizing

$$\Psi = \sum_{j=1}^{m} p_j \Delta X_j - \mu K(X_1, \ldots, X_k, X_l, \ldots, X_m). \tag{12}$$

72

If the second-order conditions are met, the maximum conditions are

$$p_j - \mu \frac{\partial K}{\partial X_j} = 0. \qquad (j = 1,..., k, l,..., m) \quad (13)$$

This implies the usual profit maximizing conditions of firms in perfect competition:

$$\frac{p_j}{p_r} = \frac{\partial X_r}{\partial X_j}. \qquad (14)$$

III

Introducing the concepts of benefits and costs, let us define the total benefit of a project to be

$$B = p_1 \Delta X_1 + \cdots + p_k \Delta X_k \qquad (15)$$

and total cost to be

$$p_l \Delta X_l + \cdots + p_m \Delta X_m. \qquad (16)$$

Then (10) can be rewritten:

$$\Delta W = B - C \qquad (10a)$$

and (12) can be rewritten:

$$\Psi = B - C - \mu K(X_1,..., X_k, X_l,..., X_m). \qquad (12a)$$

The maximum condition (13) becomes

$$\frac{\partial B}{\partial X_j} - \mu \frac{\partial K}{\partial X_j} = 0 \qquad (j = 1,..., k) \quad (13a)$$

and

$$\frac{\partial C}{\partial X_r} - \mu \frac{\partial K}{\partial X_r} = 0, \qquad (r = l,..., m)$$

which imply

$$\frac{\partial B}{\partial X_j} \frac{\partial X_j}{\partial K} = \frac{\partial C}{\partial X_r} \frac{\partial X_r}{\partial K} \quad \text{or} \quad \frac{\partial B}{\partial C} = 1. \qquad (14a)$$

In words, this condition means that marginal benefits should equal marginal cost, or that the benefit-cost ratio for marginal projects and for marginal project segments should be equal to one.

73

IV

So far we have assumed that the outputs $X_1,..., X_k$ are marketable, that their prices have been established in perfect markets, and that individuals have been able to adjust to the prices. But some of the outputs are not marketable; they are collective goods. Formally, this means that if the good G is a collective good, it will appear in the utility function as in (1), but the individual will not be free to allocate his expenditures in accordance with the maximum conditions (3). We have no assurance, therefore, that the subsequent analysis holds.

P. A. Samuelson has shown that there is no general solution to this problem, and that no voting or interviewing scheme can be devised which will elicit truthful responses about the marginal utility of a collective good.*

But for collective goods like flood control and navigation, the value to individuals can be discovered from actual expenditures on alternative methods of achieving the same objective, such as alternative transportation charges that are actually paid and post-flood repair costs. If the price paid for an amount Δx_{ia} of the alternative by individual i is p_a, then

$$\Delta y_i = p_a \Delta x_{ia}, \tag{17}$$

that is, the collective good releases income equal to Δy_i, which can be spent by i on other goods. The change in the welfare of i is $\Delta y_i \lambda_i$, or $\lambda_i p_a \Delta x_{ia}$.

The change in social welfare due to G is

$$\Delta W^G = \sum_{i=1}^{n} \lambda_i p_a \Delta x_{ia} = \lambda \sum_{i=1}^{n} p_a \Delta x_{ia}. \tag{18}$$

If a project has some marketable outputs and one which is nonmarketable, the change in social welfare can be written

$$\Delta W = \sum_{j=1}^{m} p_j \Delta X_j + \sum_{i=1}^{n} p_a \Delta x_{ia} \tag{10a}$$

and its benefit can be written

$$B = \sum_{j=1}^{k} p_j \Delta X_j + \sum_{i=1}^{n} p_a \Delta x_{ia}. \tag{15a}$$

The rest of the analysis remains unchanged.

* P. A. Samuelson, "The Pure Theory of Public Expenditures," *Review of Economics and Statistics* (November 1954), pp. 387–389.

V

We now introduce a budgetary constraint into the analysis. Let us suppose that we seek to maximize the increase in economic welfare attributable to a water-resource program, the limits of which are imposed by a constraint on the total amount of federal expenditure for this field.

We express the production relations of each project through a benefit function

$$B_l = B_l(C_{lg}, C_{lh}), \qquad (l=1, ..., n) \qquad (19)$$

where B_l is the total benefit of project l, C_{lg} is the federal cost of the project, and C_{lh} is its associated cost. The budgetary constraint is expressed by

$$\sum_{l=1}^{n} C_{lg} \leqslant D, \qquad (20)$$

where D is the total amount of federal money available. To maximize the increase in welfare, we maximize the Lagrangean expression

$$\Omega = \sum_{l=1}^{n} B_l(C_{lg}, C_{lh}) - \sum_{l=1}^{n} C_{lg} - \sum_{l=1}^{n} C_{lh} - v\left(\sum_{l=1}^{n} C_{lg} - D\right). \qquad (21)$$

The first-order maximum conditions are

$$\frac{\partial B_l}{\partial C_{lg}} = 1 + v$$

and

$$\frac{\partial B_l}{\partial C_{lh}} = 1.$$

(22

Thus the benefit of the marginal expenditure of federal funds must exceed 1 by a factor which depends on the tightness of the budgetary constraint while the benefit of the marginal expenditure of associated cost should be equal to 1. This assumes that the constraint is effective; if not, v must be set equal to zero.

VI

In the previous section we assumed that the budgetary constraint applied to all of the federal cost. Where part of the costs is reimbursable and the revenues add to funds available to the water-resource budget, the budgetary constraint takes a different form. If we assume that the tightness of the budgetary situation remains unchanged and that revenues can be considered an offset to expenditures, the constraint takes the form

$$\sum_{l=1}^{n} (1 - \alpha_l) C_{lg} \leqslant D, \tag{23}$$

where α_l is the fraction of federal cost which is reimbursable on project l. The maximum conditions become

$$\frac{\partial B_l}{\partial C_{lg}} = 1 + v(1 - \alpha_l)$$

and $\tag{24}$

$$\frac{\partial B_l}{\partial C_{lh}} = 1.$$

It can be seen that the extent to which the benefit of marginal federal expenditure must exceed 1 depends not only on the tightness of the budgetary constraint but also on the fraction of the cost which is to be reimbursable. If all the federal cost on a project were reimbursable, the benefit of a marginal expenditure should be 1.0. This model assumes that the revenues to be collected will help alleviate the budgetary situation, that is, that they will become available for further expenditures in the water-resource field. If this is not the case, the result of the previous section will apply even where costs are reimbursable. It has been contended in Chapter III that the models in the preceding and in the present section are most appropriate for benefit-cost analysis.

VII

The preceding sections have not treated the timing of the benefits and costs explicitly. All values must be discounted at the interest rate of the analysis, and then all the above reasoning applies without change.* To illustrate this aspect, we define for each project k, a benefit function

$$B_{kt} = B_{kt}(x_k),$$

---

* This section has benefitted from comments of R. Dorfman, who suggested the use of a scale variable. This formulation assumes that the different categories of costs must be incurred in fixed proportions.

where x_k is a measure of the scale of the project, either physical or perhaps total expenditure, and the four cost functions

$$O_{kgt} = O_{kgt}(x_k); \qquad O_{kht} = O_{kht}(x_k);$$
$$K_{kg} = K_{kg}(x_k); \qquad K_{kh} = K_{kh}(x_k),$$

where O_{kgt} is the federal operation and maintenance cost for project k in period t, O_{kht} is the associated operating and maintenance cost, K_{kg} is the federal capital cost, and K_{kh} the associated capital cost. For simplicity we assume that all capital cost is incurred in the first period or, alternatively, that K includes interest during construction. We seek to maximize the increase in economic welfare

$$\Delta W = \sum_{k=1}^{r} \sum_{t=1}^{T_k} \frac{B_{kt}(x_k)}{(1+i)^t} - \sum_{k=1}^{r} \sum_{t=1}^{T_k} \frac{O_{kgt}(x_k)}{(1+i)^t} - \sum_{k=1}^{r} \sum_{t=1}^{T_k} \frac{O_{kht}(x_k)}{(1+i)^t}$$
$$- \sum_{k=1}^{r} K_{kg}(x_k) - \sum_{k=1}^{r} K_{kh}(x_k),$$

subject to the budget constraint

$$\sum_{k=1}^{r} \sum_{t=1}^{T_k} \frac{O_{kgt}(x_k)}{(1+i)^t} + \sum_{k=1}^{r} K_{kg}(x_k) \leqslant D,$$

where i is the interest rate and T_k the economic life of the project. Thus we maximize the Lagrangean expression

$$\Phi = \Delta W - v \left[\sum_{k=1}^{r} \sum_{t=1}^{T_k} \frac{O_{kgt}(x_k)}{(1+i)^t} + \sum_{k=1}^{r} K_{kg}(x_k) - D \right],$$

which has the first-order conditions

$$\sum_{t=1}^{T_k} \frac{dB_{kt}}{dx_k} \cdot \frac{1}{(1+i)^t} - \sum_{t=1}^{T_k} \frac{dO_{kgt}}{dx_k} \cdot \frac{1}{(1+i)^t} - \sum_{t=1}^{T_k} \frac{dO_{kht}}{dx_k} \cdot \frac{1}{(1+i)^t} - \frac{dK_{kg}}{dx_k} - \frac{dK_{kh}}{dx_k}$$
$$- v \sum_{t=1}^{T_k} \frac{dO_{kgt}}{dx_k} \cdot \frac{1}{(1+i)^t} - v \frac{dK_{kg}}{dx_k} = 0. \qquad (k = 1, ..., r)$$

This can be written

$$\sum_{t=1}^{T_k} \frac{dB_{kt}}{dx_k} \cdot \frac{1}{(1+i)^t} - (1+v) \left[\sum_{t=1}^{T_k} \frac{dO_{kgt}}{dx_k} \cdot \frac{1}{(1+i)^t} + \frac{dK_{kg}}{dx_k} \right]$$
$$- \sum_{t=1}^{T_k} \frac{dO_{kht}}{dx_k} \cdot \frac{1}{(1+i)^t} - \frac{dK_{kh}}{dx_k} = 0,$$

and therefore the condition can be expressed as

$$\frac{\sum_{t=1}^{T_k} [(dB_{kt}/dx_k)(1+i)^{-t}] - \sum_{t=1}^{T_k} [(dO_{kht}/dx_k)(1+i)^{-t}] - dK_{kh}/dx_k}{\sum_{t=1}^{T_k} [(dO_{kgt}/dx_k)(1+i)^{-t}] + dK_{kg}/dx_k} = 1+v.$$

This is the benefit-cost criterion advanced in section V above. It will be noticed that it does not assume equal economic lives for projects or constant annual benefits or costs, the resulting criterion being a ratio of values of present worth.

If O_{kgt} and O_{kht} remain constant over time, we can factor these terms outside the summation signs. Dividing numerator and denominator by $\left[\sum_{t=1}^{T_k} (1+i)^{-t} \right]^{-1}$ and calling this term a_{iT_k}, we can write

$$\frac{(dB_{kt}/dx_k) - (dO_{kht}/dx_k) - a_{iT_k}(dK_{kht}/dx_k)}{(dO_{kgt}/dx_k) + a_{iT_k}(dK_{kg}/dx_k)} = 1+v,$$

which is the benefit-cost criterion expressed in terms of annual values and using the interest and amortization factor for annual capital charges.

If there are no associated costs, or if they are considered negative benefits, this reduces to

$$\frac{dB_{kgt}/dx_k}{dO_{kgt}/dx_k + a_{iT_k}(dK_{kg}/dx_k)} = 1+v,$$

which is the form of the criterion given in equation (2) of the preceding chapter.

In passing, it may be noted that if the constraint had been placed on all capital, that is, if we had assumed that for a suitable constant $\overline{K}$,

$$\sum_{k=1}^{r} (K_{kg} + K_{kh}) \leqslant \overline{K},$$

the resultant criterion would have been

$$\left(\frac{dB_{kt}}{dx_k} - \frac{dO_{kgt}}{dx_k} - \frac{dO_{kht}}{dx_k} \right) \left(\frac{dK_{kht}}{dx_k} + \frac{dK_{kgt}}{dx_k} \right)^{-1} = (1+v)a_{iT_k},$$

78

which is the criterion of the marginal productivity of capital. This criterion is closely related to, but is not identical with, the rate of return criterion.*

VIII

The preceding model assumes the budgetary constraint as given and thus it cannot determine expenditure levels. The size of the water-resource budget is a political choice which reflects competing claims from other fields and willingness of the people to be taxed. For the sake of completeness we present a model that yields, at least at a formal level, a benefit-cost criterion in the absence of a fixed budgetary constraint. The model is similar to that of the preceding section III, except that we make some allowance for the social cost of the distortive and disincentive effects of the taxation needed to raise the federal funds.

The coefficient δ is designed to reflect these effects and is equal to the fraction by which the decline in national income attributable to taxation exceeds the marginal tax dollars collected. We seek to maximize

$$\Delta W = \sum_{l=1}^{n} B_l - \sum_{l=1}^{n} C_{lg}(1+\delta) - \sum_{l=1}^{n} C_{lh}, \qquad (25)$$

which requires

$$\frac{\partial B_l}{\partial C_{lg}} = 1+\delta \quad \text{and} \quad \frac{\partial B_l}{\partial C_{lh}} = 1 \qquad (26)$$

in the absence of reimbursability, and

$$\frac{\partial B_l}{\partial C_{lg}} = \alpha_l + (1-\alpha_l)(1+\delta) \quad \text{and} \quad \frac{\partial B_l}{\partial C_{lh}} = 1 \qquad (27)$$

if part of the costs are reimbursable. We do not suggest that δ can be measured, though it surely is greater than zero.

---

* For fuller discussion of this criterion, see H. B. Chenery, "The Application of Investment Criteria," *Quarterly Journal of Economics* (February 1953), pp. 76–96; and O. Eckstein, "Investment Criteria for Economic Development and the Theory of Intertemporal Welfare Economics," *Quarterly Journal of Economics* (February 1957), pp. 56–85.

IX

It can be seen from these models that the form of the benefit-cost criterion depends on specific assumptions about the nature of the budgetary process. The models can be elaborated in several directions; we can assume that separate budgetary constraints apply to different fields or agencies, resulting in different benefit-cost ratios for marginal expenditures in each category. We can also assume varying severity of the budgetary constraint in different years, necessitating a criterion that attaches different opportunity costs to federal money depending on the date of the expenditure. But these complications assume information of a kind that is difficult to forecast. For this reason, the model of the preceding sections V and VI is considered to be best suited as a framework for benefit-cost analysis.

CHAPTER IV

The Benefit-Cost Criterion, continued

IN the preceding chapter we have discussed the problem of selecting a proper form for our investment criterion. Before the criterion can be applied, however, we must specify prices, interest rates, a period of analysis, and a method of depreciation. The present chapter is devoted to these questions.

1. *Some Adjustments for Risk*

Investment criteria must embody some adjustment for risk which will ensure that, other things being equal, undertakings that are relatively secure in their outcome will be favored over others that are more risky. In private industry, short payoff periods and high minimum rates of return serve this purpose. While some of the risks of private undertakings are eliminated on public projects, or at least are much less, such as the hazard of financial collapse of the organization or the risk of expropriation, other risks of projects remain, and even if we assume that governmental attitudes toward risks differ from those of management, it would be folly to ignore them altogether.

But in defining risk, we must first select the group of activities to which the concept is to apply. The risk attached to a specific project may be quite high, particularly where the output is a local product and its demand dependent on the economic development of the area. But the risks of an entire program may be much smaller. For example, while the demand for a specific local electric power project may be hard to forecast, the demand for all power projects can be determined with more assurance. Project forecasts are important for the purpose of location, for even if the national demand for electricity is projected correctly, there will be substantial waste in the form of excessive transmission costs and idle capacity. But as long as the new electrical capacity is very widely scattered, errors of project forecasts will not be additive. To some extent the insurance principle of pooling risks will be at work, and misjudged projects will be balanced by projects which paid off beyond expectations. The federal government is not in the business of running one power project but administers a large, widely dispersed, long-range program. The risks which it must consider in its project decisions are the risks which are attendant upon the program as a whole, plus, to a more minor degree, the risks of possible net social loss due to the deviation of the actual development pattern from an ideal pattern as seen on an *ex post* basis. The most important risks of the power program as a whole are that the technology will make the plants obsolete, that economic development will slow down or will take a turn which will not require as much power as anticipated, and finally that serious depressions may reduce the demand.

The insurance principle can be applied to an even higher degree. The risks of the power program can be pooled with the risks of all the other programs in the resources field, again permitting some cancellation of errors, reducing the aggregate risk. The government could pool the risks of all its operations in all fields, permitting the maximum amount of cancellation of errors.

A workable procedure for allowing for risk must strike some balance between the amount of pooling that is conceptually possible on the one hand, and treatment of each project in isolation on the other. Conservative adjustments can be made in physical standards, in project-evaluation procedures, in price projections, in broad budgetary allocations, and so on. But it is important that there be no excessive pyramiding of risk allowances. The general standards must take some cognizance of the cancellation of errors; one of the advantages of federal participation in resource development is the reduction of risk through the diversification of projects both by purposes and by area. The procedures must not be so conservative that this intrinsic gain from governmental intervention is lost.

Within the benefit-cost framework, risk adjustments can be injected in at least three ways: (1) by shortening the period of analysis; (2) by including a risk factor in the interest rate; and

(3) by making safety allowances on the cost or on the benefit side. The first device has been used extensively. The Subcommittee on Benefits and Costs recommended an upper limit of one hundred years on the period of analysis, even if the economic life is expected to be longer. The limit is imposed for two reasons. First, with many projects having a more or less indefinite physical life, it is important that all agencies use the same limit on the period of analysis in order to produce comparable benefit-cost ratios. Second, the risks of benefits remote in time are extremely large and should therefore be disregarded altogether. For the same reasons *Circular A-47* limits the period of repayment to fifty years and states that benefits and costs be evaluated for the same period, thus effectively limiting the period of analysis to fifty years as well. The fifty-year figure has now been almost universally adopted. We shall examine whether this method is a good rule of thumb for allowing for risk.

Any project which has an economic life which is less than the specified limit will be immune to the adjustment. A project which has an economic life that is longer than the limit will, essentially, not be given any credit for benefits which accrue after the cutoff date. The more durable a project, the larger will be the share of benefits which cannot be included in the analysis. It is generally agreed that the more remote the expected date of a benefit, the more risky it will be and the less credit should be given for it. But simply denying any credit for benefits after a certain date is an extremely crude adjustment, and implicitly assumes that benefits before the cutoff dates are certain and benefits thereafter are so uncertain as to be worthless.

Figure 5 and Table 4 make this effect clear. They show the extent to which the benefit-cost ratios of projects of different economic lives are depressed by this form of risk allowance. Each project would have a ratio of 2.0 if it were granted credit for its benefits to the end of its life. By cutting off benefits after fifty years, the ratios are reduced by amounts which depend directly on the excess of the economic life beyond fifty years and on the capital intensity. A ratio of 2.0 was chosen as a typical example. The effect would be proportionate for other ratios; if the original ratio were twice as high, the ratio after the imposition of the limit would also be twice as high.

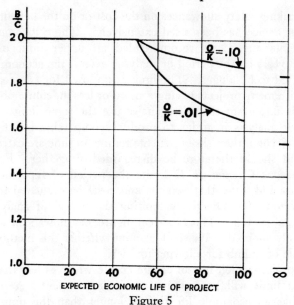

Figure 5

Table 4. Effect of limit on period of analysis on a benefit-cost ratio equal to 2

Expected economic life	Resultant benefit-cost ratio	
	$O/K=0.01$	$O/K=0.10$
50	2.00	2.00
60	1.87	1.95
70	1.78	1.93
80	1.72	1.91
90	1.68	1.89
100	1.65	1.88
∞	1.55	1.85

The values are derived as follows:

Let B/C be the original ratio, B'/C' the new ratio, a the capital charge with the expected period of analysis, a' the capital charge with a limited period of analysis. Then

$$\frac{B}{C} = \frac{B}{(O/K+a)K}; \quad K = \frac{B}{(B/C)(O/K+a)}.$$

$$\frac{B'}{C'} = \frac{B}{(O/K+a')K} = \frac{B}{(O/K+a')} \cdot \frac{(B/C)(O/K+a)}{B} = \frac{B}{C}\left(\frac{O/K+a}{O/K+a'}\right).$$

With B/C, O/K, a, a' known, B'/C' is easily evaluated.

Capital-intensive projects, with ratios of operating and maintenance costs to fixed costs of 0.01 or so, are much more affected than others. The values of O/K of the graph are typical for the projects in this field, representing capital intensities near the extremes of the range commonly found. Since it is the fixed investment that is risky, the operating costs always being subject to suspension, it is sound that the capital-intensive projects should be penalized more by the risk adjustment, and this is one advantage of the method.

A limit of a hundred years has a much smaller effect and for practical purposes can be ignored. A project with an eternal expected life, an O/K ratio of 0.01, an interest rate of $2\frac{1}{2}$ percent, and a benefit-cost ratio of 2.0, will have a ratio of 1.88 under the hundred-year limit.

There are two serious drawbacks to this device for adjusting for risk. First, it is capricious, since it only penalizes projects with an economic life longer than an arbitrary number of years. Fifty years, which is the currently favored limit, is a long time, and projects which are a little shorter are also risky. In fact, extremely durable projects, such as dams with low siltation rates, may be less risky than fairly durable installations with a clearly defined physical end, since the genuinely permanent installation may find uses in the future of which we cannot even conceive with present technology. In any event, there is no significance to the fifty-year figure, and it merely obscures the true relative merit of different projects where there are differences in the expected economic life.

The limit on the period of analysis can also lead to systematic misplanning in the formulation of projects. Many installations, including most reservoirs, can be planned for different economic lives. Over the years, silt accumulates in back of dams, and once the silt passes a certain height, it starts to reduce the possible benefits of a project, finally filling the reservoir and leaving it worthless. In the original plan of a reservoir, provision is made for siltation in the form of dead storage space set aside for future silt accumulation. The more space that is incorporated in the design of the dam for this purpose, the longer will the reservoir be serviceable. But if a fifty-year limit is imposed on the period of analysis, all benefits which accumulate thereafter are worthless, and if an agency is operating in accordance with its benefit-cost criterion, it will not incur any extra costs for "worthless" benefits, and so it will plan projects to last no longer than fifty years.

Yet there will often be opportunities to prolong the useful life of an installation far beyond fifty years at relatively little extra cost. If a separate analysis were performed for this choice of durability, using an appropriate interest rate, the extra durability might be justified. Furthermore, an important part of the ideology and motivation of resource development is the thought that future generations will reap large benefits through federal programs, and that only the government can undertake these activities because the payoff comes so very late. The fifty-year limit works completely at odds with this rationale for government intervention.

It is doubtful whether in actual practice the engineers and technical experts who design installations let the limit on the period of analysis mislead them and make them pass up good opportunities. But the official rules definitely put pressure on the agencies to slight benefits after the cutoff date and to make the installations less durable than an optimal calculation on marginal principles would suggest or than a stronger consideration of benefits for future generations would call for.

While an arbitrarily short limit to the period of analysis has little to recommend it, some upper limit must be specified. There are many projects whose economic life appears to have no foreseeable end. If the benefit-cost ratios of such projects are to be comparable, the same economic life must be assumed for all of them. Specification of an upper limit, to be adhered to by all agencies will assure this result.

An alternative to the limit on the period of analysis is the introduction of a risk premium into the interest rate. If it is found that riskless investments should be planned on the basis of a pure rate of interest of $2\frac{1}{2}$ percent, perhaps reflecting the rate of social time preference, a premium on the order of $\frac{1}{2}$ percent or 1 percent can be added to this basic rate. A relatively small premium will have quite a large effect on the benefit-cost ratio.

Figure 6 and Table 5 are comparable to Figure 5 and Table 4. They show the influence of risk premiums on projects of different economic lives, all of which would have a benefit-cost ratio of 2.0

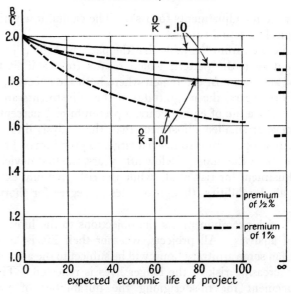

Figure 6

Table 5. Effect of risk premiums on the benefit-cost ratios of typical projects with different economic lives

Economic life	Risk premium			
	½ percent	1 percent	½ percent	1 percent
	(O/K=0.01)		(O/K=0.10)	
0	2.00	2.00	2.00	2.00
10	1.95	1.91	1.97	1.95
20	1.92	1.84	1.96	1.93
30	1.90	1.80	1.96	1.92
40	1.87	1.75	1.95	1.90
50	1.85	1.72	1.95	1.90
60	1.84	1.69	1.95	1.89
70	1.82	1.67	1.94	1.88
80	1.81	1.65	1.94	1.88
90	1.80	1.63	1.94	1.87
100	1.79	1.62	1.94	1.87
∞	1.75	1.56	1.92	1.85

These values are computed by the same method as in the previous table, except that different values of a' are applied.

if there were no adjustments for risk. The capital intensities are again typical of actual values.

It can be seen from the table that the pattern of the adjustment is different than the pattern which results from a limit to the period of analysis. In the region where both are effective, above a life of fifty years, the magnitudes of the adjustments are comparable. For a life of eighty years, a premium of $\frac{1}{2}$ percent leads to a somewhat smaller adjustment than the analysis limit, while a premium of 1 percent is somewhat larger; a premium of $\frac{3}{4}$ percent would be about the same. Below fifty years, the first device leads to no adjustment for risk at all, while the risk premium exerts its effect at all durabilities, though to a lesser degree for short-lived projects.

Thus a risk premium meets the objections to the limit on the period of analysis. All projects, whether their life is longer or shorter than some arbitrary limit, will be subject to the adjustment, yet the increasing risk of the longer lives is reflected. There is no inducement for misdesigning the durabilities of projects systematically; instead there may be a slight tendency to reduce the durability of all projects because of the higher interest rate, but this is an explicit change to reduce the risk of the investment. At the same time, capital-intensive projects are penalized in accordance with their larger riskiness, since their larger fixed investment commits more resources irrevocably.

The pattern of this adjustment corresponds to the general nature of a large part of the risks. Technological change is probably the biggest source of risk for long-range projects, and, even though it is extremely difficult to forecast the exact nature of technological progress, historical experience seems to indicate that there is a fairly steady rate of advance and that it permeates all industries to a larger or smaller degree. From the moment a project is finished, it can be expected to become more and more obsolete as compared to the current state of technology, and as time passes, it will lag further behind current best practice for achieving the same purpose. And so as the benefits become more remote in time they become more problematical and should be discounted more heavily. A risk premium in the interest rate is the clearest way of making the appropriate adjustment.

Present practice, as reflected in the report of the Subcommittee on Benefits and Costs, makes some small use of the risk premium. On the whole, the report favors the use of the long-term government bond rate of interest, which at the time it was written was $2\frac{1}{2}$ percent. But in calculating the net worth of deferred benefits, and in calculating the cost of private capital to be associated with a project, it provides for an interest rate of 4 percent or higher.

The report is not very clear on its rationale for using the 4 percent rate for deferred benefits. There are hints of two different reasons:[1] deferred benefits are particularly risky, and therefore they should be subject to a special adjustment. In fact, the adjustment is very large; a benefit to be received in fifty years which is worth \$1 now if discounted at $2\frac{1}{2}$ percent, is only worth 43¢ if discounted at 4 percent, and a capital-intensive project with a regular benefit-cost ratio of 2.0 would only score 1.6 under this rule.

The other reason for applying a higher rate to deferred benefits is related to the question of private participation. The report states that "this higher rate would be in keeping with the values attached to deferred benefits by beneficiaries and approach the rate of return needed to induce private investment and participation."[2]

This argument is not acceptable. It would introduce a bias against those projects that involve private costs, since a higher rate of discount is applied to benefits which are to be paid for as against those which are gifts. Second, in most instances it is generally understood that a satisfactory benefit-cost ratio does not imply that local participation is assured.

Exactly the same argument applies to the other instances in which the report prescribes a higher rate of interest, the calculation of the annual cost of the private investments which must be undertaken in order for the public project to become effective. The report prescribes the use of a rate of interest of 4 percent or higher to assure private participation. "This rate corresponds to the minimum current costs to private borrowers for obtaining funds through mortgage loans secured by real property or other substantial assets."[3] This rate is relevant for estimating the expenses the beneficiaries are willing to incur, but is not an

[1] Subcommittee on Benefits and Costs, *Proposed Practices...*, p. 23.
[2] *Proposed Practices...*, p. 23.   [3] *Proposed Practices...*, p. 23.

appropriate rate for the social valuation of capital. Presumably all project valuations should use an interest rate determined by social policy, for otherwise inconsistent results will emerge, depending on the fraction of cost borne privately. Just as in the case of deferred benefits, the higher rate of interest on private capital biases the benefit-cost ratio against those projects which have a large share of private financial participation, and while the actual rate paid by private borrowers must be considered in the financial analysis for setting user charges and for determining the local contribution to construction costs, it should not intrude into the benefit-cost analysis. Nor can the higher interest rate be justified on the grounds that it is a risk premium, since there is no reason to suppose that the benefits associated with privately borne costs are any more risky than the rest.

The third method of allowing for risk is the safety allowance, a flat percentage reduction of benefits or increase of costs. It is suitable for compensating for those risks which are not correlated with the passage of time, and is widely applicable on the cost side, where it takes the form of contingency allowances which are a part of the estimates of construction costs.[4] Fewer of the risks of benefits are independent of time. Conservatism in projecting output prices is a kind of safety allowance. But in the evaluation of individual projects, safety allowances are difficult to apply because it would be necessary to make different safety allowances for different types of projects, and it is not clear from what kind of considerations such allowances could be derived.

In conclusion then, a premium in the interest rate appears to be the most useful adjustment for risk in project evaluation. Safety allowances have some application on the cost side, while an arbitrary, brief limit to the period of analysis has little to offer, though some limit must be specified to assure that all projects with more or less indefinite physical lives be evaluated with the same standards. Of course, if inadequate provision for obsolescence and other risks is made, then a limit on the period of analysis of, say, fifty years serves a useful purpose. Under present evaluation standards, the fifty-year limit may be well justified.[5]

[4] See Chapter V, Section 12.
[5] This also appears to be the situation in the Soviet Union. An authoritative textbook on hydroelectric-power design states, "Massive structures, for example massive dams, can exist for a period of many

2. *Depreciation and Amortization*

Where private industry employs depreciation accounting to allow for the use of capital in production, federal agencies use amortization instead.[6] Formally the two concepts are the same, with amortization corresponding to the sinking-fund method of depreciation,[7] a method that calls for making sufficient annual payments into a sinking fund in order to replace the original equipment at the end of its economic life. The sinking-fund method differs from the straight-line method in that it assumes that interest is earned on the money in the sinking fund. This interest helps in the accumulation of a sufficient sum of money for replacement, and so the amount of depreciation charged is somewhat less than under the straight-line method.

In the late 1930's, when the federal practice was evolved, the

---

decades and even centuries. The use of such service lives would be equivalent to burdening future generations with the obligation of compensating a certain share of construction expenditures, [a practice] which in many cases cannot be considered a reality, and which would be an expression of excessive self-confidence on the part of our generation in the correctness and unchangeability of its technical decisions for future generations. The factor of 'obsolescence' must not be left out of consideration....In connection with this we can hardly consider it justifiable to establish planning service lives or norms of amortization greater than the average duration of productive activity of one and one-half to two generations, that is greater than 40–50 years." F. F. Gubin, *Gidroelektrichste stantsii* (Moscow–Leningrad, 1949), pp. 675–677, cited in R. W. Campbell, "Accounting for Depreciation in the Soviet Economy," *Quarterly Journal of Economics* (November 1956), p. 503.

[6] The use of the word "amortization" is misleading in this context, since its general meaning is related to repayment of debts, while the usage in this field has nothing to do with payments at all.

[7] The annual sinking-fund charge is equal to

$$\frac{i}{(1+i)^T - 1}.$$

The annual charge for interest and amortization in federal practice is equal to

$$\frac{i}{(1+1)^T - 1} + i,$$

which is seen to be identical to the sinking-fund charge plus interest. Under the sinking-fund method, interest must be charged on the entire original investment because the amount of investment which has been written off in depreciation has theoretically been placed in the sinking fund, where it accumulates interest of its own. From the point of view of economic theory, this is the correct method of depreciation.

sinking-fund method was not atypical of private practice.[8] But the large increase in corporation income taxes has made business much more eager to depreciate its plant and its equipment heavily and rapidly. The Tax Code of 1954 has encouraged the use of two depreciation methods other than straight-line: the method of declining balance and that of the sum of the years-digit. These call for large depreciation allowances in the early years and for smaller allowances later on. Figure 7 shows the depreciation allowances per dollar of investment that are set aside each year on a project with an economic life of fifty years. Four methods are contrasted, straight-line, declining balance, sum of the years-digit, and the sinking-fund method to which federal practice corresponds. It can be seen from the figure that federal practice calls for considerably smaller allowances, particularly in the early

---

[8] The following table summarizes the depreciation practice of the private electric utilities industry for 1937:

Method	Percent of total plant	Depreciation expense as percent of total plant
Percentage of various classes of plant	2.09	2.91
Percent of total depreciable plant	10.11	2.41
Percent of operating revenues	9.80	1.66
Percentage of operating revenue less maintenance	7.11	1.75
Mills per kilowatt-hour sold	1.39	2.38
Sinking fund	6.53	*1.91*
Combination of several	3.02	1.90
Orders of and agreements with regulatory bodies	4.03	1.98
Arbitrary amounts	52.02	1.62
Not stated	3.90	1.75
Total	100.00	1.79

Source: Twentieth Century Fund, *Electric Power and Government Policy* (1948), p. 269.

This table shows that federal amortization practice calls for a somewhat larger annual amortization charge than the average depreciation actually imposed by this industry in 1937.

years. This is strong reason for setting the limit to the period of analysis conservatively as a partial offset.

However, it would be wrong to have public agencies adopt private practice in this matter, for little normative significance should be attached to the latter. The increase in depreciation allowances is justified in part on technological grounds, particularly the high rate of obsolescence. But this, in my view, is not

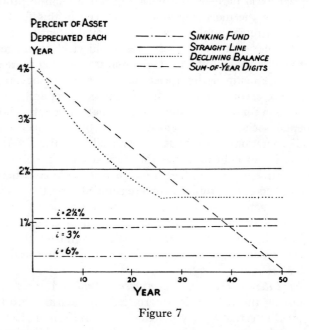

Figure 7

the main reason for the changes. Rather, their purpose is to offset the impact of the high corporation income tax on the internal supply of investable funds of business. Due to the risks and imperfections of the capital market, firms find it difficult or unpleasant to finance more than a moderate fraction of their expansion from external funds, and therefore the rate of investment of private business is very much affected by the internal supply of funds. The liberal depreciation allowances permit internal accumulation of investable funds despite the high tax on profits. But these considerations have no relevance for public projects, since the rate of public investment does not hinge on the internal accumulations of revenues of the agencies. It is only insofar as private depreciation practices may better reflect the true rate of obsolescence of capital that it holds any implications for public practice.

3. What Interest Rate?

The choice of interest rate for the design and evaluation of public projects is perhaps the most difficult economic problem and yet one of the most important ones faced in this field. In view of the extreme durability and high capital intensity of most projects, the use of a low interest rate would yield an altogether different kind of program than a high interest rate. Far more projects would be justified; hydroelectric power would be favored over steam; reservoirs would be designed to be larger and to make more provision for siltation, and so on. Choice of a rate involves fundamental social value judgments about benefits accruing to different generations and about the over-all objectives. At the same time, it can help to assure that capital channeled into this field of investment yields as high a return as it would elsewhere.

Three aspects of the problem will be examined: first, the rationale for the rates actually used and for some other rates that have been seriously proposed; second, a statistical investigation into the opportunity cost of federal capital; and finally the value judgments which must underlie this expression of social time preference.

(a) *The Interest Rate of Government Bonds.* Interest rates approximating the rate on long-term federal securities are typically applied in actual agency practice. The Bureau of Reclamation has employed a rate of $2\frac{1}{2}$ percent,[9] the Corps of Engineers a rate of 3 percent.[10] The Subcommittee on Benefits and Costs recommends a rate of $2\frac{1}{2}$ percent, "which approximates the interest rate on long-term government bonds,"[11] while Budget Bureau *Circular A–47* specifically recommends

A rate based upon the average rate of interest payable by the Treasury on interest bearing marketable securities of the United States outstanding at the end of the fiscal year preceding

[9] Department of the Interior, Bureau of Reclamation, *Reclamation Manual*, vol. XIII, 3.1.7, March, 1952.
[10] Subcommittee on Benefits and Costs, *Proposed Practices...*, p. 78.
[11] *Proposed Practices...*, p. 24.

such computation which, upon original issue, had terms to maturity not more than twelve months longer or twelve months shorter than the economically useful life of the project....Where the economically useful life of the project is expected to be longer than 15 years, the rate of interest shall be calculated at a rate based upon the average of interest payable by the Treasury on obligations, if any, outstanding at the end of the fiscal year preceding such computation, which upon original issue, had terms to maturity of 15 years or more.[12]

The Presidential Advisory Committee on Water Resources Policy of 1955 also endorses the federal long-term borrowing rate.[13]

Does the government bond rate measure the social cost of the capital employed in water-resource projects? If the government sought to raise investable funds for water-resource development in the capital market it would find lenders who are willing to supply the money at the going federal bond rate and this might be taken as evidence that the social cost of the loan is measured by this rate. But this line of reasoning overlooks two fundamental factors which make the argument invalid.

The first factor is the social cost of risk bearing. We must distinguish between borrower's risk and lender's risk.[14] The former is determined by the riskiness of the venture, whether or not the expected income stream will materialize; the second risk is related to the financial strength of the borrower, whether or not he will be in a position to repay the loan when it is due. The two risks will only be the same if the repayment ability of the borrower is entirely determined by the success of the one venture for which he borrowed. In general, borrower's risk is determined by the accuracy of the forecasts of prices and of production conditions, while lender's risk is determined by the moral character of the borrower, the nature and success of his general business, his other financial resources, the seniority of the loan in his financial structure, and so on.

It cannot be stated a priori which of the two kinds of risk is

---

[12] Bureau of the Budget, *Circular A–47*, Section 15, p. 14.

[13] The President's Advisory Committee on Water Resources Policy, *Water Resources Policy*, Dec. 22, 1955, p. 27.

[14] See J. M. Keynes, *General Theory of Employment, Interest and Money* (1936), p. 144.

larger. In the case of small, one-venture business, lender's risk will often be larger because repayment of capital requires not only that the business be successful, but also that the borrower is honest. For large, multiproduct firms, lender's risk will usually be smaller than borrower's risk because the entire financial resources of the firm stand in back of its obligations.

In the case of federal investment projects, lender's risk is very small. The holder of a federal bond need not be concerned about the success of a specific water-resources project, nor even about the success of all the reimbursable programs of the government. The credit of the federal government is determined by its taxing power and is as firm as the political system itself. The interest rate on federal securities, as compared to other rates in the economy, is determined by the extremely low lender's risk. If a project should fail to produce the expected benefits, the loss is socialized; it is the taxpayer who makes up the loss, not the bondholder where costs were intended to be reimbursable, while it is the disappointed beneficiaries of the project who suffer the loss where costs were nonreimbursable. Thus the federal bond rate does not measure the full social cost of capital since it makes no allowance for the risks of the project.

Second, the argument in favor of the government bond rate assumes that the money is actually raised through voluntary bond sales to the public, which is not, in fact, the case. An increase of the federal water-resources program in time of full employment will require an increase of taxation or a curtailment of other expenditures if the government pursues fiscal policies designed to help stabilize the economy. There is no voluntary individual choice about payment of these taxes and the social cost of money raised in this way depends upon the circumstances in which the households and businesses who pay the taxes find themselves and upon their desires. Should the alternative to the increase of expenditure in this field be curtailment in another, the social cost of capital would depend on the value of marginal expenditures in the alternate field.

(b) *The Rate of Return on Private Investments.* It has also been suggested that public projects should earn a rate of return equal to good private investments, and hence that an interest rate equal to private rates of return be used in the benefit-cost analysis. It is argued that the capital employed in public projects could be used in fields of private investment instead, where it would earn a high rate of return, and therefore that an optimal allocation of investment in the economy would require that the rate on public investment should be as high as the rate in the private sector in order to maximize the total increase of national income that the country's investment in any period can produce.

This line of reasoning assumes that an expansion of public investment leads to a contraction of private investment in equal amount, or that a contraction of public investment would result in an equal expansion in the private sector. In fact, since public investment is financed primarily out of taxation, much of which is paid by households, its expansion would at least in part be at the expense of consumption. And insofar as it is investment that is affected, it need not be the best investments, but only marginal undertakings in enterprises whose growth is particularly constrained by federal business taxes. Thus the rate of return on good private investments also holds little normative significance for public projects.

(c) *The Opportunity Cost of Capital.* Having rejected both the government bond rate and the rate of return on private investment, what rate would be an appropriate measure of the social cost of federal capital? This rate can only be estimated by tracing the capital to its source and by discovering its value in the use to which it would be put in the absence of the public project. Since the money is actually raised by taxation,[15] the incidence of the marginal taxes necessitated by a project must be assigned to various businesses and households. Specific increases (or forestalled reductions) of taxes must be assumed and assumptions about the incidence of these taxes must be made. Once the tax money is traced to its source, its value in the alternative use can be estimated. In the case of taxes falling on business, there will be some decline of investment, representing a percentage of the taxes, the exact magnitude of which will depend upon the availability of investable funds in relation to the firm's opportunities.

[15] This assumes that the government runs a countercyclical fiscal policy which necessitates an increase of taxes sufficient to release the resources for a project. It also assumes that the project is not at the expense of other public expenditures. We also continue to adhere to our assumption of full employment.

Some ascertainable rate of return would have been earned on these investments. The rest of the business taxes presumably reduce the liquidity of the firm and will tend to reduce the funds available in the general capital market. As for the taxes falling on households, in order to impute a rate of return to the money raised from this source it is necessary to accept consumers' sovereignty with regard to intertemporal decisions; whatever time preference individuals attach to the marginal dollars which they borrow or lend reflects the relative satisfaction of present consumption versus a consumption stream in the future, and the marginal borrowing or lending rate at which they voluntarily exchange present versus future consumption is the best measure of this time preference. A household which is willing to borrow at an interest rate of 10 percent in order to increase its present consumption must be assumed to have that time preference; and income which is taxed away for the sake of a public project represents a social cost measured by that interest rate, for it would take a rate of at least that magnitude to have the consumer voluntarily lend his money in order to permit the public investment. Taxation is backed by the coercive power of government; to measure the social cost of the forced loan which taxation for public investment represents we must look to the interest rate at which the household operates in its market transactions.

Elsewhere I have published the results of an extensive statistical investigation following the methods outlined above.[16] Two alternative tax changes were assumed, one affecting consumption, consisting of a change in the personal exemption of the income-tax and of excise-tax rates, the other primarily affecting investment through changes in the corporation income tax plus a proportionate change of personal income-tax payments. For both tax changes, a distribution between large and small businesses and between households in different income classes was worked out. The effects of the taxes on investment were estimated for small and large business, and empirically derived rates of return were assigned. Each income class of households was divided into subgroups according to the interest rates at which they made their lending-borrowing decisions. To estimate the interest rate

[16] J. V. Krutilla and O. Eckstein, *Multiple Purpose River Development, Studies in Applied Economic Analysis* (1958).

applicable to any particular set of tax changes, a weighted average of the relevant interest rates and rates of return was taken, with the weights determined by the distribution of incidence of the taxes among businesses and among households. The estimates for the social cost of the funds for public investment raised through taxes ranged between 5 and 6 percent; under alternative tax cuts and various assumptions about the incidence of taxation the estimate remained very close to this range. Thus if we accept consumers' sovereignty with regard to intertemporal choices, then, under conditions of full employment, the social cost of federal capital appears to be on the order of 5 to 6 percent.[17]

(d) *The Social Rate of Time Preference.* An interest rate of 5 or 6 percent in benefit-cost analysis would preclude the justification of most projects. The high capital intensity and the very long economic lives of resource-development projects make interest cost a larger part of total cost than in most other fields of investment. Under a high interest rate the federal government would reduce its efforts in the resource field.

While there is little doubt that the opportunity cost of the capital is at least of the order of magnitude indicated, there are good reasons for not accepting the policy implications blindly. The study was predicated on the assumption that the time preferences of the present generation be accepted for intertemporal decisions. Social policy, as derived from the political process, may prefer rejection of present intertemporal preferences in favor of a redistribution of income toward future generations. Much of the conservation philosophy can be interpreted in these terms. Resource development is a field particularly suited to this kind of redistribution because there are genuine opportunities for making investments, part of the benefit of which will accrue in the far future. And perhaps equally important is the fact that it is in the resource area that the idea of making provision for the future of the country has caught the imagination of the public. It is not logically inconsistent for the same person to be willing to borrow at high interest rates to increase his present consumption while voting to spend tax money to build a project from which

[17] For a fuller discussion of the methods and assumptions which yielded these estimates, see Krutilla and Eckstein, *Multiple Purpose River Development*, chap. V.

future generations will benefit, for in the case of a vote to tax, he can be sure that the other individuals in the society will be compelled to act similarly. Also, the distribution of voting power differs from the distribution of economic power in the market.[18] Our notion of efficiency is relative to a distribution of income; should we seek to redistribute income to future generations, the interest rate loses its usual meaning as an efficient price.[19]

To some extent, a low interest rate is also a substitute for increased saving. In private business, capital should be invested where the return is highest because the depreciation allowances which are accumulated become available for reinvestment in other projects with high rates of return. In the case of public projects, with their very limited reimbursability, the capital in the project gradually disappears as the project wears out; the government collects no funds which would become available for a replacement of the project, nor do the beneficiaries make any such provision. Thus the addition to the nation's capital stock represented by public projects is only temporary, lasting as long as the projects last. A low interest rate will favor more durable projects, and thus the addition to the nation's capital stock, while still only temporary, is for a longer period of time.

But these lines of argument must be pursued with caution. If a low interest rate is used in benefit-cost analysis, it will not only favor particularly durable and capital-intensive projects; it will also lead to the justification of projects of little economic value. It must be remembered that the critical variable for distributing income toward the future is not so much the interest rate as it is the level of investment. An optimal policy from this point of view would call for an increase of investment to take advantage of the best available opportunities, wherever they may be in the economy. The development of resource projects yielding low rates of return for a long period is only justified if no way can be found to earn a higher return with the funds raised for public investment.

[18] See Baumol, *Welfare Economics and the Theory of the State*, pp. 91–93.
[19] For a more detailed discussion of this point, see O. Eckstein, "Investment Criteria for Economic Development and the Theory of Intertemporal Welfare Economics," *Quarterly Journal of Economics* (February 1957).

Use of a low interest rate can also be justified on the grounds that most private investment decisions contain an inherent bias toward short-lived projects. The use of payoff periods is just one of a number of private criteria that on the one hand serve as an adjustment to reflect the riskiness of durable investments, but on the other also produce a systematic underdevelopment of areas of investment in which the technology happens to call for long-lived projects. Were the government to follow private practice slavishly, it would overlook the very opportunities which are most suited for public development.

I propose the following compromise, which is designed to preserve the long-time perspective of the federal program, yet would assure that only projects are undertaken in which capital yields as great a value as it would in its alternative employments: *let the government use a relatively low interest rate for the design and evaluation of projects, but let projects be considered justified only if the benefit-cost ratio is well in excess of 1.0.* In order to assure that the average rate of return in this use is as high as in the alternatives, a combination of interest rates and minimum benefit-cost ratios should be selected which will correspond to a rate of return of 6 percent for a project of average capital intensity. Under this procedure projects would continue to be designed to be capital intensive and remote benefits would have a significant value. But the marginal projects which would be undertaken would not represent a misallocation of capital into a use in which it is incapable of earning a satisfactory rate of return.[20]

Following the above principle, Figure 8 and Table 6 show all the combinations of interest rates and benefit-cost ratios which correspond to a rate of return of 6 percent for typical capital intensities and economic lives. It can be seen from the figure how higher benefit-cost ratios can compensate for lower interest rates. In Table 7 similar combinations are represented for projects of average capital intensity, that is, for values of O/K of 0.05. If an interest rate of 3 percent is used, it should be combined with a minimum benefit-cost ratio of about 1.3. A rate of

[20] The excess of benefits over costs can also be considered a risk adjustment in the form of a safety allowance. It is an adjustment that does not penalize more durable and capital-intensive projects, as they ought to be, but that may be desirable in order to preserve the long-time perspective.

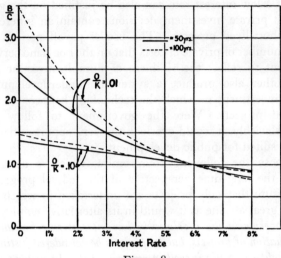

Figure 8

Table 6. Combinations of benefit-cost ratios and interest rates
which are equivalent to a private rate of return of 6 percent

Interest rate	Benefit-cost ratio			
	Economic life 50 years		Economic life 100 years	
	$O/K = 0.01$	$O/K = 0.10$	$O/K = 0.01$	$O/K = 0.10$
0	2.45	1.36	3.50	1.46
1	2.07	1.30	2.71	1.38
2	1.76	1.24	2.11	1.30
$2\frac{1}{2}$	1.62	1.21	1.88	1.26
3	1.50	1.18	1.69	1.22
$3\frac{1}{2}$	1.40	1.15	1.52	1.18
4	1.30	1.11	1.38	1.14
5	1.13	1.06	1.16	1.06
6	1.00	1.00	1.00	1.00
7	0.88	0.95	0.88	0.94
8	0.80	0.90	0.77	0.89

The method of computation is the same as in Table 5, except that the
expression which is evaluated is

$$\frac{B'}{C'} = \frac{O/K + a_{.06}}{O/K + a_i}.$$

102

$2\frac{1}{2}$ percent should be combined with a ratio of 1.4 or so. Combinations in this range appear most appropriate for the evaluation of resource projects.

Table 7. Some combinations of benefit-cost ratios and interest rates which correspond to a rate of return of 6 percent for projects of average capital intensity (O/K 0.05)

Interest rate (percent)	Benefit-cost ratio	
	Economic life = 50	Economic life = 100
2	1.39	1.51
$2\frac{1}{2}$	1.33	1.43
3	1.28	1.35
$3\frac{1}{2}$	1.22	1.28
4	1.17	1.21
5	1.08	1.10
6	1.00	1.00

Earlier, in the preceding chapter, it was argued that the cutoff point to the benefit-cost ratio should be determined on the basis of a fixed-budget constraint. It was assumed there that the constraint would be effective, that is, that there would be sufficient good project opportunities to exhaust the budget ration of funds. The considerations raised in the present section determine standards by which a project can be considered justified if the budget does not limit the program. As long as the cutoff point in the ratio imposed by the budgetary constraint lies above the lower limit suggested by the present considerations, the latter limit does not dominate. It will act as a constraint on the program in the event that the better opportunities have been used up and the budgetary constraint has become ineffective.

To summarize: (1) no particular significance attaches to the government bond rate for project evaluation; (2) the rate of return on the best private investments also is inappropriate; (3) the opportunity cost of capital raised by federal taxation is on the order of 5 to 6 percent, accepting private time preference; (4) there are good reasons for rejecting private time preference and using a lower interest rate for planning resource development; (5) but if a low interest rate is used it must be coupled with a minimum benefit-cost ratio greater than 1.0 in order to assure that capital is not wasted. An interest rate of 3 percent and a benefit cost ratio of 1.3 or an interest rate of 2½ percent coupled with a ratio of 1.4 are combinations which will produce an average rate of return for the entire federal program of about 6 percent, and therefore are appropriate minimum justification standards.

4. *Price Projections*

The benefit of several types of water-resource projects consists of an increase of output of agricultural commodities. For example, irrigation projects permit intensive farming in dry areas which results in a very drastic increase in the value of product grown, while flood-control projects often reduce the damage inflicted on crops.

The effect of a project on the quantities produced is primarily a physical question, depending on the change in yields due to irrigation, the percent of crops that can be expected to be destroyed by floods, the degree to which a project will reduce the frequency and severity of flooding, and so on. While there is considerable controversy about the relevant physical constants, and in some instances the forecasts of quantities are more uncertain than the forecasts of prices, we shall not enter into a discussion of this range of issues. These physical uncertainties produce an equal uncertainty in benefits, but economics can shed little light on them, except to indicate the high cost of planning programs without adequate physical assumptions.

If the benefit-cost analyses of projects are to be comparable, their output estimates must be valued at the same prices. In recent years, all agencies, including the Corps of Engineers and the Bureau of Reclamation, have accepted common price projections supplied by the Bureau of Agricultural Economics and the successor agencies in the Department of Agriculture, based on principles laid down by the Subcommittee on Benefits and Costs. In a statement issued August 28, 1951, the Subcommittee recommended that prices used in the analysis should reflect "real" costs and "real" benefits, and should therefore assume that the price level as a whole remains constant over the lives of the projects.[21] It recommended that current prices be used for costs to be incurred in the near future, such as construction, and that average long-term prices be used for other costs and all benefits. The Subcommittee suggested that the statistical approach of an earlier study by the Department of Agriculture,[22] entitled "Long-Range Agricultural Policy," could be used to derive the long-term estimates. That study projected population growth, rise in per-capita income, increase in national demands for different foods, and rates of productivity improvements on three different assumptions about the overall level of activity. The Subcommittee recommended that the projections be based

Table 8. Parity ratio of price projections and actual ratios

	Three projections			Actual			
	1950	1951	1956	1950	1951	1953	1956*
Prices paid	175	215	265	256	282	279	287
Prices received	155	215	235	258	302	258	234
Parity ratio	86	100	89	101	107	92	82

Source: U.S. Department of Agriculture, Agricultural Research Service and Agricultural Marketing Service, *Agricultural Price and Cost Projections for Use in Making Benefit and Cost Analyses of Land and Water Resource Projects, Analyzing the Repayment Capacity of Water Users,* June 1956.
* October 1956.

on the assumption of high employment. Projections to be followed were first announced in April 1950 and were revised in November 1951 and June 1956. The critical number for projecting the level of prices for agricultural output is the parity ratio, the ratio of prices received to prices paid by farmers. Table 8 summarizes the parity ratios of the three projections and contrasts them with the actual experience. The projections of

[21] This assumption was not made universally before. The Corps of Engineers had used price projections which included allowances for general price increases which raised estimates about 20 percent above the B.A.E. projections. (Reported in Order of Chief of Engineers of 21 July 1953, ordering use of B.A.E. projections.)

[22] U.S. Department of Agriculture, *Long Range Agricultural Policy* (1948).

1951 were too optimistic; the parity ratio proved to be worse than projected. But this error in the anticipated relation between the level of prices paid and received was more than offset by the agency practice of measuring construction costs at current levels. The parity projection, while overoptimistic for the ratio, anticipated a general fall of all prices. As long as benefits and costs are both valued at this low price level, their relative magnitudes

Table 9. Projections of relative prices for major product groups and actual relative prices for 1955

Product group	1951 projection as percent of 1951 prices*	Actual 1955 prices as percent of 1951 prices†	1951 projection adjusted to average 100‡	1955 prices adjusted to average 100
Food grains	94	71	108	90
Feed grains	80	80	92	102
Commercial vegetables	87	73	100	93
All fruits	117	91	134	116
Meat animals	61	66	70	84
Dairy products	88	85	101	108
Poultry and eggs	83	81	95	107

* U.S. Department of Agriculture, Bureau of Agricultural Economics, pamphlet of price data, November 1951; revised August 1952.
† *Agricultural Price and Cost Projections*, Department of Agriculture, p. 8.
‡ Columns 3 and 4 are derived by multiplying columns 1 and 2 by constants.

are unaffected. But with the construction costs measured at the much higher current price levels, an asymmetry is introduced; benefits are related to a much lower general price level than construction costs. With the parity ratio too high by only about 10 percent and with the construction costs that would be consistent with the projections at least 30 percent below the current cost figures that were used in benefit-cost analyses, the over-all effect was to err on the conservative side by about 20 percent. For the moment, this asymmetry has been eliminated. The projections of 1956 extrapolate the price levels prevailing at that time, with just a slight decline in the prices to be paid by farmers. Should the general rise of prices in the economy continue above the levels of 1956, the conservative bias will be reintroduced as the long-term projected price level falls short of the current price level at which the construction costs are valued.

The Department of Agriculture also provides price projections for individual commodities for each state in which they are grown and for the United States as a whole. These projections serve to establish the relative prices among various project outputs and thus play an important part in the relative evaluation of projects with different outputs. The projections of 1951 stood up well in the first four subsequent years. Table 9 shows the projections for major product groups, expressed as a percentage of the average price in 1951, and contrasts them with actual prices for 1955, expressed in a similar manner. In order to bring out the implicit relative prices, columns 3 and 4 convert both sets of prices to an average of 100. It can be seen that the most serious price changes, the increase in the price of fruit and the decline in meat prices, were foreseen correctly. As for the minor price changes of the other groups, in four out of five cases the projection had the wrong sign.[23]

The projections for the individual commodities which make up the major product groups had a somewhat larger error, as might be expected, but they are not as serious because the possibility of switching production from commodities with particularly low prices to those with higher prices is larger. The large price increase in apples and the large decreases in cattle, sheep, lambs,

[23] A test of these projections against a naïve model can easily be made from the above data. If the projections are better than simple extrapolation of the relative prices prevailing in 1951, then columns 1 and 2 (or 3 and 4) should be positively correlated. The actual correlation coefficient is 0.66, a high figure that can be explained by the small number of observations and by the presence of two extreme values. Despite the qualifications, there is no doubt that the projections are better than the naïve model.

and wool were anticipated correctly; the increases in the prices of peanuts, grapefruit and sweet potatoes were not foreseen.[24]

Our crude check of the projections against the experience of 1955 can certainly not be considered conclusive by any means, since there is a large random element in the prices of one year, and since the projections were designed to be valid over the fifty-year period typical for projects. Also, the relative price relationships were upset by the various price-support programs which boosted some of the prices above their natural levels. But it is reassuring that the projections were not far from the mark for the brief period over which they could be verified.

The projections of 1955 indicate a rise in the prices of meat, poultry, and feed grains, and a fall in the prices of wheat, rice, cotton, peanuts, apples, grapefruit, and tobacco. This is consistent with the assumption that the United States will gradually increase its consumption of meat at the expense of other foods. The projections also contain an offsetting factor to price supports; the prices of commodities in which there are large government surpluses are assumed to fall 20 percent below the levels of 1955. While the social benefit of commodities that end up in storage is still overstated, the new projections contain at least some bias against projects which will yield outputs that are already in surplus.

5. *Annual Values and the Typical Year*

Most benefit-cost analyses employ one annual value for benefits and costs which is assumed to apply throughout the project's life. But in some instances, such as flood-control projects in growing regions, navigation projects where traffic will slowly be generated by plants located on the stream after it is made navigable, and irrigation projects which sell their products in expanding local markets, some allowance must be made for the general growth of benefits. A benefit-cost analysis in terms of present values can easily handle this situation. But if annual values are preferred, it is possible to make allowance for the growth by estimating the

---

[24] Repeating our test against a naïve model, we find a correlation coefficient of 0.38, a coefficient that is significant at the 0.95 probability level and that indicates that the projections are superior to the naïve model.

benefits of a year not in the immediate future, but later in the life of the project after some of the growth has occurred. Generally, the higher the anticipated rate of growth of benefits, the later should be the typical year that is selected for analysis. Figure 9

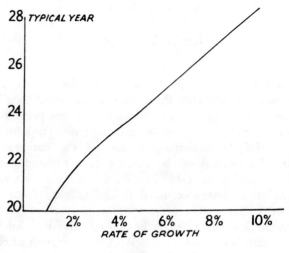

Figure 9

shows the relationship between the rate of growth and the proper typical year, assuming a period of analysis of fifty years and an interest rate of 3 percent. It will be seen that the typical year remains in the relatively narrow range of twenty to twenty-eight years for rates of growth from 1 to 8 percent.

CHAPTER V

Flood Control

ALTHOUGH the rivers of the United States have been a great source of economic strength, their tendency to exceed their banks has caused great damage over the years and has provided our government with the traditional and expensive task of flood control.[1] Table 10 indicates the size of the nation's flood damages.[2] All sections of the country have suffered losses at one time or another, as Table 11 shows, but it can be seen that 60 percent of all losses occurred in the valleys of the Ohio, Missouri, and Mississippi rivers.

Only in the last twenty years has an effective national flood-control program been developed. With the exception of control measures on the alluvial valley of the Mississippi for which Congress established the Mississippi River Commission in 1879, of some work in the Sacramento–San Joaquin river valley begun in 1917, and of a project on Lake Okeechobee authorized in 1930, there was no federal flood-control policy or program until Congress passed the Flood Control Act of June 22, 1936. Whatever protective works were built, were projects of state and local

[1] The most extensive discussion of the flood-control program of the Corps of Engineers can be found in Appendix F of "Report on the Federal Civil Works Program as Administered by the Corps of Engineers, U.S. Army," submitted by the chief of engineers to the Subcommittee to Study Civil Works in 1951, which has been published as Part 1, Vol. 3 of the *Annual Report of the Chief of Engineers, U.S. Army,* 1951. This section draws heavily on that report and subsequent references in footnotes are to this report. For a general survey of the flood problem, see W. G. Hoyt and W. B. Langbein, *Floods* (1955).

[2] The figures are based on surveys which are made after all floods by the U.S. Weather Bureau. Since many of the data are obtained from questionnaires filled out shortly after a flood, when hysteria leads people to overstate their losses, the figures cannot be taken to be more than an indication of the orders of magnitude.

Flood Control

Table 10. Approximate damages by floods in the United States
(in millions of dollars)

1927	348	1940	40
1928	44	1941	40
1929	63	1942	98
1930	16	1943	200
1931	3	1944	102
1932	10	1945	166
1933	36	1946	71
1934	10	1947	272
1935	127	1948	230
1936	232	1949	94
1937	441	1950	176
1938	101	1951	1,029
1939	14	1952	254
		1953	122

Average, 1927–1953: $160,000,000

Source: U.S. Weather Bureau, *Climatological Data, Annual National Summary*, 1928–1953.

Table 11. Regional distribution of loss of property from floods
(millions of dollars)

Region	Total losses 1924–1953	Percent
Great Lakes	107	2.0
North Atlantic	313	5.8
South Atlantic	49	0.9
East Gulf	50	0.9
Ohio Valley	804	14.8
Upper Mississippi	1,344	24.8
Lower Mississippi	229	4.2
Missouri	1,630	30.1
Arkansas	236	4.4
Red	147	2.7
West Gulf	199	3.7
Colorado	4	0.1
Pacific	297	5.5
Great Basin	14	0.3
Total, U.S.	5,423	

Source: U.S. Weather Bureau, *Annual National Summary*, 1953, p. 90.

governments, and were locally financed.[3] The outstanding local works of this era were the projects of the Miami Conservancy District in Ohio, where effective flood-control dams and levees were built with funds raised through local assessments on property which stood to benefit. This program was organized during a period of intense interest in flood control after the disastrous flood of the Ohio in 1913 which caused damages of over $200,000,000. But there are only a few isolated instances of effective control, which can perhaps be explained by the fact that flood control usually involves work throughout a river basin, particularly in the upstream area, often at great distances from the points where the flood damages are suffered.

The River and Harbor Act of 1927 called on the U.S. Army Corps of Engineers to prepare a series of comprehensive plans for improving America's major rivers for navigation, for power development, for flood control, and for irrigation. The Army Engineers thereupon prepared the famous "308" surveys which showed that there were many opportunities to control floods at costs that were far short of flood damages. Thus, when the Flood Control Act of 1936 officially acknowledged flood control to be a federal responsibility and designated the U.S. Army Corps of Engineers to prosecute a large-scale program, much of the basic planning had already been done, and the program gained momentum very rapidly. This act also assigned responsibility for upstream flood control to the U.S. Department of Agriculture, though this program got under way more slowly. World War II interrupted the Engineers' program, of course, but it was resumed on a large scale and has continued almost undiminished under President Eisenhower. Table 12 shows the annual expenditures for flood control by the Army Engineers.

To indicate the scope of remaining flood-control opportunities, Table 13 summarizes the status of the Corps' program in 1955. At the present rate it would take eighteen years to complete authorized work. Some of the authorized projects will never be sufficiently attractive to receive actual appropriations; on the other hand, the continued economic development of the river

[3] Except for funds that were the proceeds of sales of public swamp lands, which Congress turned over to local authorities in the Swamp Land Acts of 1849, 1850, and occasional later acts.

Flood Control

Table 12. Expenditures of the Corps of Engineers for flood control and multipurpose projects

(fiscal year—thousands of dollars)

1929	25,053	1943	125,473
1930	26,455	1944	104,476
1931	37,892	1945	76,387
1932	29,229	1946	88,238
1933	39,577	1947	180,489
1934	48,143	1948	245,507
1935	38,767	1949	400,759
1936	51,069	1950	437,059
1937	55,146	1951	424,690
1938	64,221	1952	404,844
1939	81,724	1953	442,856
1940	102,656	1954	416,000
1941	125,266	1955	383,000
1942	114,908	1956*	373,000
		1957*	397,000

Source: Compiled from *Annual Reports of the Chief of Engineers,* 1929–1953, Part I, "Appropriations and Expenditures;" later years from *Budget of the United States Government for Fiscal Year* 1956, 1957.

* Estimate.

Table 13. Status of authorized flood control projects in active program

	Number of projects			
	Total	Completed	Under construction	Not yet started
Flood control	763	341	95	327
Multipurpose (including power)	63	21	23	19

	Estimated cost in millions			
	Total	Spent to June 30, 1955	Fiscal 1956	Fiscal 1957	Balance to complete
Flood control	4827.1	1502.5	104.9	140.4	3079.3
Multipurpose (including power)	5439.1	2271.1	211.4	168.4	2788.2

Source: *Budget of the United States Government,* 1957, p. 6.

113

valleys will create growing possibilities of flood damages and will result in further flood control needs. Thus, new projects can be expected to continue to be authorized.

1. *Flood Control Upstream*

About half of all flood damages are agricultural, in the form of destruction of growing crops, of live stock, of farm property, and of damage to the soil,[4] Much of this loss is suffered upstream, on small tributaries which are far above the big dams on the main stems of the big rivers. It is the mission of the U.S. Department of Agriculture to reduce these damages. As Table 14 shows, this program has developed much more slowly; but it now promises

Table 14. Appropriations for flood prevention programs of the Department of Agriculture (in millions of dollars)

Fiscal year	Flood prevention program under Act of 1936	Watershed protection program under Act of 1954
1937	0.5	—
1938	7.0	—
1939	3.0	—
1940	2.0	—
1941	1.0	—
1946	2.1	—
1947	3.0	—
1948	6.0	—
1949	9.5	—
1950	6.1	—
1951	6.6	—
1952	7.8	—
1953	7.3	—
1954	7.0	5.0
1955	7.5	7.2
1956	10.0	12.0
1957	10.7	16.0

Source: Committee on Public Works, *Report of the Subcommittee to Study Civil Works, The Flood Control Program of the Department of Agriculture*, House Committee Print No. 22, 82 Cong., 2 sess., p. 3 for data to 1952. For subsequent years, *The Budget of the United States Government*, 1954, 1956, and 1957.

---

[4] Hoyt and Langbein, *Floods*, pp. 78–84.

to reach much larger proportions than it has heretofore. Most of the funds spent before World War II were devoted to planning; after the war the program remained surprisingly small.[5] This was partly due to the nature of the projects proposed, which were usually comprehensive land-treatment programs in which flood control was only one of several agricultural benefits. Thus, of ten projects proposed in 1952, flood-control benefits ranged from 3 percent to 22 percent of total benefits.[6] The public-works committees which considered these projects were reluctant to give their approval to work which was more closely akin to soil conservation than to flood control. In 1954 Congress terminated the program except for completion of the relatively small number of projects authorized earlier. To take its place a new program of watershed protection was authorized by the Watershed Protection and Flood Prevention Act of 1954,[7] which calls for small projects in watersheds covering less than 250,000 acres. Subsequent amendment limits installations to a total storage capacity of 25,000 acre-feet of which no more than 5,000 acre-feet can be devoted to flood prevention.[8] Appropriations for the new program are rising rapidly, as can be seen in Table 14, and there is strong reason to believe that if the Soil Conservation Service can submit a large number of projects that have economic feasibility, funds much in excess of present levels will be made available.

A major controversy has arisen between the Department of Agriculture and the Corps of Engineers and their proponents about the relative merits of upstream and downstream flood control. I shall not discuss or try to evaluate the issues of this controversy, which has been done in considerable detail in the

[5] For some of the reasons for this failure of the program to expand see A. Maass, "Protecting Nature's Reservoir," C. J. Friedrich and J. K. Galbraith, eds., *Public Policy* (1954), III, 71–106.

[6] U.S. Congress, House Committee on Public Works, *Report of the Subcommittee to Study Civil Works*, Pt. 2, *The Flood Control Program of the Department of Agriculture*, House Committee Print No. 22, 82 Cong., 2 sess., p. 38.

[7] 68 Stat. P.L. 566 Aug. 4, 1954.

[8] 70 Stat. P.L. 1018 Aug. 7, 1956. This amendment of the Act of 1954 revises the limit of size of structures upward and extends the possible scope of projects to the "conservation, development, utilization and disposal of water." The Act also requires that the Secretary of Agriculture determine whether benefits exceed costs of projects.

recent book by Leopold and Maddox, *The Flood Control Controversy.*[9]

The procedures used by the Department of Agriculture for the evaluation of projects are quite similar to those of the Corps of Engineers. There are few differences in the concepts of benefits and costs themselves, though the figures which are produced by means of them show no such agreement. For example, the flood damage estimates of the two agencies for one small agricultural area on Mulberry Creek, Colorado, differed by 600 percent, with the Corps' figure equal to $6,000 a year and the figure of the Soil Conservation Service equal to $38,000. In subsequent joint investigation the agencies agreed on $10,000 a year.[10] Despite agreement on fundamental concepts, such inconsistencies can emerge because of different assumptions about the frequency of floods, the crop yields of the land, and the degree to which crops would be damaged. It should be noted that these important differences are not due to the method of economic analysis but lie in the realm of hydrology and agronomy, and, in some instances, of engineering.

A recent study undertaken by F. A. Clarenbach for the second Hoover Commission has brought the validity of the estimates for agricultural flood damages produced by both agencies into serious question.[11] Clarenbach cites several examples in which the value of the damages prevented by protective works is estimated to be so large that the increase in land value derived by capitalizing this benefit far exceeds the total value of the land. In our study we shall confine ourselves to the concepts of benefit and cost

[9] L. B. Leopold and T. Maddox, Jr., *The Flood Control Controversy* (1954).

[10] Cited in I. Picken and I. K. Fox, *The Upstream-Downstream Flood Control Controversy in the Arkansas–White–Red River Basins Survey.* It should not be concluded from this example that the estimates of the Engineers are always lower. Instances in which their figures are much higher than those of the SCS can also be cited.

[11] F. A. Clarenbach, "Reliability of Estimates of Agricultural Damages from Flood," in Commission on Organization of the Executive Branch of the Government, *Task Force Report on Water Resources and Power* (June 1955), vol. III, pp. 1275–1298. An amendment to Corps regulations now requires that benefit estimates be checked against the changes in land value that are implicit in them. U.S. Army Corps of Engineers, *Examinations and Surveys, Relation of Flood Damage and Flood Control Benefits to Market Value of Land*, EM, 1120-2-111, 13 June 1957.

without endeavoring to evaluate the performance of the agencies in applying the concepts to specific assumptions about flood frequencies, crop yields with and without the project, and the changes in production costs induced by flood protection. Since the concepts of benefits and costs of the two agencies are quite similar, we shall only take up the procedures of the Corps of Engineers. It must be stressed, however, that failure to adopt common physical standards results in benefit-cost analyses which are not comparable. This, together with the administrative separation between upstream and downstream work, precludes the development of consistent, much less optimal, flood-control plans for our river valleys.

A. Economic Analysis

2. *The Estimation of Floods*

Flood-control benefits only accrue if floods are prevented and so they depend on the frequency with which a river would over-flow its banks in the absence of preventive works. Thus, the estimation of flood-control benefits requires that the frequencies of floods of different magnitudes and the damage that they would cause be estimated.[12] With the frequencies and potential damages known, measures of benefit can be constructed.

The probability of a flood of given dimensions is expressed in terms of a flood frequency. If a flood is very probable, say of a magnitude which has been occurring every other year, it will have a flood frequency of 2, meaning that it can be expected once in every two years. An extremely large flood, such that it has been recorded only once in the last hundred years, has a frequency of 100, and is called a hundred-year flood.

Floods are usually measured by their maximum rate of discharge of water, either at the peak instant or during the peak period. The rate of discharge is measured in cubic feet per second, or ft³/sec. Figure 10 shows a typical discharge-frequency curve, which applies to a portion of the Connecticut River near Spring-field, Massachusetts.

[12] A much more detailed discussion of the technical aspects of the problem can be found in H. K. Barrows, *Floods, Their Hydrology and Control* (1948).

Since damages from floods depend on the number of feet by which the river exceeds its banks, usually called the flood stage, it is necessary to compute the stage at the important centers of potential damage. A rating curve indicates the relation between the rate of discharge and the flood stage at a specific point. Figure 11 shows a rating curve for an index station, a curve which

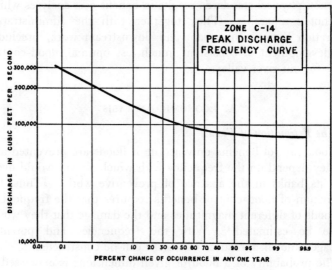

ZONE C-14 PEAK DISCHARGE FREQUENCY CURVE

Figure 10

Note : Figures 10 to 14 are reproduced from a paper prepared by the New England Division of the Corps of Engineers for the New England–New York Inter-Agency Committee, included in its report, *The Resources of the New England–New York Region, Part III, Reference Data*, Vol. 3, Section 19, "Hydrologic and Economic Analysis for Flood Control," 1955, unpublished.

was actually derived from hydrological records. The index curve can be applied to other localities after suitable correction for differences in the river beds, permitting the construction of stage-frequency curves for each damage center.

Most American rivers have relatively short stage records, which makes it difficult to derive reliable discharge-frequency or stage-frequency curves by statistical means. If the stage or other stream-flow data are inadequate, a priori formulas can be used as an approximation. There are a number of such formulas, usually incorporating such factors as size and shape of drainage basin and rainfall. But as meteorological and hydrological data improve and become available for smaller rivers, there need be less recourse to synthetic methods of frequency estimation.[13]

The reliability of the flood-frequency estimates for forecasting purposes depends upon two factors. First, is the number of observations large enough to yield reliable estimates, that is, is the historical record long enough and does it exist for enough points

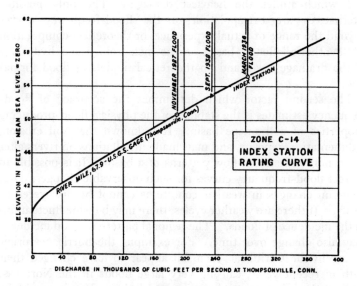

Figure 11

on the river? The Committee on Standards for Basic Data of the President's Water Resources Policy Commission recommended that the number of gaging stations in the United States be increased from 6,300[14] to 12,100 in order to get the kind of

[13] The most complete discussion of methods for estimating flood frequencies may be found in the Department of the Interior, Geological Survey, *Floods in the United States*, by C. S. Jarvis and others, Water-Supply Paper 771 (Washington, 1936).

[14] These stations are run by the Water Resources branch of the U.S. Geological Survey, Department of the Interior; their records are published in the Water-Supply Papers.

stream-flow data which the magnitudes of the river-development programs require.[15] It also recommended a comparable increase in the number of precipitation gages and snow courses, which provide data for estimating the runoff in a drainage basin. These recommendations imply that in the judgments of these experts, the estimates can be significantly improved in many places. But even if more data are collected in coming years, the paucity of the historical record will preclude good estimates for the frequency of very large floods, ones which occur only once in several decades and which inflict the heaviest damages. The only possible alternatives are extrapolation of the flood-frequency curves beyond the range of actual experience, or theoretical computation of "synthetic" floods, based on the meteorology and hydrology of the drainage basin and on theoretical models of flood formation.[16]

The second factor which determines the accuracy of flood-frequency estimates is the stability of the physical flood-producing properties of a drainage basin. It is known that soil erosion, sedimentation deposits, and man-made installations on rivers alter the runoff and stream-flow patterns of a basin. It is possible to correct flood-frequency curves for such observable changes. But long-run changes in weather conditions cannot be discovered so easily. If there are weather cycles, there may be wide fluctuations in the incidence of floods. The regional pattern of flood incidence may also change over time. For example, the hurricanes originating in the Caribbean each fall appear to have changed their path in recent years, causing very large floods in the Northeast while reducing average damages in Florida. Yet it would be dangerous to assume that such a change is permanent, for it is possible that yet another pattern may succeed the present one. Our history is too short, the record too incomplete, and our understanding of the underlying factors which determine the weather too inadequate to permit us to employ models of flood formation which incorporate changing flood frequencies over time. Under these conditions there is little choice but to assume that

[15] The President's Water Resources Policy Commission, *A Water Policy for the American People*, Appendix 3, p. 326.
[16] See *Floods in the United States*, Water-Supply Paper No. 771, especially pp. 421–461.

the variables which produce the flood-frequency distribution remain constant.[17]

3. *Estimating Flood Damages*

Once the frequency of different floods has been estimated, it becomes necessary to estimate how much damage would be done at each flood stage.[18] Sometimes stage-area curves are drawn to indicate what areas, given a certain flood stage, will be inundated. Within the flooded area, it can be determined how many feet of water will cover different sections. Through surveys conducted by the division offices of the Engineers, the actual damages to property in the area can be estimated.

The techniques[19] of the surveys depend on the problems of the specific area and on the funds available. Questionnaires are sent to the major industrial firms, railroads, governmental units, and public utilities after each flood. Residential areas may be surveyed completely or, more commonly, may be subject to sample surveys of typical homes, using representative sampling. In some instances, stage-damage curves may be worked out for typical structures of the area, indicating what percent of the real value of assets will be destroyed by flooding of different heights. Food stores, for example, which keep large inventories in basements, will be hard hit by small flooding, while multistory residences may suffer relatively minor damages even with flooding of the first floor if adequate warning is given to the inhabitants to remove as many of their belongings as possible to higher floors.

[17] C. S. Jarvis (main author of *Floods in the United States*, the definitive paper on flood frequencies) contended in 1939 that floods were becoming more frequent. This argument was based on examination of the historical record of the then most recent years, which were particularly bad. The succeeding years (1939 to 1942) had relatively few floods, however, casting doubt on Jarvis' hypothesis. C. S. Jarvis, "Symposium on Flood Control," *Geophysical Union Transactions* (1939), p. 157. Also see Barrows, *Floods, Their Hydrology and Control*, p. 2.

[18] The amount of damage also depends on the duration of the flood, the nature of sediments deposited in the flooded area, and other factors. The procedures are adapted to include these factors.

[19] Survey techniques are discussed in J. B. Lampert, "A Study of Methods of Determining Flood Control Damages and of Evaluating Flood Control Benefits," unpublished master's thesis (M.I.T., 1939), chap. 3. Also see Barrows, *Floods, Their Hydrology and Control*, pp. 140–159.

Stage-damage curves for typical buildings can be combined with listings of the buildings by type and by elevation to derive a stage-damage curve for the area as a whole. Figure 12 shows a typical stage-damage curve.

Once the stage-frequency curve and the stage-damage curves are known, they are combined into a damage-frequency curve. Figure 13 contains this curve before control measures are installed, with natural conditions.

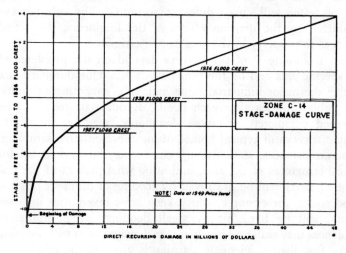

Figure 12

Annual flood losses are calculated by computing the mathematical expectation of flood losses, that is, by multiplying the probability of each stage by the corresponding damage, and adding up these expected values.[20] Damages which are averted can be estimated by constructing a new damage-frequency curve, which shows the damages that can be expected to occur after the projects have been built. Since flood control lowers the stage which results from a given set of meteorologic conditions, the frequency of a certain stage will become smaller; the damage of that stage

[20] If the data do not warrant computation of damage-frequency curves, annual flood losses may be estimated by averaging annual flood losses during the past fifty or one hundred years. *Annual Report of Chief of Engineers* (1951), Pt. I, Vol. III, p. 375.

will remain the same, so that the new damage-frequency curve only requires the new set of stage frequencies.[21]

Figure 13 summarizes the computation. The frequency scale of the damage-frequency curves is divided into three ranges, for each of which a different damage scale is used in order to facilitate reading of the charts and in order to show what share of the damages can be attributed to the different kinds of floods. Range A, consisting of floods likely to occur less than once in a hundred years, contains 19 percent of the damages; Range B, which includes floods expected once every twenty years to once every hundred years, contains 26 percent of all damages; and Range C, floods occurring more than once in twenty years, contains the remaining 55 percent of all damages. Damage-frequency curves are also drawn for four different degrees of protection, where the degree is defined by the percentage by which the peak discharge is reduced.

To show the effect of increased efforts to reduce the peak discharge, Figure 14 indicates the benefits that result from the decrease of floods in each of the three ranges. It can be seen that all the possible benefits accrue if the peak discharge is reduced 50 percent. It is clear that it would be a waste of resources to provide more control, a result peculiar to this example.

If it were the objective of the program to maximize net benefits, that is, the difference between benefits and costs, it would be possible to construct a cost curve for different reductions in peak discharge, and to compare it with an aggregate of the three curves in Figure 14, as is done with hypothetical values in Figure 15. The difference between benefits and costs is maximized with that reduction of the peak for which the slopes of the two curves are the same, at point P in the figure, where marginal benefit equals marginal cost. Or, applying the principles of the preceding chapter, the degree of protection might be pushed to the point where the benefit of the marginal expenditure exceeds its cost by an amount appropriate to the tightness of the budgetary constraint, a degree of protection short of point P, such as Q. But as we shall see,[22] the Corps does not accept any of these principles fully and employs other criteria to determine the scale of

[21] If control measures change the time pattern and duration of floods at different stages, a new stage-damage curve may become necessary.

[22] Section 9 below.

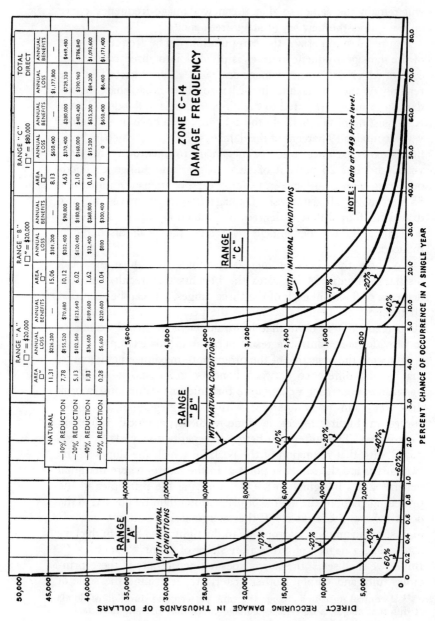

ZONE C-14
DAMAGE FREQUENCY

NOTE: *Data at 1949 Price level.*

	RANGE "A" 1 □ = $20,000			RANGE "B" 1 □ = $20,000			RANGE "C" 1 □ = $80,000			TOTAL DIRECT	
	AREA □"	ANNUAL LOSS	ANNUAL BENEFITS	AREA □"	ANNUAL LOSS	ANNUAL BENEFITS	AREA □"	ANNUAL LOSS	ANNUAL BENEFITS	ANNUAL LOSS	ANNUAL BENEFITS
NATURAL	11.31	$226,200	—	15.06	$301,200	—	8.13	$650,400	—	$1,177,800	—
—10% REDUCTION	7.78	$155,520	$70,680	10.12	$202,400	$98,800	4.63	$370,400	$280,000	$728,320	$449,480
—20% REDUCTION	5.13	$102,560	$123,640	6.02	$120,400	$180,800	2.10	$168,000	$482,400	$390,960	$786,840
—40% REDUCTION	1.83	$36,600	$189,600	1.62	$32,400	$268,800	0.19	$15,200	$635,200	$84,200	$1,093,600
—60% REDUCTION	0.28	$5,600	$220,600	0.04	$800	$300,400	0	0	$650,400	$6,400	$1,171,400

RANGE "C"

WITH NATURAL CONDITIONS

-10%

-20%

-40%

RANGE "B"

WITH NATURAL CONDITIONS

-10%

-20%

-40%

-60%

RANGE "A"

WITH NATURAL CONDITIONS

-10%

-20%

-40%

-60%

PERCENT CHANCE OF OCCURRENCE IN A SINGLE YEAR

DIRECT RECURRING DAMAGE IN THOUSANDS OF DOLLARS

Figure 13

124

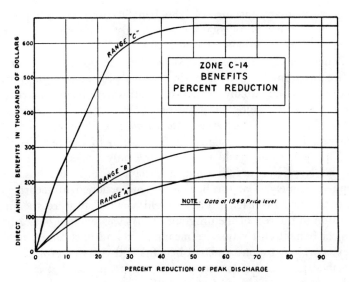

Figure 14

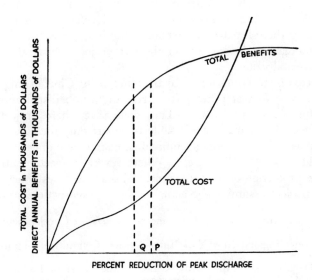

Figure 15

projects in many instances. The benefit-cost ratio of a project only states the ratio of total benefits to costs for whatever degree of protection the project plan provides.

Benefits are usually calculated not for one project, but for an entire program for a river basin. Since projects are submitted to Congress individually, benefit-cost ratios have been constructed for them by assigning the total benefit by means of convenient rules of thumb. The *Orders and Regulations*[23] suggest that the program benefits be assigned in proportion to the benefits that each project would yield if it were the only project to be built. In the New England division, a variant of this rule has been applied, namely, that the benefits be apportioned in accordance with the benefits each project would yield if it were the final addition to the rest of the program.[24] As was pointed out earlier, project benefit-cost ratios are meaningless and misleading, unless they represent the incremental benefits and costs of projects in a specified plan of development. Since in many cases it is official policy to provide a degree of protection greater than the amount that would result if the incremental benefits had to exceed their costs, it is likely that the final projects in a program produce less benefits than costs. Either of the two rules of thumb for assigning program benefits to projects acts as a leveler among projects, reducing the estimates of benefits of the first projects to be built and increasing the benefits of the last projects above their true incremental value.

Recent instructions issued by the office of the Chief of Engineers represent a first step away from rule of thumb distributions of benefits among projects.[25] They state that where projects are interrelated, "it may be advisable to report only the ratio of the group as a whole," though "individual justification of each project should be checked" as well. Where several projects contribute to the protection of the same area, ratios are to be established for each project assuming the actual order of construction, provided

[23] U.S. Army, Corps of Engineers, *Orders and Regulations*, par. 4208.24.
[24] New England-New York Inter-Agency Committee, unpublished report.
[25] Department of the Army, Office of the Chief of Engineers, 27 August 1954. "Certain Supplemental Guidance With Respect to Flood Control Projects," section 3. Internal paper.

the order is known; if the sequence of construction is unknown, benefits should be divided "equitably," in accordance with the old rule of thumb. While this memorandum represents some progress toward incremental decision making, it raises a new host of difficulties by relating project ratios to the order of construction. Since this order is usually determined politically, the resultant ratios will still not indicate the true relative merit of various projects in an area. While the procedure assures that each additional project can pass a valid test of economic justification, it does not yield the optimum combination of projects. To achieve the latter aim, an optimal combination of projects must be derived first; once the optimal set has been identified, the best sequence of development should be selected. In the event that the order of construction must be determined politically, as is frequently the case, this procedure helps to accomplish the objective of providing the optimal combination of projects once all of them have been built. To provide some check on the rationality of the actual sequence of construction, incremental benefit-cost ratios based on the actual order can be computed and presented when appropriation requests are being processed.

4. *Direct Flood-Control Benefits: Decline of Direct Flood Losses*

Aversion of flood losses is the major flood-control benefit. The Corps of Engineers considers two types of damages: *direct* and *indirect*. Direct damages are largely physical damages to property by flood waters, and are measured by the cost of restoration to preflood condition. They also include agricultural losses, which are measured by the change in net revenue of farmers.

Each division office of the Corps has considerable autonomy in the evaluation of these losses. There is no uniform set of categories for damages, though the systems of different divisions are quite similar. A typical set of categories and its components is reproduced below.[26]

(a) *Residential losses*, such as damage to grounds, trees, shrubbery, fences, walks, dwellings, garages, furnishings, equipment, utilities, personal effects, and vehicles.

[26] Reproduced from Federal Inter-Agency River Basin Committee, Subcommittee on Benefits and Costs, *Qualitative Aspects of Benefit-Cost Practices*, pp. 2–3.

(b) *Commercial losses* affecting business, industrial and other private commercial enterprises, such as damage to land, buildings, equipment, supplies, stock, utility plants and distribution works, mines, wells and other resources and transportation facilities.

(c) *Public losses* such as damage to public land, buildings, churches, schools, playgrounds, parks, roads, bridges, water supplies and distribution systems, dams, reservoirs, canals, waterways and other property of federal, state, municipal and other public agencies.

(d) *Agricultural losses*, such as loss of crops and livestock, damage to stored crops and livestock products, costs of replanting, damage to buildings, equipment, and supplies, damage to land through scour, caving and deposition.

On the basis of economic principle, the prevention of any of these direct losses is a genuine benefit. We saw in Chapter II that willingness to pay is a good indicator of the value of a service to consumers. In the case of flood control there are no voluntary market revenues because the service cannot be withheld from an individual who refuses to pay for it; that is, it is nonmarketable. Thus market revenue cannot be used to determine the benefit. But we can ask what price people would be willing to pay for flood control if it could be sold in the market place. If consumers behaved rationally, they would purchase flood prevention if it were offered at a price equal to or less than the cost of desired repairs. The sum of all the repair costs which are averted is therefore equal to the value of protection and can be used as a measure of benefit. If it is assumed that all damages would be repaired, then the damage figures indicate the benefit, since damages are defined in terms of repair cost. The use of this measure of benefit implies that those projects will be justified which prevent more damages than their cost. Failure to pass the benefit-cost criterion implies that less resources are lost through floods in the area than would be used in constructing the project. In the event that consumers would not repair the damages completely, the benefit is smaller, of course, equal at least to the actual repair expense they are willing to make, and at most equal to the sum of money they would be willing to pay to be protected from floods.

The first three categories of direct flood-control benefits are clearly in the nature of prevented damages. The fourth, reduction in agricultural losses, is in part also a reduction of damages, in this instance of crops, livestock, and other property. A rational farmer would be willing to pay an amount equal to such damage if he could be sold flood control, since the loss of marketable outputs represents a loss of revenue to him, while repair of property will be necessary for operation of the farm; only the benefit of prevention of damage to consumer goods, including his dwelling, may be limited by his willingness to actually incur the repair expense. Part of the loss from floods will not be damage to property but an increase of the cost of production; there may be need for replanting, additional harvesting costs, and so on. If flood control reduces these costs, factor services are released for other purposes (including leisure) and there is a corresponding increase in the real national income.

5. *Indirect Flood-Control Benefits: Reduction of Indirect Flood Losses*

Indirect flood losses are "the net economic losses of goods and services to the nation due to the interruption of business, industry, commerce, traffic, communications, and other activities, both within and outside the area subject to flooding, and the cost of activities made necessary by the flood such as emergency flood-fighting measures and relief, care, and rehabilitation of flood victims."[27] The most important of the items in this category are: (1) loss of goods and services in the area because of cessation of production; (2) loss of wages and other incomes, which is sometimes used as an approximation of the value of lost production (if wages are paid in connection with flood work, the amount is subtracted from the wage loss); (3) loss of stock due to spoilage; (4) increased cost of business operations, including higher transportation costs; (5) costs of evacuation, reoccupation, temporary quarters, emergency flood-protective work, and relief and care of flood victims.

[27] *Annual Report of Chief of Engineers* (1951), p. 372.

Many items on this list are of the same type as the direct losses. Items included in (3), (4), and (5) are genuine social costs that detract from the income which is available to the nation. But the other item, loss of production, whether measured by (1) or (2), poses some very serious issues. The chief of Engineers, in his report to the Subcommittee to Study Civil Works, writes:[28]

> One of the principal difficulties involved in measuring indirect flood losses is determination of the point in the chain from producer to consumer at which the successive effects of a specific item of flood loss will be felt...it is the practice of the Corps of Engineers to evaluate as indirect flood losses only those effects which cannot be avoided or compensated for by adjustments or procedures other than flood control. For example, in tracing the indirect losses arising from loss of a cotton crop due to flooding, it is considered proper to assume that a cotton ginning enterprise that depends on the cotton crop from the area in question would suffer a business loss. However, it is reasoned that the mills to which the cotton is normally shipped for further processing, can, and in all probability do, adjust their supply arrangements so as to preclude any loss to them when expected shipments are not received from the area in question.

The Corps recognizes, according to this paragraph, that at some point fairly early in the production chain there will be substitution of alternative supplies, thus definitely terminating the possibility of loss due to floods.

How far in the productive process should the indirect losses be traced, and to what extent can their prevention be considered a benefit of flood control? To answer this question we shall again make use of the principle that economic benefit can be measured by the amount of money which rational producers would be willing to pay if flood protection were marketable. We continue to assume that the economy is in a state of general full employment.

Farmers who lose crops should be willing to pay an amount for flood protection that is equal to the value of the crops which

[28] *Annual Report of Chief of Engineers* (1951), p. 373.

are saved from destruction or that is equal to the production expenses which they are saved by eliminating replanting of crops. Their benefit is measured entirely by the direct agricultural benefits.

Businesses located in the flood area, in addition to incurring the direct losses of property damage, will suffer losses from interruption of operations. If a plant is forced to close there will be a loss of profits, which in many cases cannot be made up later on. Stores that are forced to close will also lose some of the sales permanently, with their loss measured by the change in profits.

Workers in the area who are made idle by a flood will value protection to be equal to the wage payments which they would lose, except for one minor qualification. If the flood makes them idle, it gives them an opportunity to enjoy leisure instead of working. Since workers are not likely to value leisure highly during a flood, and since the surprise of the sudden loss of income involves real costs of its own, particularly for heads of families, it is probably safe to ignore the value of the extra leisure, leaving the reduction in wage losses as the benefit.

Processors who depend entirely on farms or other sources in the flooded area should be willing to pay an amount for flood protection which is as great as the operating profit they would earn on the commodities that are lost through the flood. Since their fixed costs continue during periods of idleness, they value flood protection to be the difference between the change in the value of output and the change in their current costs.

Firms in still later stages of production are likely to be able to substitute other sources of supply. These sources may involve somewhat higher costs, particularly higher transportation costs. The willingness to pay of firms at these stages will be limited to these differences in costs.

Businesses which sell to the flooded area will suffer some loss of profits, but much of this loss is likely to be made up after the flood is over. In the case of perishables the loss of sales is permanent, but it is already measured by the direct loss of "loss of stock due to spoilage."

In addition to these businesses that suffer reductions in profit and who would therefore value flood protection, we must consider firms who benefit from the flood. Processors outside the affected region will have some extra business because of the reduced output of their competitors in the flood plain. Workers elsewhere will receive some extra wages, and similarly for the other factors of production. In order to measure the net indirect benefit of flood control we need to isolate those indirect losses which are not offset elsewhere. Where the direct physical effect of the flood leads to a reduction of output and a reduction of factor payments, there is a genuine loss of national income which cannot be offset elsewhere. Any reduction of output at subsequent stages must be presumed to be offset unless the contrary can be shown. Even in the case of the processor wholly dependent on the flooded area for his supply, there will generally be processors elsewhere who will fill the gap in meeting the total demand for the product. The costs of the alternate processors may be slightly higher and their profits lower, but there is no reason to suppose that the profit on their extra output would be zero.

Whether offsetting production elsewhere is possible depends on the nature of the product. If it can be shipped, the offset is likely. Some outputs, however, particularly personal services, cannot be transported any great distances. For example, barbers' services elsewhere will not be substituted for haircuts foregone because of flood conditions. The wages and profits thus lost are genuine, indirect flood losses. If a flood is large and affects commercial areas, losses of this kind become significant.[29]

There are severe problems in the estimation of these benefits. Indirect damages of floods are usually estimated from surveys of local chambers of commerce and of local businessmen which are undertaken shortly after a flood. Hysteria and the American desire to surpass all previous records are likely to lead to excessive damage estimates. In the case of indirect losses, the organizations that are surveyed are likely to be particularly sophisticated about the very limited reimbursability of flood control and about the advantages which accrue to local businessmen from the construction activity caused by a project.

---

[29] The New England division of the Engineers confines indirect benefits to a fraction of their usual values in the case of small floods, following the reasoning that the losses in production and sales are more likely to be made up later.

Although the *Orders and Regulations* of the Corps caution against the use of constant indirect loss factors,[30] it has been found in the New England division that it is impractical to survey the indirect losses after each flood, and particularly after small floods. The division undertook detailed surveys after the very large floods of 1938, when it had the funds and the manpower to make a thorough canvass. From these surveys, the indirect loss factors shown in Table 15 were derived. These values are still

Table 15. Indirect loss factors, New England division

Category of damages	Indirect losses / Direct losses
Industrial, including utilities	1.2
Urban—commercial, residential, and public	1.5
Rural	0.2
Highways, railways	1.0

Source: New England–New York Inter-Agency Committee.

in use. Total indirect loss can be computed by multiplying the direct loss in each category by the corresponding indirect loss factor.[31]

6. *Flood-Control Benefits: Higher Utilization of Property*

Benefits from averted flood losses are usually calculated on the assumption either that the current use of the land subject to flooding is unchanged or that the land will participate in the general growth of the area. But if flood control is provided, it often becomes possible to put the land to a higher use because it becomes feasible to make substantial capital investments which had been precluded by the flood hazard. The Corps has generally confined this benefit to agricultural land,[32] perhaps because new

[30] *Orders and Regulations*, par. 4208.13.
[31] In other cases indirect damage estimates have been prepared for specific projects. For an example, see *Report on West Branch of the Susquehanna River, Pa.*, House Doc. 29, 84 Cong., 1 sess.
[32] Federal Inter-Agency River Basin Committee, Subcommittee on Benefits and Costs, *Qualitative Aspects of Benefit-Cost Practices*, p. 5.

uses of urban land generally involve mere diversion of activity from other sites.

The benefit of higher utilization of property, often called "enhancement of property value," is measured by the increased net earnings of the land. The cost of private investment which must be made to yield the higher income is deducted to derive the net figure. It is considered preferable to measure directly the change in annual net income. Sometimes, however, it is only possible to measure the change in the value of the property. If so, an annual figure is derived by applying that interest rate to the property which similar private investments in the area would yield.[33] Since the property value itself is determined through private capitalization of income at the private rate, the annual social benefit is derived by applying the private rate.

Benefits in this category can become quite large. For example, they constitute 10 percent of all flood-control benefit of the Main Control Plan on the Columbia River, $1,700,000 annually out of $16,200,000.[34]

The Corps is careful to prevent double counting of the same benefits by measuring them as prevented flood losses and as enhancement of land value.[35] If it is assumed that the land will be put to more intensive use for calculating the decline of flood losses, then the other category will be omitted altogether.[36]

This category of benefits is in accordance with the principles

[33] *Orders and Regulations*, par. 4208.23; and Federal Inter-Agency River Basin Committee, Subcommittee on Benefits and Costs, *Measurement Aspects of Benefit-Cost Analysis*, p. 60.

[34] *Report on Columbia River and Tributaries*, House Doc. 531, vol. I, p. 121.

[35] The error of counting both the change in income from land and the resultant increase in land value was made on some occasions in the past, but now seems to be eliminated. Barrows cites an example of such double counting in a report on the Connecticut River of 1938. (*Floods, Their Hydrology and Control*, p. 153). The TVA report on a flood-control project on the Upper French Broad River is another instance of it. This error was more common in the past when the "depreciation method" of benefit estimation was widely used. This method tried to estimate flood losses from changes in property value before and after a flood. Since these values drop excessively in postflood hysteria, and since the valuations may be quite capricious even in ordinary times, this method is no longer widely used.

[36] For example, this practice was followed in the *Report on the Upper Iowa River*, House Doc. 375, 83 Cong., 2 sess., p. 29.

of this study.   If the reduction of flood risk permits the exploitation of intrinsic natural advantages of a piece of land, the national income is increased.   Since it can be assumed that the extra output replaces output of marginal land on which no return can be earned, any rise in net income on the land is a genuine economic benefit from the point of view of the nation as a whole.

7. *The Probabilistic Nature of Flood-Control Benefits: The Use of Mathematical Expectation*

It has been shown that annual flood-control benefits are computed by subtracting the annual flood losses with the project from the annual flood losses without the project, where the annual losses were computed from the damage-frequency relationship.   The figure which is calculated in this manner represents the expected average annual change in losses, given the assumptions of constant flood probabilities, of reliable stage-damage relationships, and of correct operation of reservoirs.   On those assumptions, this expected average figure will turn out to be the true average after a period has elapsed which is long enough to permit the laws of chance to even out good years and bad.

This use of mathematical expectation, of maximizing the average expected net benefit, is open to serious challenge, because it is not clear that the people and the Congress really desire that the average expected benefit be the variable to be maximized.[37]   The policy, if scrupulously practised, would mean that flood-control installations and operations be planned with those floods in mind which provide the largest share of the annual damages.   The frequency-damage curve of Figure 13, which is fairly typical, shows that very large floods do not contribute much to the total because they are so very rare.   Yet the Flood Control Acts of

---

[37] For a theoretical challenge to the principle of maximizing expected benefits, see J. Marschak, "Why Should Statisticians and Businessmen Maximize Moral Expectation?" *Proceedings of the Second Berkeley Symposium on Mathematical Statistics and Probability*, pp. 493–506. Marschak suggests alternative principles for business but does not deal with governmental decisions.   But the negative part of his argument applies with equal force to public policy.   See especially pp. 495, 497. For an application of the use of mathematical expectation in flood-control design, see D. V. Dantzig, "Economic Decision Problems for Flood Prevention," *Econometrica* (July 1956), pp. 276–287.   Also see M. Allais, "Discussion," *Econometrica* (April 1955), pp. 212–213.

1936 and 1938, which are the basic legislation in the field, were obviously passed in response to the disastrous floods of those years, to bring the full potential of federal intervention to bear to prevent recurrence of such national calamities. The control of many little floods with primarily local impacts was surely a subsidiary aim. Further, ideas held by the public about flood control run in terms of a disaster type of large flood, not of small ones. On many rivers, if the Engineers carried out all their construction and operations with the objective of maximizing the expected annual net benefit, they would not attempt to provide protection against large floods but would concentrate on those with greater frequency.[38]

In practice, the Engineers do not use strict computations based on mathematical expectations of damages except in the benefit-cost analysis itself. The *Engineering Manual for Civil Works Construction*,[39] which provides detailed guidance to field offices, explicitly rejects complete acceptance of the principle of maximizing mathematical expectation. For example, in the chapter on reservoir regulation the *Manual* states[40]

> The storage capacity requirements of a reservoir might be determined by a mathematical analysis of benefits and costs and adopting the criterion that an economically justified reservoir would give a high ratio of benefits to costs. Since unusually large floods, or series of floods, occur infrequently and require much more reservoir capacity than the smaller and more frequent floods, this procedure might indicate that operation for regulation of the larger floods is questionable. Hence it is a fallacy to base reservoir storage capacity entirely on the benefit-cost ratio....

The paragraph also stresses that capacity must be increased somewhat to allow a safety factor in view of the short historical records of flood frequencies.

The *Manual* also cautions against the use of pure mathematical expectation in the operation of reservoirs, such as in the allocation of storage space and in the setting of release schedules.

---

[38] *Orders and Regulations*, par. 4208.11 and 4208.18.
[39] U.S. Army, Corps of Engineers, *Engineering Manual for Civil Works*.
[40] *Engineering Manual for Civil Works*, pt. CXXXVI, chap. 1.1.03.

First, it points out that flood-water releases cannot always be scheduled optimally because public opinion at time of flooding downstream from a dam will not permit the release of water which is necessary to provide space for insurance against a second flood, and therefore capacity must be somewhat larger than optimal operation would require. The *Manual* discusses three methods of reservoir operation. Method A calls for "maximum beneficial use of available storage during each flood event,"[41] and aims to minimize the damage of the flood currently occurring. This is the method that is taken as synonymous with maximization of expected benefit.[42]

Method B is based on the control of a standard project flood. It is recommended especially where protection is provided for large urban centers which would only be affected by a very large, and hence very rare, flood. In this case, Method A might prescribe similar operations, since presumably most of the expected damage would be due to large floods, and hence most of the storage space would be assigned to that purpose. But it is true that Method A, especially in the specified operational form in which it ignores all floods but the current one, will tend to yield much control of little floods and consequently leave a relatively large hazard for large floods, since the reservoirs may well be filled when a large flood takes place. Method B tends to let small floods take their course undisturbed, saving the reservoir capacity for the possibility of a disaster type of flood.

Method C is a combination of A and B and considers both objectives. For example, Method A might be used during the growing season if agricultural benefits are large at that time and the possibility of gigantic floods is relatively small; Method B could be applied the rest of the year. Though no one method is

[41] *Engineering Manual for Civil Works*, pt. CXXXVI, chap. 3.
[42] It should be noted that this is incorrect. If there is a possibility that two floods will occur with not enough interval to permit complete runoff of the first flood, then operation according to mathematical expectation would require that some portion of a reservoir be set aside for the possibility of a second flood, the share to be determined by the magnitude of the current flood, the probability of a series of two floods, and the expected magnitude of damage of a second flood. Thus the *Manual's* objection to Method A, that it does not allow for the possibility of a second flood, is not well taken and is based on an incorrect operational interpretation of the principle of maximizing expected benefit.

recommended for universal use, the *Manual* indicates that Method C may be an appropriate compromise.

Though the design and operation of projects do not maximize expected net benefits, the benefit-cost evaluations reflect only expected average values. The measure of benefits that results is conservative and leaves a substantial area to be filled by verbal evaluation of intangibles if the objectives implicit in the procedures correspond more closely to popular desire than pure maximization of expected net benefits.

8. *Determination of the "Degree of Protection"*

Since the design of a project uses principles other than maximization of net benefit, the use of benefit-cost analysis at the design stage is rather limited. Let us look briefly at the procedures actually employed to determine the scale of a project. The size of flood which an installation is designed to control will determine its scale, and the "degree of protection" indicates how large a flood is to be controlled. Thus a project which protects against a flood expected to occur once in a hundred years has a higher degree of protection than a project designed to cope with a fifty-year flood.

In planning flood protection in an area, the Corps of Engineers first studies the historical record of rainstorms and identifies the standard project storm,[43] a storm approximating the most severe flood-inducing conditions considered "reasonably characteristic" in the area. This storm will reflect the nature of the drainage basin, the potential snow belt, and a particularly adverse geographic pattern of rainfall. The standard project storm yields the standard project flood, assuming adverse but reasonably possible runoff conditions, a flood which is used as a reference standard against which the degree of protection is measured. Where potential loss of life and of highly valued property is great, but where some risk can be taken, the standard project flood may be accepted as the design flood; that is, the plans will provide protection against a flood of this magnitude. Even more severe conditions are described by the maximum probable flood,

[43] Department of the Army, Office of the Chief of Engineers, Civil Works Engineer Bulletin 52–58, 26 March 1952: "Standard Project Flood Determinations."

which reflects the worst possible combination of circumstances that could conceivably occur. This concept will not be accepted as the design flood except in extraordinary cases, but will serve as the basis of spillway design to assure that the project will survive under the worst of conditions even if it fails to control. No definitive policy exists for the selection of the design flood and hence of the degree of protection. Instructions issued in 1952[44] state that it may exceed or fall short of the standard project flood, "depending to an important extent upon economic factors and other practical considerations governing the selection of design capacity in a specific case." Annual tangible benefits are also rejected as the sole criterion; "intangible benefits, resulting from provision of a high degree of security against floods of a disastrous magnitude, including the protection of human life, must be considered in addition to tangible benefits that may be estimated in monetary terms." Yet the standard project flood is to play some part in design. With uniform physical standards prescribed for its estimation, protection against it would provide a uniform degree of protection everywhere, defined in terms of the frequency of the flood to be controlled. It is thus considered a standard of comparison for the actual protection provided, and should serve to promote "a more consistent policy."

The Memorandum of 1954[45] is a little more specific. It reasserts that the degree of protection "must be a matter of judgment," to be determined on the basis of "costs, benefits, the nature of the threat," and so on, with a low degree of protection more acceptable where there is relatively little property or danger to human life. It also sets down three principles: (1) a project must provide "a reliable and fully understood degree of protection," adequate to meet the foreseeable needs of the area; (2) there should not be excessive protection "at the expense of sound economics," though it is not necessary to limit protection to the degree that will "give the highest benefit-to-cost ratio." Protection should be limited to the degree, however, where the "added increment of cost exceeds the expected increment of benefit, except in cases where that increment of protection is necessary to obviate some threat to life, threat to public health,

[44] *Engineering Manual for Civil Works*, p. 6.
[45] "Certain Supplemental Guidance," p. 3.

or danger of widespread economic dislocation." (3) Finally, the memorandum cautions against excessively detailed computations of benefits and costs based on inadequate data and suggests that brief analyses should be sufficient to determine the degree of protection. On the basis of these considerations, the memorandum suggests that small agricultural projects protecting only land may be built to provide against floods no bigger than a ten-year flood, though protection against a twenty-five-year flood is expected to be more typical. Larger agricultural projects, protecting some physical improvements, may provide against twenty-five-year floods, though protection against fifty- or seventy-five-year floods will be more normal. Finally, in the case of highly developed areas, protection against a flood expected to occur once in several hundred years may be warranted.

These instructions still leave the fundamental decision about the design of a project a matter of judgment to be resolved by responsible officials in the field, perhaps in consultation with central authorities. The guidance which is provided is very incomplete and the principles on which federal flood-control policy rests remain unclarified. At least two distinguishable strands of thought appear to run through the various instructions. First, projects are to reduce the expected damages, an objective reflected in the benefit-cost calculation and suggesting that the degree of protection be limited to the point where incremental benefits equal incremental costs. Second, projects are to reduce the flood hazard in the sense that floods below a certain frequency be eliminated. This principle is closely akin to insurance; floods, like other risks against which the federal government provides some protection, such as unemployment, lack of income in old age, and so forth, are a public responsibility, and measures must be undertaken to reduce this risk, with both human life and property at stake.

Whether one or the other of the principles should govern federal flood-control policy has never been specified by Congress nor has the President ever resolved this issue. It is not surprising that in the absence of any policy the Corps of Engineers should endeavor to pursue both objectives—the reduction of damages and the reduction of risk—without facing the possible conflicts. Yet this situation leaves an undesirable amount of administrative discretion in the hands of the Corps, much of which is exercised at the field level. It also places a severe strain on benefit-cost analyses, since there is considerable pressure to design projects with the intent of removing risk, yet have them show mathematically expected benefits in excess of cost. So far the Corps has brought these two objectives into consistency by posing the economic test in terms of total benefits and total costs without applying the benefit-cost technique on an incremental basis; but it has done so at the price of bad economics, for this form of the criterion has little economic rationale. Yet until the fundamental objectives of the federal flood-control program are defined more clearly, the benefit-cost technique cannot be applied rigorously to the design of projects.[46]

9. *Intangible Benefits*

Intangible benefits are those benefits for which no appropriate monetary measure can be constructed. The Corps of Engineers usually includes a very brief statement in each project report which summarizes verbally some of the main intangible benefits. The chief categories are reduction of loss of life, enhancement of the general welfare and security of the people, improvement of sanitation, and protection against epidemics.[47]

In the popular mind, the prevention of loss of life is certainly one of the most important benefits of flood control. Yet, strangely enough, the loss of life from floods in the United States is relatively small, and even that loss is difficult to avert through

---

[46] Abandoning our assumption of a constant marginal utility of income would permit us to bring the insurance aspect of flood control within the framework of benefit-cost analysis. If the marginal utility of income falls for all individuals, yet is the same for all individuals before floods, then the loss of utility suffered by those affected by floods will exceed the loss of utility caused by the marginal dollars of taxation incurred to build protective works. Under these assumptions the equality of marginal benefits and costs would occur at a point at which the money value of costs exceeds the money value of benefits. (I owe this point to Prof. J. K. Butters.) The degree to which the money value of costs should exceed the money value of benefits at the margin will depend on the elasticity of the marginal utility of income and the percentage by which the income of flood victims is reduced. For an application of this conceptual framework in a different context, see R. J. Freund, "The Introduction of Risk into a Programming Model," *Econometrica* (July 1956), pp. 253–263.

[47] *Orders and Regulations*, par. 4208.23.

141

control measures. The total loss of life from 1902 to 1941 was 3,186 deaths, or 83 a year.[48] Since then the loss has been even smaller, as Table 16 shows. This is an almost insignificant part of the loss of life from accidents in the United States. In 1953, 95,000 people died because of accidents, 38,000 in auto accidents alone.[49]

Table 16. Loss of life from floods in the United States

1946	28	1950	93
1947	55	1951	51
1948	82	1952	54
1949	48	1953	40
		1954	55

Average 1946–1954: 52.
Source: U.S. Weather Bureau, *Climatological Data, Annual National Summary*, 1950, p. 61, 1953, p. 64, 1955, p. 95.

The small annual loss of life seems to be quite contradictory to the number of deaths which are reported at the time of major floods. But the paradox is easily explained; when the loss of life is high, such as in the hurricanes of the fall of 1954 when more than 800 people were reported killed, most of the loss of life is due to the immediate impact of the tornado itself, with its high winds and extraordinary rainfall. The floods, which are the only element of the process which can be controlled, do not occur until the rainfall has run off into the streams and these have exceeded their banks. By that time, the alarm has been spread and there has been time for such emergency precautions as evacuation. Some floods do occur during the storm itself and cause loss of life, but these are flash floods of small rivers in small areas, and these are the floods that are least subject to control.

The loss of even eighty lives a year is not a matter to be brushed aside as unworthy of federal attention; and of course the figure is as low as it is because all vulnerable major centers of population are protected by flood-control works at least to some degree.

[48] U.S. Weather Bureau; cited in G. F. White, *Human Adjustment to Floods* (1945), p. 62.
[49] Press release of the National Safety Council, reported in the Boston *Globe*, October 19, 1954.

Insofar as protection of life is a genuine benefit and one of the objectives of public policy, flood-control design and operation must be adapted to the policy. In practice, the most important provision of the Engineers in this regard is the high degree of protection which is the aim of the design of local levees and flood walls in urban areas. Extraordinary large floods striking suddenly in urban areas can cause deaths; the Engineers' rejection of the principle of maximizing expected net benefit partly rests on cognizance of this objective.

Enhancement of the general welfare and of the security of the people is an intangible benefit, which was validated by the conservative practice of measuring benefits on the basis of mathematical expectation, while operating installations in a manner designed to abolish the flood hazard altogether for large centers of population and decreasing the hazard beyond the value justified by expectations for others. The magnitude of this immeasurable benefit is circumscribed by the fact that the loss of life from floods is small, thus implying that the increased feeling of security is either restricted to people's feelings about their property or else is based on an exaggerated notion of the dangers to life.

At this time, project reports contain no supporting information for this benefit, although most projects provide for it to some extent. If it could be established that some projects yield this benefit to a larger extent than others, it would be worth while to indicate it by some means. One might include a statement of the proportion of the total expected benefit which is anticipated from the damage done by rare floods; and one might add how many lives would actually be given significantly larger protection against floods.

Of course, there are many other aspects of the "general welfare and security of the people" which not only are immeasurable, but are even beyond specific description. No doubt the net balance of these effects is harmful, and there are genuine intangible benefits of this kind from the prevention of this experience for the community. But these are intangibles of the truest sort, which each citizen and each legislator must judge for himself.[50]

The third group of intangibles is related to public health

[50] An interesting discussion of the nature of the community experience can be found in White's *Human Adjustment to Floods*, p. 155.

conditions in areas which are flooded. There may be deterioration of services of sanitation, such as failure to collect garbage, breakdown of sewage disposal, pollution of the water supply, and so on. Years ago, the resultant danger of epidemics was acute. But today, mass inoculations make epidemics very unlikely. Thus, since the cost of the inoculations is among the indirect measurable losses, only the discomfort of inoculation can be considered an intangible health benefit, plus the inconvenience of delayed garbage disposal and the annoyance of plugged sewers.

The conclusion which can be drawn from this examination of the intangible benefits of flood control is that the intangible benefits are real but not very large. The loss of life is relatively small, and the health hazard is not very significant. As for increasing the security of the people, there is certainly a real benefit, but frequently it is related to the security of property more than of persons.

The value which is placed on these benefits is a judgment for which no objective principle can be prescribed. The author would make the judgment that the intangibles can be no more than a minor part of the justification of flood-control expenditures and that the main justification for the investment of the nation's economic resources must lie in measurable economic benefits. There are much more efficient ways for the federal government to save human lives and to promote the health of the people. And yet the intangibles must be considered, and, especially among projects which are financed by the nation's taxpayers, those should be favored which involve substantial protection of life and increase of personal security as against projects which yield merely pure economic benefit. In practical terms, projects which only yield increased crops or only protect industrial and commercial property should be subjected to the most rigorous economic tests, including a benefit-cost ratio of 1.3, which will assure that the resources in this use are employed as productively as they would be elsewhere in the economy. On the other hand, protective works for dense residential areas may be justified even if the benefit-cost ratio is substantially less. In such instances, full description of the reduced hazard to human life must supplement the benefit-cost analysis as a basis for project evaluation.

144

10. *The Definition of Cost in the Criterion*

The Corps of Engineers bases the cost aspect of the benefit-cost ratio on project costs, which include the total investment and the cost of operation and maintenance, both federal and local, which must be incurred to permit the project to function. Cost does not include associated costs which must be incurred in the area to reap all the benefits, such as the private investments needed for the higher utilization of land. Associated costs are subtracted from benefits.

We saw in Chapter III that if we assume that it is federal expenditure that places the limit on total activities and that must be considered to be the scarce, rationed component, then the benefit-cost ratio should be expressed in such a way that federal costs are the only item on the cost side of the ratio. The Corps of Engineers' practice of including project costs contributed locally results in a lower benefit-cost ratio, but the degree to which the Corps' ratio falls short of a ratio based on federal cost alone is relatively small. For the program as a whole, local costs are only about 4 percent of total cost,[51] which is explained by the legal provision that all flood-control reservoirs and all flood-control allocations of multipurpose reservoirs are financed entirely by the federal government.[52] In some projects the local contribution may run as high as 30 percent,[53] which leads to a larger effect on the benefit-cost ratio. A ratio of 2.0 would rise to 2.43; a ratio of 1.5 would rise to 1.71, and a ratio of 1.2 would rise to 1.28. Projects which involve such large local contributions are rare, for they must not include reservoirs, yet must involve large expenditure for lands and easements; typically, it might be a local project involving diversion of a stream. Nevertheless, we can conclude that from the conceptual point of view, the definition of costs in the ratio is biased in a conservative direction.

---

[51] *Annual Report of Chief of Engineers* (1951), pp. 51, 55.

[52] *Annual Report of Chief of Engineers* (1951), p. 55.

[53] For example, the Arkansas River and Tributaries project at Enid, Oklahoma, where annual costs of $1,020,000 include local costs of $295,000. The benefit-cost ratio is 1.18, which would be raised to 1.24 if local costs were treated as negative benefits. *Report on the Arkansas River and Tributaries*, House Doc. 81, 83 Cong., 1 sess., p. 22.

11. *The Cost of Agricultural Land*

There are few conceptual difficulties in identifying cost. Since they must actually be paid, they are generally measurable and tangible. The only important exception is the cost of acquiring land for reservoirs. Many of the reservoirs formed by large dams have been built over the most violent protest of the residents of the area, who have been forced to move from their homes. Dams for flood control are particularly likely to run into local opposition because they must be located within a reasonable distance from the cities and towns they are to protect. These valley floors are likely to be in high-intensity agricultural uses, whereas dams for other purposes can often be located in remote and sparsely settled mountainous areas. Since the landowners are compensated at a price that is considered fair in the light of market prices for similar property, the intensity of the opposition is very strong evidence that the land has a greater value to its owners than the cash they receive. Often they have lived there for many years and have been part of a community pattern, which they are unwilling to surrender. These costs are intangible but very real. Project reports usually contain a summary of the position taken by interests which opposed a project in public hearings, which usually includes the people who will be flooded out. It would appear logical and consistent to give a verbal statement of these intangible costs with an emphasis equal to statement of tangible costs. The clearest way to do so would be to include an intangible analysis, featured as prominently as the economic and financial analyses.

In addition, the value placed on property by real-estate appraisals[54] understates the real cost of the property within the benefit-cost framework. In Chapter II we discussed the way in which privately held assets are valued by capitalizing the future income stream at the rate of time preference of the owner. If the cost is measured by the private-asset values while the benefit-cost analysis uses a low public rate of interest, there is an asymmetry which understates the cost. Consistency could be achieved by measuring the cost of assets directly by the annual income that

[54] The valuation method prescribed by the *Engineering Manual for Civil Works*, pt. CXIII, par. 1.28f.

they yield, or else by applying the same rate of interest in the capitalization of the asset in both the private and the public use.

To illustrate the problem, let us examine a project that has been fought to the utmost by the residents of the area to be flooded, the Tuttle Creek Dam on the Big Blue River, a tributary of the Missouri. The reservoir will flood 55,000 acres, decreasing agricultural output by $6,000,000 a year.[55] In return, the reservoir will protect 5,000 acres and will contribute to the protection of another 65,000 acres in the flood plains of the Kansas and Missouri rivers. It will also contribute to the protection of Kansas City, Missouri. Landowners were to be paid $110 an acre for land to be flooded,[56] an estimate of market value. The benefit-cost analysis justifies the project, as Table 17 shows.

Table 17. Summary of benefits and costs of Tuttle Creek Dam

Costs	
Total federal cost (est. 1951)	$79,132,000
including relocations and lands	28,831,000
Annual charges	3,047,000
Benefits	
Flood control	4,279,000
Low flow regulation	389,000
Total	$4,668,000

Benefit-cost ratio: 4,668,000/3,047,000 (1.53)

Source: *Hearings...Civil Works*, p. 134.

In typical reservoir projects in that area, about 75 percent of the cost of relocation and land represents cost of land (and associated property), indicating this cost for this property to be about $21,500,000. Although the rate of return on agricultural land has fluctuated very widely, ranging from less than 5 percent to 9 percent at different times, the rate at the time of the analysis

---

[55] *Hearings...Civil Works*, testimony of Secretary of Agriculture Brannan, p. 210.

[56] *Hearings...Civil Works*, testimony of W. Breidenthal, p. 357.

was at least 7 percent.[57]   If this rate is applied to the estimated land cost, we find that the income stream which is produced by the land to be flooded is about $1,500,000.   The official analysis applies an interest rate of 3 percent[58] to the land cost in order to derive the annual cost, implying an annual cost of land of only $650,000.   Thus the analysis understates the annual social cost of land by about $850,000.   If the annual cost is raised by that amount, the benefit-cost ratio falls from 1.53 to less than 1.2, which indicates the project to be marginal or worse.

I do not believe it wise to include this kind of estimate in the usual analysis; the figure would be too much dependent on the choice of estimate for private rates of capitalization; that is, some sort of survey would have to be made to see how the market value of land in the area is related to the annual net income.   A simpler approach, and one which would be symmetrical with the procedures used on the benefit side, would be to estimate the annual net income which accrues to the owners of the land.   It is certainly easier to estimate net incomes that are actually being realized than to estimate net incomes to be achieved after the use of land has been changed because of flood protection, and so it can be assumed that this is a feasible procedure.

To be sure, there is an attractiveness about a cost figure which is actually expected to be paid.   But if the market value of land is to be the criterion, then, in order to avoid a systematic upward bias of considerable proportion, it would be necessary to measure the benefits in the same way, by merely measuring the change in land value of all land affected.   If an annual figure is desired, the difference in land value with and without the project can be put on an annual basis by applying the interest rate of the analysis to the net change in value.   Because private asset valuations use much higher interest rates in the process of deriving the change in land value, the resultant benefit figure would be smaller and would underestimate the social benefit.

[57] I owe these estimates to Professor D. Gale Johnson.   See his "Allocation of Agricultural Income," *Journal of Farm Economics*, Nov. 1948, pp. 732–745.

[58] Although the interest and amortization factor which is used to compute the annual charge is 3.89 percent, to allow amortization over fifty years, the effective rate for land is only 3.0 percent, since it is assumed that the land will have a scrap value equal to the purchase price at the end of the project's economic life.

148

12. *Estimating Flood-Control Costs*

In the ordinary private construction project, the estimation of costs is primarily a technical question. If the engineers are able to draw up a plan that is physically feasible and appropriate and if they allow for contingencies in a manner based on long experience, they can estimate the total cost either with existing prices, or else on the basis of a forecast covering a very brief period. But cost estimation of public projects is a much more difficult task.

The reasons are not far to seek. The period from planning to construction may exceed a decade. The magnitude of the project may multiply through changes in the authorization or through administrative decision.

The Corps of Engineers takes cognizance of the technological uncertainties. At the preliminary planning stage it provides for a contingency allowance of at least 25 percent.[59] The estimates at the project survey stage, which are the figures used in the benefit-cost analysis, allow 15 percent or more for contingencies, and even at the plans and specification stage, which is not reached until construction is anticipated in the very near future, at least 10 percent is allowed for.[60] But there can be no allowances for the larger uncertainties that are injected by the political nature of the decision process.

For example, the total estimated cost of the authorized civil-works program of the Army Engineers, including both flood control and rivers and harbors work, rose 99.5 percent from the time the projects were authorized to January 1952.[61] This doubling of costs, which is the cause of a good deal of Congressional criticism, has been analyzed by the Corps, and has been explained to be due to the following causes in the proportions listed in Table 18. The largest item, changes in construction costs, is explained by the fact that many of the projects were authorized before World War II and have had their costs inflated in the 1940's. The second cause, changes authorized by Congress, presumably led to extra benefits, and should have been subject to separate

---

[59] *Manual*, pt. CXIII, par. 1.11.
[60] *Manual*, pt. CXIII, par. 1.32.
[61] Committee on Public Works, *Report of the Subcommittee to Study Civil Works*, Part 1, *The Civil Functions Program of the Corps of Engineers*, *U.S. Army*, House Com. Print No. 21, 82 Cong., 2 sess., p. 18.

benefit-cost analysis. The other causes, adding up to 25 percent above original cost, indicate that the contingency allowances included in the original estimates were not large enough, on the average, to compensate for the actual contingencies. But better performance can be anticipated in the future, because many of the old authorizations were based on very sketchy cost data, in some instances on the general survey data of the original "308" Reports. Today, project reports on which authorizations are based include more refined cost estimates, which, according to

Table 18. Analysis of components of cost increases

	Percent
Price changes	57.8
Changes authorized by law	17.6
Engineering modifications	6.3
Changing local needs	4.1
Unforeseen conditions	8.5
Inadequacy in planning	5.7
	100.0

Source: *Hearings...Civil Works.*

the *Orders and Regulations*, must be compiled by the same personnel that are in charge of the final planning and design in order to assure that the quality of the cost estimates which are submitted to the Bureau of the Budget and the Congress will be of the highest professional standard. The Presidential veto of the Rivers and Harbors Bill of 1956 on the grounds that it authorized projects without sufficient advance investigation indicates that the problem persists, however.

The Corps of Engineers hires contractors for most of its work, and, insofar as possible, lets the contracts on the basis of sealed bidding. To make sure that the bids are of the right order of magnitude, the Corps constructs an estimate of fair and reasonable cost to the contractor for the part of costs which he incurs. This figure, which takes into account the labor practices of the area, including feather bedding and premiums for particularly scarce skills, and which allows the contractor the usual private rate of return on working capital, is compared with the lowest acceptable bid.   If the difference between the government estimate and the sealed bid is large, further investigation must be made.[62]

B. Financial Analysis

13. *Required Local Coöperation*

The Flood Control Act of 1936 required that local communities make certain contributions to the cost and upkeep of flood-control installations.   The act required that no federal appropriation be spent until states or local governments have committed themselves to meet their share of the cost.   The requirements of the 1936 act for local contributions were (a) to provide without cost to the United States all necessary lands, easements, and rights-of-way; (b) to assume responsibility for all damages inflicted during construction; and (c) to maintain and operate the project after it is finished in accordance with rules laid down by the Secretary of the Army.   The limits imposed on this local contribution were that if the cost of land exceeded the cost of construction, 50 percent of the difference would be paid by the federal government, thus effectively limiting the local cost to less than 50 percent of the total.   Also, if more than 75 percent of the benefits accrued outside the state, the Secretary of the Army could, with the permission of the state in which the project is located, try to collect the land cost from the states that would benefit.   If the state and local governments failed to commit themselves to supply the land within five years of the authorization, the project was to be automatically deauthorized.[63]

The Act of 1938, written on the basis of the initial experience of the program, reduced the required local contribution drastically by exempting all dam and reservoir projects, and all channel improvements and rectifications, the entire cost of which was to be assumed by the federal government.[64]   Since all large projects fall into these categories, the local contributions are now confined primarily to local protective works, such as levees and flood walls, which clearly yield only local benefits.

[62] *Orders and Regulations*, par. 4216.13f.
[63] President's Water Resources Policy Commission, *Report*, Vol. 3, *Water Resources Law* (1950), p. 144.
[64] *Water Resources Law*, p. 145.

Table 19 indicates the magnitude of the local contributions to flood control. Local interests pay about 5 percent of the total investment, the federal government paying the remaining 95 percent. Local interests pay a larger share of the operation and maintenance costs, since they pay all of it on local protective works. The Engineers estimate that these current costs will be about half as large as the local investment, which would raise the total cost to about 7 percent of the total.[65] All of the local

Table 19. Federal and local investment costs of the flood control program

Status	Federal investment (to 1951)	Local investment (to 1950)*	Local cost as percent of total cost
	Millions of dollars		Percent
Completed or in operation	3,057	176	5.4
Under construction, not in operation†	2,162	97	4.3
Authorized, not yet started†	4,817	206	3.9
Total	10,036	480	4.6

Source: *Annual Report of Chief of Engineers*, 1951, p. 337.

* It should be noted that the total federal investment cost is inclusive of 1951, while the local investment cost is only given to 1950, thus slightly understating the ratio.

† Includes expected costs.

contribution is concentrated in about 20 percent of the program, and represents about 30 percent of that part. To these figures must be added another $150,000,000 which local governments invested in protective works that became part of federal projects or that were necessary adjuncts,[66] raising the local share of the program to approximately 8 percent.

14. *Could Flood Control be Financed Locally?*

The policy of the present administration in the water-resources field rests on the "partnership approach" to development, which

[65] *Water Resources Law*, p. 348.   [66] *Water Resources Law*, p. 348.

stresses local initiative and transfer of more of the cost to local communities.

Whether costs should be borne locally or by the federal taxpayer involves a value judgment about the proper distribution of national income. The present division of the burden, under which the federal government has paid 92 percent of the cost, has no particular economic justification and can only be explained by the historical setting in which flood control became a federal responsibility. In 1936, after some very severe floods in several sections of the country, and after the American people had become aware of the possibilities of federal programs through the many New Deal measures, it was decided that flood control was a task that the federal government ought to undertake. Since floods are determined by the flow of rivers, and since all our major rivers flow through several states, it was impossible for a state acting in isolation to do more than put up local protective works which would speed the flood waters downstream to inundate some other area. The original law, the Act of 1936, recognized that many of the benefits accrued to specific localities, and required the trio of local contributions discussed above. A provision of the Rivers and Harbors Act of 1920, which was applied to flood control as well, requires that if much of the benefit accrues to a few individuals, a statement to that effect must be included in the project report; such beneficiaries may also be required to make contributions in cash, though this practice has not become extensive.

After the Act of 1936 went into effect it was discovered that it was extremely difficult to get those communities which were at some distance from the reservoirs, and which received only partial protection,[67] to assume the required local obligations. There were delays of programs, and when 1938 brought more severe floods, the Act of 1938 eliminated the local requirements for reservoirs. There was a feeling of urgency, of removing obstacles, and, at the same time, flood control was part of a public works program designed to put the country's idle workers and resources to productive use. Under these circumstances, the present low requirements for local contributions were evolved.

There is much to be said in favor of more local financing. The

[67] *Water Resources Law*, p. 347.

pressure by local interests for new projects would be diminished; as long as projects are essentially free goods to the communities, they will bring their political power to bear on the Congress to receive projects, and will try to show that large benefits will be produced. If there were substantial local costs one could be fairly sure that the benefits would at least equal the local costs.

But complete self-financing will never be possible. There are great political obstacles, among which the most significant may be the precedent of the past twenty years of the federal program. Local governments will be most unwilling to shoulder a burden which past policy has made a federal responsibility, unless the federal government also evacuates some corresponding field of taxation.

Voluntary local contributions by communities which are at a distance from the protective works, which receive only partial protection, and which are only secondary beneficiaries, will not be forthcoming because of their bargaining position. Since flood control cannot be withheld from them if they do not join the plan, they know that they will receive the benefit whether they pay for it or not. Just as flood control is not a marketable commodity to individuals, it is not marketable to many communities since they are almost equally free to enjoy the service without payment. Municipalities are in this fortunate position with regard to all projects except local works, and even states can be in the same relation to comprehensive river-control plans. As a result, the bargaining among communities about their relative assessments is likely to be a very drawn-out process, and likely to end in such a way that the primary beneficiaries, such as the communities that are particularly vulnerable, or large cities with a substantial flood hazard, will shoulder all of the cost.

The nature of some of the flood-control benefits also precludes complete application of the principle of local financing. It will be recalled that some of the benefits, especially of the indirect variety, are caused by the interruption of economic activity. These losses are in the form of wages and profits. But local contributions must come from local taxes, and these are primarily on property. Thus, while the benefits from averted property damage might well be financed out of general local property taxation or out of special assessments on property that receives protection, the changed local incomes in the form of wages or profits do not produce any significant amount of local taxation. On the other hand, federal taxes on private and corporate income do recapture some of these benefits. This means that there is no tax inducement for local government to provide the benefits which it cannot tax. In theory, the community should be willing to vote to expend an amount of money equal to all local benefits, including the loss of wages, but since the actual tax burden will be borne by the property owners, and since they are usually the most influential pressure group on local governments, the decision will not reflect indirect benefits to any great degree.

Finally, the probabilistic nature of the benefits places another limitation on local participation. With human nature as optimistic as it is, people will not be willing to make provision against floods which are extremely rare. The exception is in areas where a hundred-year flood has just taken place; but providing flood protection after the hundred-year flood is like closing the barn door after the horse is gone. There have been many instances where communities knew from hydrologic data that they could be victims of a disaster flood, yet did nothing about it till it was too late. The great flood on the Columbia River of 1948 is one example of a flood to which there was a reaction of hurt surprise, though historical data showed that there had been similar floods early in this century. The City of Chattanooga, Tennessee, has refused to participate in local flood-control works despite years of warnings by the Tennessee Valley Authority that a flood on the Tennessee so severe as to cause disaster damage despite the functioning of the present dam system is a possibility unless local works supplement the river system. Thus the part of the benefits which arises from averted losses of floods of frequency of, say, greater than twenty years will never become subject to assessment, except after such a flood has taken place.[68]

15. *Some Criteria for Determining the Local Contribution*

We have seen a number of limitations to the possibilities of complete local financing. But the considerations which have

[68] Though a wider adoption of the practice of the City of Los Angeles of making available a technical appraisal of the flood hazard of property would lead to greater awareness of rare floods and would make property owners more willing to bear special assessments.

been raised also suggest some criteria for determining the share of costs which should be borne locally, since the absence of these conditions or their applicability to only a part of all the benefits and beneficiaries leave the remainder subject to the imposition of financial charges.

At least three criteria suggest themselves. First, local contributions can only be expected from the primary beneficiaries of a project. Benefits which accrue far downstream and are widely dispersed among many communities cannot be considered reimbursable, since there is no way in which the beneficiaries can be made to pay except by the unacceptable method of federal coercion.

Second, the local contribution should be related to the direct benefits of flood control, which are largely the averted damages to property. Other benefits are not a part of the local tax base, and hence offer little inducement to local governments to agree to make the local contribution. Finally, only the benefits which are produced by the prevention of fairly frequent floods should be considered reimbursable, since benefits from rare floods are usually not recognized by the beneficiaries.

For each of these criteria operational definitions and rules of computation must be devised. For the first criterion, primary beneficiaries might be the people of those communities that can expect flood losses large enough to constitute a serious problem, perhaps defined as a percentage of all property value, and for which protection would reduce the expected loss by at least 50 percent. In this way, only those communities which will have a substantial stake in flood control will be asked to participate financially.

Primary beneficiaries must be defined from the point of view of an entire program and not for each individual project. In the typical case, a flood-control program will call for several reservoirs and numerous local protective works. The latter clearly can be made, at least in part, the financial responsibility of the protected community. But the reservoirs usually will contribute to the protection of many communities, with each individual reservoir providing only partial protection. Therefore it is difficult to get local financial coöperation for the construction of one reservoir. But if the community is given the choice of helping to pay for the entire program or else receiving no protection at all, it is more likely to participate.

The present project-by-project decisions on appropriations make it very difficult to draw up the agreements between federal and local bodies which would commit the communities to help pay for an entire program and which would commit the federal government to construct all of it. But if the federal government plans to extend the "partnership approach" very far in the field of flood control, the appropriation procedures must be adapted to permit the federal government to commit itself to the execution of an entire program in a river basin, rather than just to individual projects.

The second criterion has an obvious operational implication; local contributions can only be based on direct benefits. The financial requirement should be some fraction of the direct benefits to the community. Since considerable inducement is required to assure speedy local coöperation, probably not more than 50 percent of the direct benefit can be collected through the local contribution.

The final criterion exempts another group of benefits from the financial base for the local contribution. Benefits that accrue from floods that can be expected to occur less than once in twenty years or so must be excluded. In the case of the program on the Connecticut River which was used for illustrative purposes above, about 45 percent of all direct benefits came from floods of lower frequency. To compute this financial base, one need only add up the damages in the damage-frequency curve up to the cutoff point, and assume that all rarer floods cause damages equal to those of a flood of the specified frequency.[69] The latter adjustment must be made to make some allowance for the damages of rare floods to frequently flooded property.

If the local contributions are set to be rather high, it may become impossible to collect the entire amount over a short period. Since the benefits accrue over many years and remote benefits are valued with an interest rate of 3 percent in the benefit-cost analysis, it may become necessary to set up a contractual payment schedule which corresponds to the time pattern with

[69] Diagrammatically, this implies that the damage-frequency curve becomes horizontal at that point.

which the benefits are expected to accrue. If the entire contribution must be paid in the first year of the project, local beneficiaries will value the benefit to themselves at their rates of time preference, which will be higher than the public rate of interest. If they must pay at once they may find that the present value of future benefits is not high enough to warrant their participation. If they pay over many years and the interest charge is computed at the public rate of interest, they should be willing to participate if the annual benefits to them exceed the annual costs. Should the local contribution remain only a moderate percentage of benefits, the federal government can continue to insist on prepayment.

Political and administrative processes must also be specified which will serve to bring about the local participation. For local works, the problem is simple, and present procedures for providing local commitments can be applied, though the contribution itself may differ. Where a small group of towns is involved, individual community negotiations and commitments may also be practical, provided there are no holdouts in the group. If a set of bilateral negotiations between the Corps and the towns does not bring unanimous consent, resort may be made to the organization of flood-control districts which may be able to raise the local contribution through direct assessments on the property owners to be protected. The constituents of the district would be the affected property owners. Perhaps a vote of owners representing 80 percent of the property to be assessed might be defined by state or federal law to constitute sufficient assurance to satisfy the requirement.

If several states are involved and the flood control district is not a feasible device,[70] the federal government may insist that the states which contain a high percentage of the primary beneficiaries enter into a flood-control compact and commit themselves to make the local contributions. The states will be free to raise the funds as they see fit. Presumably they would have recourse to special assessments on the property, acting perhaps through local authorities. In the case of large river basins, the

[70] Flood control districts would be created by state legislatures in a manner similar to irrigation districts. It would be difficult to have a district include land in more than one state.

interstate compact device may offer the only possibility of getting the local interests to share in the costs of protection, since the number of communities which would have to be brought into a flood-control district would be too large and the possibility of holdouts too great. Unless the states are brought into the picture, only federal compulsion of local communities could bring about the participation of all beneficiaries.

CHAPTER VI

Navigation

THE improvement of the nation's rivers and harbors, a traditional function of the federal government throughout our history, has been carried on by the Corps of Engineers of the U.S. Army since early in the nineteenth century, and it continues to remain a little-challenged activity of this agency.

The federal waterway program[1] concerns itself with five separate transportation systems: (1) ocean harbors, (2) the Great Lakes system, (3) the Mississippi River system, (4) the coastal rivers of the country, and (5) intracoastal waterways.[2] Investment in new routes and in new facilities in recent decades has been concentrated in the inland waterway system other than the Great Lakes, since the harbors and the Great Lakes have been the subject of federal development for a long time. In these older parts of the program, the Corps of Engineers still engages in dredging, in deepening channels, and in other incremental investments, and these are also subjected to economic analysis. But the most important economic problems are related to the new parts of the program, and so we shall concentrate our attention on them. The economic analysis of harbor improvements has few difficulties which we will not encounter in our discussion of inland waterways; we shall treat it briefly in section 5.

As early as 1820, Congress appropriated funds for a survey of parts of the Mississippi and its tributaries.[3] In the first half of the nineteenth century, inland waterways were the most impor-

---

[1] A brief survey of the system and the history of the program can be found in P. D. Locklin, *Economics of Transportation* (3rd ed., 1949), pp. 735–752.

[2] Besides the federal system, there is the New York Barge Canal, which is one of the most important canals now in use, but which was built by the State of New York.

[3] *Annual Report of Chief of Engineers* (1951), p. 263.

tant arteries of trade. The state governments and private companies supplemented the natural waterways with a large number of canals, totalling about 4,400 miles.[4] But after 1860, the development of the railroad network halted the development of the waterway system. For example, total port-to-port traffic on the Mississippi River system fell from 28 million tons, in 1889, to 16 million tons in 1916.[5] This decline of waterway traffic was partly due to the diversion of most freight of medium or high value and of much bulk freight to the railroads because of their inherent advantage and because of the inefficient organization of the water-carrier industry; the rest must be attributed to practices of the railroads designed to ruin the water carriers.[6] In that era of relatively ineffective regulation, the railroads were free to cut the rates on routes that were competitive with the waterways to levels that would drive the water carriers out of business, making up temporary losses on the higher rates they could charge elsewhere. The railroads also refused to establish through routes and through rates for shipments that used both means of transportation, thus making it very difficult for the waterways to carry traffic other than bulk shipments along the river. And in some areas the railroads even obtained control of much river-front property, hampering the development of terminal and storage facilities.[7]

From 1906 to 1920 a number of regulatory steps were taken which ended some of these practices and made possible a revival of waterway transportation. The Hepburn Act of 1906 forced the railroads to accept maximum joint rates for rail-water transportation. In 1910 it was ruled that rate cuts which had been enacted to meet water competition could not be raised after the competitors' throats had been cut. And in 1912 the Interstate Commerce Commission was given authority to force railroads to participate in the installation of links between rail systems and the waterways.[8] At the same time, continued popular dissatisfaction with the railroads, plus the expanded transportation needs

[4] Locklin, *Economics of Transportation* (3rd ed.), p. 73.
[5] Federal Coördinator of Transportation, *Public Aids to Transportation* (1939), vol. III, p. 17.
[6] *Public Aids to Transportation*, p. 18.
[7] *Public Aids to Transportation*, p. 18.
[8] *Public Aids to Transportation*, p. 19.

of the country during World War I, led to revived interest in the waterway system.

The Transportation Act of 1920 stated that it is the policy of the federal government "to promote, encourage and develop water transportation, service and facilities," and called on the Secretary of War to carry on investigations toward these ends. It also placed further restrictions on the competitive practices of railroads. With substantial federal expenditures every year, the inland waterway system has again participated in the growth of the transportation industry, as Tables 20 and 21 show.

Table 20. Freight traffic carried by the major transportation systems (in billion freight ton miles)

Year	Inland waterways	Rail	Truck	Pipelines	Total
1920	76	414	5	n.a.	495
1929	106	450	19	n.a.	575
1932	33	235	19	n.a.	287
1940	118	375	51	60	604
1950	159	641	88	119	1,007
1955	217	631	226	203	1,278

Source: Senate Committee on Interstate and Foreign Commerce, *Progress Report of the Subcommittee on Domestic Land and Water Transportation*, 82 Cong., 1 sess., Sen. Report No. 1039 (1951), p. 76; data for 1954 from U.S. Interstate Commerce Commission, *Annual Report*, 1956.

Table 21. Percentages of relative shares of the major systems of total freight traffic

Year	Inland waterways	Rail	Truck	Pipelines	Total
1920	15.4	83.6	0.9	—	100
1929	18.4	78.3	3.3	—	100
1932	11.5	81.9	6.6	—	100
1940	19.5	62.1	8.4	9.9	100
1950	15.9	63.6	8.7	11.8	100
1955	17.0	49.4	17.7	15.9	100

Source: Table 20.

Out of the total ton miles carried on the inland waterway system, a substantial part was carried on the Great Lakes. As can be seen in Table 22, this traffic was relatively static, except for a collapse during the Great Depression, when iron-ore shipments, which are its biggest component, became very small.

Traffic on the other inland waterways, that is, the improved rivers, canals, and intracoastal waterways, which have been the main subject of federal development since 1920, have shown a

Table 22. Freight traffic carried on the Great Lakes and connecting channels

(in billion freight ton miles)

1929	97	1940	96
1932	25	1950	112
		1953	127

Source: *Annual Report of Chief of Engineers*, 1951, pp. 278–279.

much more dynamic growth. Table 23 shows the freight ton miles carried on this portion of the waterway system, and its share of the total domestic transport load in the United States.

This growth was distributed over the major systems in different parts of the country with all of them showing a multiplication of traffic between 1928 and 1953, as Table 24 illustrates, though two thirds of the traffic remained on the Ohio–Mississippi system.[9]

But the resurgence of the competitive strength of the system has been confined to bulk commodities, which is easily explained by some of the disadvantages of shipment by water. It is a very slow form of transportation, moving at a few miles an hour and often over circuitous routes; some waterways are closed occasionally by ice; others suffer unpredictable interruptions because of drought or flood. Perhaps most important of all, there are high

[9] For a geographic analysis of waterway traffic, see D. Patton, "The Traffic Pattern on American Inland Waterways," *Economic Geography* (January 1956), pp. 29–37. Patton foresees further growth on the Mississippi–Ohio system, but little elsewhere.

Table 23.   Freight traffic carried on inland waterways,
excluding the Great Lakes system

	Billions of ton miles	Percent of total domestic freight traffic		Billions of ton miles	Percent of total domestic freight traffic
1925	8.4	1.6	1940	22	3.6
1926	9.5	1.7	1941	27	3.6
1927	9.0	1.7	1942	26	2.8
1928	9.2	1.6	1943	26	2.6
1929	8.7	1.5	1944	31	2.9
1930	9.1	1.8	1945	30	3.0
1931	7.8	2.0	1946	28	3.2
1932	7.9	2.8	1947	35	3.5
1933	10.2	3.1	1948	40	4.0
1934	9.4	2.7	1949	42	4.5
1935	13.4	3.6	1950	52	5.2
1936	15.4	3.3	1951	58	5.1
1937	17	3.0	1952	59	5.2
1938	18	4.0	1953	75	6.7
1939	20	3.8	1955	98	7.7

Source: compiled from *Annual Report of Chief of Engineers*, 1926 to 1953, Part II, *Commercial Statistics*, table of ton mileage carried on inland waterways.   Total ton mileage for all means of transportation is given in *Progress Report of Subcommittee...*, Senate Report 1039, p. 76; data for 1951–53 from ICC, *Annual Reports*.

Table 24.   Growth of traffic on major waterway systems

System	1928	1953
	(millions of ton miles)	
Atlantic Coast rivers	1.4	9.7
Gulf Coast rivers	0.3	1.2
Pacific Coast rivers	0.7	4.5
Mississippi river system including Ohio and tributaries	5.7	42.4
Canals and connecting channels excluding Great Lakes system	1.1	10.8
Total	9.2	68.6

Source: ICC *Annual Reports*, 1929, 1954.

handling costs for most freight if it must be taken to and from the waterway by truck or by rail.[10]

Table 25 gives an indication of the nature of the traffic. The figures must be interpreted with caution, since they are given in tons rather than in ton miles, but they do show pretty clearly that petroleum, coal, sand, and gravel constitute most of the traffic.

Table 25. Domestic, internal, water-borne commerce in the United States, 1951, by commodities

Commodity	Millions of tons	Percent of total tonnage
Petroleum, crude, and processed	66	31
Coal, anthracite, etc.	52	24
Gas, oil, and distillation fuel oil	10	5
Sand, gravel, crushed rock	35	16
Logs	15	7
Seashells, unmanufactured	7	3
Grains	4	2
Wood and pulp	3	1
Industrial chemicals	2	1
Other	18	8
Total	213	100

Source: *Annual Report of Chief of Engineers, Commercial Statistics,* 1952, pp. xxll–xxiv.

Transportation of bulk commodities has a relatively low economic value, as measured by the revenue that is collected. Table 26 shows the revenue per ton mile for different means of transport, as estimated by Barger in 1939. It can be seen that while inland waterways carried about 2.4 percent of all traffic, they produced only 1.6 percent of the revenue, and even the height of this figure is partly due to the very short average length of haul, which was only 61 miles in that year. But it must also

[10] Locklin, *Economics of Transportation* (3rd ed.), pp. 751–752. But the possibility of "piggy-back" operation of truck trailers on barges may give waterways a share of high-value traffic in the future.

Table 26. Freight revenue in the United States, 1939,
domestic and international shipments

System	Revenue per ton mile (cents)	Percent of total freight revenue	Percent of ton miles
Steam railroads	0.983	64.4	41.0
Intercity trucking (commercial)	4	17.3	2.7
Oil pipelines	0.38	3.7	6.0
Waterways (total)	0.17	13.9	50.2
Coastwise	0.13	4.4	21.3
Intercoastal	0.157	1.6	6.4
Great Lakes	0.107	1.4	8.4
Inland	*0.4*	*1.6*	*2.4*
Noncontiguous	0.5	1.6	1.9
International, American-flag	0.200	3.3	9.7
Other		0.8	0.4
		100.0	100.0

Source: H. Barger, *The Transportation Industries, 1889–1946* (New York: National Bureau of Economic Research, 1951), p. 21.

be remembered that these revenues were based on rates set on the basis of costs that did not include the improvement of the waterways themselves. Presumably the average rates could have been somewhat higher.

The magnitude of the federal program can be seen from Table 27, which gives the annual expenditures for the entire rivers' and harbors' program, including the Great Lakes' system and the seaports. Operating and maintenance costs are quite a large part of these expenditures, since the Corps of Engineers does not turn over these functions to local interests as it does in the case of flood control, and since the upkeep of a waterway is quite expensive because of the frequent need for dredging. Little more than half of the expenditures represent new investment in the inland waterway system.

Table 27.   Annual expenditures by the Corps of Engineers for
rivers and harbors
(in millions of dollars)

1880	6	1936	185
1899	15	1937	179
1905	22	1938	136
1910	30	1939	116
1916	35	1940	107
1920	47	1941	87
1921	57	1942	89
1922	43	1943	84
1923	47	1944	64
1924	62	1945	57
1925	70	1946	80
1926	63	1947	89
1927	61	1948	116
1928	70	1949	160
1929	50	1950	190
1930	74	1951	121
1931	72	1952	106
1932	76	1953	113
1933	70	1954	102
1934	99	1955	108
1935	155	1956	135

Sources: For 1931–1949, *Annual Report of Chief of Engineers*, 1951,
p. 279; earlier years, *Annual Reports of Chief of Engineers*, Part I, paragraph on appropriations and expenditures. Later years, *The Budget of
the United States Government*. These figures understate total expenditures, especially in recent years because multipurpose projects are not
included. Years prior to 1928 include some flood-control expenditures.

A. ECONOMIC ANALYSIS

1. *Present Practice: Navigation Benefits on Inland Waterways*[11]

All benefits which the Corps of Engineers attempts to estimate
for navigation projects are of the same type: savings in the cost of
transporting the nation's commerce. For improvement of ports,
the saving will come primarily from lower handling costs and from
use of more efficient equipment. On rivers, the saving will be

[11] For detailed examination of the evaluation of several major systems,
see "Evaluation of Federal Navigation Projects," by C. D. Curran, in
Commission on Organization of the Executive Branch of the Government, *Task Force Report on Water Resources and Power* (June 1955),
vol. III, pp. 1317–1394.

estimated by comparing the cost of shipments on the river with the cost of the cheapest alternative, both estimated from the point of view of shippers. Thus, most of the procedures are concerned with deriving the estimates of alternative costs, and with predicting the flow of traffic on which the unit savings are to be realized. For example, if shipment of coal on a certain route a hundred miles long currently costs $1.20 a ton by the cheapest method, say by rail, and if it would cost $0.75 a ton to ship by water, a saving of 0.45¢ a ton is realized. If 500,000 tons a year are expected to be shipped, the benefit on the shipment of coal will be $225,000 a year.

The cost of shipment by rail can be derived from published rates. Costs of shipment by water must be constructed synthetically by estimating the requisite capital equipment and its cost, the line-haul cost of moving the commodity, the costs of possible delays caused by drought or other contingencies, and the handling costs at terminals. These costs do not include construction and maintenance of the waterway, which are not charged to the barge lines or to the shipper. Instead, the cost of the waterway is compared with the navigation benefits, a comparison that essentially consists of comparing the savings in transportation costs which can be attributed to the investment in the waterway with the cost of the investment itself. The calculation is logically equivalent to the computations on the basis of which a firm would decide on a cost-saving investment such as a new machine to replace an old one; the firm would make the investment if the savings of cost exceeded the cost of the investment, including the cost of interest on capital.

The validity of this procedure for measuring the economic benefit from the national point of view depends on two factors: the conceptual appropriateness of the cost-saving measure and the ability to forecast the flow of traffic on the waterway. We shall examine them in turn.

In Chapter III, we discussed how savings in the cost of producing the national output are a genuine economic benefit from the national point of view. Resources are released for other purposes, making it possible to increase the total output. Therefore, in order to accept the present measure of navigation benefit, it must be shown that the savings in cost which present procedures measure are savings in cost for the nation as a whole besides being savings from the point of view of the shippers. There is strong evidence that present procedures do not measure the cost savings from the national point of view.

Since the cost without the project is assumed to be measured by the rates currently charged by the most economical alternative means of transport, which is usually the rail system, the issue turns on the question whether railway rates reflect the social costs to the nation of hauling certain commodities. If railways were ordinary private enterprises operating under conditions of increasing costs and in competition, they would maximize their profits by charging at least the incremental cost of hauling a commodity; the competition would preclude a charge much above it.

But railways are not competitive enterprises; they are natural monopolies. Their rates are regulated so that they will earn a rate of return which is reasonable and no more. Since total revenue must equal total cost, including this reasonable return on capital, the rate structure as a whole must bear some relation to costs as a whole. But this does not necessarily imply that specific rates correspond to the costs of hauling specific commodities between specified points.

Rate making is a very complex art, practiced by both the railways and the Interstate Commerce Commission. At the risk of oversimplification, the principles of rate making can be classified into two categories: principles related to charging "what the traffic will bear," and principles related to specific costs of hauling commodities. Throughout the history of railroad regulation, both ideas have found much favor.[12]

From the point of view of economic efficiency it would be desirable to have rates correspond to long-run out-of-pocket costs, since in this way the shipper would be charged the true social cost of his shipments. The price of each commodity would reflect a transportation charge corresponding to the social cost of transport services actually embodied in it. Consumers would purchase indirectly these transportation services, and, through their choices in the market place, they would allocate resources to

[12] See I. L. Sharfman, *The Interstate Commerce Commission* (1936), Part III–B, pp. 311–329.

the various forms of transportation and to the specific routes where they ought to be used. Through the market mechanism, transportation services would be arranged in such a way as best to meet consumers' desires.

But rate making in accordance with the incremental costs of hauling a commodity over a certain route runs counter to another and more fundamental principle—that railroads are entitled to charge rates that cover their total cost and that give them a fair rate of return on the value of their assets. The Transportation Act of 1920 prescribed a rate of return of $5\frac{1}{2}$ percent a year as a fair rate of return on railroads; in fact, competitive conditions have not permitted the railroad system as a whole to earn above $5\frac{1}{2}$ percent in any year since then, except briefly during World War II, and in most years the return was much lower.[13] With the growth of trucking, pipelines, waterways, and airlines, the railroads have been forced to price many of their services sufficiently low to keep at least a part of the traffic in the commodities for which competing systems also bid. It can be assumed that the railroads will not lower such rates below out-of-pocket expenses since such rates would lead to financial losses on every shipment; it is also a basic principle of rate regulation that any rate below out-of-pocket costs is unreasonable, a view consistently upheld by the Interstate Commerce Commission.[14]

The general overhead of the system must be financed by rates which are above out-of-pocket costs, and so the railroads and the Interstate Commerce Commission face the problem of maintaining a rate structure that includes sufficient gaps in rates above out-of-pocket costs[15] to yield an excess of revenue that is sufficient to cover the common costs. The determination of these gaps must be in the light of competitive conditions, and will vary from commodity to commodity and from route to route. These gaps are all a form of price discrimination, but they are the inevitable result of the cost structure of the railway industry and of the

[13] Senate Committee on Interstate and Foreign Commerce, Senate Report 1039, p. 74.

[14] Locklin, *Economics of Transportation* (3rd ed.), p. 435.

[15] Throughout this discussion it is assumed that long-run out-of-pocket costs are a close approximation to long-run marginal cost, or to what A. W. Lewis calls "long-run escapable cost." See A. W. Lewis, *Overhead Costs* (1949), chap. 1.

requirement that total revenues equal total costs. There are legal and administrative limitations on the patterns of these discriminatory gaps, prescribed by the Congress and the Interstate Commerce Commission. But the growth of competition has shifted much of the regulatory emphasis toward permitting the railroads to maintain their share of the transportation load, even at the expense of worsening discriminatory patterns.[16]

Thus, the principle of "what the traffic will bear" continues to play an important role in setting these gaps. Since the competitive conditions on particular routes and for particular commodities determine what the traffic will bear, the gaps above out-of-pocket costs and thus the contribution of a rate toward the system overhead will be determined in substantial degree by the nature of the competition for the haul. As a result, the pattern of railway rates is influenced by the presence or absence of competitive means of transport.

When a new waterway is built, the railroads usually reduce their rates on parallel routes for commodities which are in danger of being diverted to the new competitor. The pressure on railway rates engendered by a waterway is one of the main reasons for shippers' support for waterways and was one of the important historical reasons for the revival of interest in the navigation program in the first decades of the century.

But if railroad rates are adjusted in this manner, two serious questions are raised about navigation benefits. First, insofar as rate cuts prevent the diversion of traffic, no savings in real costs are achieved for the nation as a whole. The savings in transportation charges of shippers are offset by the loss of revenue of railroads, or, in the event that the latter can make compensatory increases on other rates, are offset by higher charges on other shippers. The nation as a whole continues to incur exactly the same real cost of resources to move its commerce as it did without the waterway.

Second, and more important, this practice of the railroads is an indication that the gap between rail rates and out-of-pocket costs for specific shipments which exists before the waterway

---

[16] A brief survey of the changing regulatory patterns of recent years can be found in Locklin, *Economics of Transportation* (3rd ed.), pp. 253–274.

project is built is substantial. But this gap represents an excess of railway rates over the real social costs of the shipments. Since the benefits are supposed to measure cost saving from the national point of view, it is the out-of-pocket expenses, or, as an approximation, the rates after the competitive rate cuts have been made, that represent the alternative social cost. And this must be the base line for measuring the cost saving, for only those real costs of resources which cease to be incurred because of the waterway represent a social saving.

The conceptual picture of the rate structure which has been used in the above argument presupposes the existence of increasing returns in the railroad industry, based on the existence of two kinds of costs: out-of-pocket costs which vary directly with output, and common costs which remain constant. If there were constant or decreasing returns, the rate structure could not deviate far from out-of-pocket costs, and only in compensatory ways in view of the regulatory limit on total revenue. Thus the magnitude of the deviation between social cost and the railroad rates, the present measure of alternative cost employed in the calculation of navigation benefits, depends on the degree to which returns increase with output in the railway industry.

We shall approach this question, upon which the issue of navigation benefits really turns, in two ways: we shall examine the statistical evidence as presented in some very detailed studies of the question; and we shall examine some instances of rate cutting in response to the improvement of waterways.

The usual assumptions of statistical studies have been that variable, or out-of-pocket, costs vary in direct proportion with output,[17] with all other costs constant. The question then is posed, what percent of total cost is out of pocket? There have been many answers to this question,[18] including three detailed statistical examinations. The first of these, done by M. O. Lawrence in 1916, showed 72 to 88 percent of all costs to be

---

[17] This assumption is born out by statistical analysis. See *Explanation of Rail Cost Findings Procedures and Principles Relating to the Use of Costs*, ICC, Bureau of Accounts and Cost Finding (Washington, 1948), p. 38.

[18] The best survey of the question can be found in *Rail Freight Service Costs in the Various Rate Territories of the United States*, Senate Doc. 63, 78 Cong., 1 sess., pp. 41–44, 63–70.

variable.[19] The second, done under the direction of Ford K. Edwards in the Bureau of Accounts and Cost Findings of the Interstate Commerce Commission, found 70 to 80 percent of all costs variable in the short run, and 65 percent of the investment variable in the long run.[20] The most recent study, by G. H. Borts, produced estimates ranging from 55 percent to 103 percent, with estimates for most cases well below the upper figure.[21] It would appear, then, that the typical true value lies somewhere in the range of 65 to 85 percent. Since these values are average values for railways, they need not necessarily imply that the specific gap above out-of-pocket costs on the commodities to be affected by a new waterway need be of the same order of magnitude, but it does indicate unambiguously that there are increasing returns, and that the average gap between out-of-pocket costs and freight rates must be on the order of 15 to 35 percent of the total rate.

Let us now examine the amounts by which railroads actually have cut rates in response to water competition. To ascertain the exact amounts is rather difficult, of course, because the rate structure is constantly adapted to other changing circumstances as well, but a few examples will yield an idea of the orders of magnitude.

The rate on petroleum shipments from Portland, Oregon, to Pasco, Florida, dropped from $5.60 per ton to $3.50 after a competing portion of the Columbia River became navigable;[22] this is a drop of 38 percent.[23] The rate on coke from Ironton, Ohio, was reduced from $3.25 a ton to $2.35 a ton to meet competition on the Ohio River; the shipper notified the railroad that he would ship by water for $2.10, but was willing to pay $2.35 for the more prompt and convenient rail service. The

---

[19] Cited in G. H. Borts, "Increasing Returns in the Railway Industry," *Journal of Political Economy* (August 1954), p. 323.

[20] *Rail Freight Service Costs*, Senate Doc. 63, pp. 56–60.

[21] G. H. Borts, "Production Relations in the Railway Industry," *Econometrica* (January 1952), pp. 71–79.

[22] Reported in a study done by the Corps of Engineers for the Department of the Interior, Bureau of Reclamation. *Columbia Basin Joint Investigations*, Problem 21, *River Transportation*, p. 15.

[23] This drop occurred before this particular study was made, so that the reduced rail rate became the alternative cost. The study foresees still further rail-rate reductions.

railroad had to petition to the ICC because the cut was in violation of the principle that long hauls must have higher rates than short hauls on the same route, and the ICC ruled that the discrimination was necessary to meet the imminent water competition.[24] The rate was cut by 36 percent. The rate on carload lots of asphalt to Fulton, Missouri, and Arrowhead, New York, was cut from 21 to 18.5¢ a hundred pounds with the permission of the ICC in a similar situation, a cut of 12 percent.[25]

We can be fairly sure that the resultant rates were not below out-of-pocket costs, since they would be noncompensatory and hence unreasonable if the ICC held them to be so. But we cannot assume that the railroads were forced to reduce the rates by the entire excess above out-of-pocket costs, since the cut was determined by the severity of the threat of competition. Thus these rate cuts only indicate a lower limit to the typical gap between the rates and the out-of-pocket costs.

The behavior of the railroads in these instances is empirical support for the findings of the statistical studies. We can therefore conclude that there is strong evidence to indicate that the usual railway rate exceeds the marginal cost of a specific haul by 15 to 40 percent or so. The benefits of navigation, as measured currently by the Corps of Engineers, therefore substantially overstate the saving of cost realized by the nation as a whole.[26] The savings to the benefitting shippers are much larger than the savings for the country, because there is an offsetting loss of income to the railways or else an offsetting loss to the shippers on other routes and of other commodities.

The quantitative impact on benefits is much larger than the percentage of change of the railroad rates. An arithmetic example will make this clear. Suppose a commodity is shipped

[24] *Coke from Ironton, Ohio, to West Henderson, Ky.*, 258 ICC 264, 266 (1944).

[25] *Asphalt to Fulton and Arrowhead, N.Y.*, 238 ICC 531, 534 (1940).

[26] For a different view, see *Annual Report of Chief of Engineers* (1951), pp. 318–322. This report argues in favor of using the old competitive rate on the grounds that the savings to the "public" be measured. But "public" is defined implicitly to be all the people except the railroads and their stockholders, and other shippers whose rates are raised in compensation. For an analysis similar to that found in this Chapter, see E. F. Renshaw, "Measurement of Benefits from Navigation Projects," *American Economic Review* (September 1957), pp. 652–661.

for $3.60 a ton, but with real out-of-pocket cost of $2.40; if a waterway could be used to ship the same commodity for $1.50, the navigation benefit would be calculated to be $2.10 a ton, the transportation saving of the shipper, although from a national point of view the cost saving is only $0.90. Thus, even though the rail rate includes a gap of 33 percent above out-of-pocket cost, the difference in the two benefit figures is 57 percent. If the project in question had a benefit-cost ratio of 2.0 under present concepts, it would only have a ratio of 0.86 from a national point of view.

The findings of this chapter can be given operational meaning by abandoning the use of the existing rail rate structure as the baseline for computing transportation savings. Instead, an approximation of long-run out-of-pocket expenses must be used. The rate at which railroads are willing to meet waterway competition would serve this purpose, particularly since it would also reflect differences in service.

This procedure would entail new problems of estimation which need investigation. If it should turn out to be impossible to make these estimates (and there is no reason to believe that it is harder to estimate them than it is to project traffic or to estimate the rates which water carriers will charge), then a rule of thumb, such as a reduction of the rail rate by 20 percent could be used.

The actual rates have the attractiveness of concreteness. They can be discovered by simple procedures. But since they yield benefit estimates that are clearly too high from the national point of view, they should be abandoned.

2. Present Practice: Projecting Future Waterway Traffic

The Corps of Engineers has a staff of transportation specialists who estimate the size of the traffic that can be expected on a waterway and the savings to be realized thereon. Such economic studies are part of the surveys authorized by Congress.

These studies assume that the proposed waterway will have a specific reliable depth and width, that adequate barge service will be established, and that terminal facilities will be provided.[27] The study defines the area that can be expected to supply traffic, it surveys existing facilities and freight rates, and it estimates

[27] *Annual Report of Chief of Engineers* (1951), pp. 295–300.

the cost to the public of shipment by waterway for different commodities. All commerce flowing into and out of the area is then surveyed in order to see what components of it would flow by waterway. Questionnaires are sent to samples of shippers and receivers to see how much traffic they would generate. From these questionnaires and from other data, such as surveys of resources and of economic activities of the area, a list of those commodities is compiled which will provide most of the volume, and more detailed studies are made for them to estimate the future expected traffic. Though the possibility of competitive rate cuts for such commodities by railroads is recognized, it is not incorporated explicitly into the procedures. All the extra traffic, including new traffic on connecting waterways, is credited to the project.[28]

For commodities which already move in substantial quantity, the difference in freight charges per unit is applied to the expected flow of commodities, usually on a commodity-by-commodity basis, to derive the navigation benefit. For undeveloped traffic the procedure is quite similar, except that the per-unit benefit is determined by comparing the expected rate by water with hypothetical rail or truck rates that would be charged if such transport facilities were provided.[29] This procedure will overstate the benefit in cases where the higher alternative cost would have precluded shipments by pricing the commodities so high that they could not be competitive in their markets.

The economic study of each project poses particular problems of its own. To illustrate the nature of the task, we shall examine two projects, one an incremental addition to an existing system, the other, a very large new system.

3. *A Small Navigation Project: Columbia Slough, Oregon*[30]

This project is to make navigable a slough running into the Willamette River near its junction with the Columbia River. The slough runs through an industrial area near Portland; several shingle mills are located on it. Without the project, logs

---

[28] *Orders and Regulations*, par. 4206.23.
[29] *Annual Report of Chief of Engineers* (1951), p. 300.
[30] *Report on Columbia Slough, Oregon*, House Doc. 270, 81 Cong., 1 sess.

are shipped to the mouth of the slough in standard rafts which are 800 feet by 65 feet; the rafts have to be broken up and smaller tugs have to pull them up the slough. The slough is to be made navigable to a depth of 10 feet, with a width of 100 feet, which would permit standard rafts to be hauled to the shingle mills.

Four different plans of improvement were considered, but only one of these held the promise of generating benefits in excess of costs. From data submitted by local interests and on the basis of an independent survey carried out by the Engineers the prospective commerce for each of the plans of improvement was estimated. The transportation savings were derived by com-

Table 28. Transportation savings on Columbia Slough, Plan 3

Commodity	Savings per ton	Tonnage	Saving
miscellaneous rafted logs	$0.08	341,700	$27,200
coke	0.28	10,000	2,800
sand and gravel	0.33	21,900	7,200
steel	1.00	15,600	15,600
pig iron and scrap	0.50	1,700	800
shingles	1.10	4,100	4,500
carbide	1.00	6,500	6,500
concrete pipe	1.00	1,900	1,900
glue and wood prod.	0.50	6,500	3,200
miscellaneous items	0.80	3,200	2,600
		413,100	$72,300

Source: *Report on Columbia Slough*, p. 18.

paring rates on the most economical alternative with rates that barge lines would have to charge to cover all their costs. Table 28 summarizes the computation for the feasible plan.

The transportation savings were used as the estimate of direct benefits. In addition, paralleling the estimation procedures of flood-control benefits, the project was credited with certain indirect benefits, which in this case were attributed to the enhancement of property values and to the stimulation of business and industry. Table 29 summarizes the benefit-cost analysis for the four alternative plans.

Plan 3 was recommended by the district engineer and was endorsed by the Board of Engineers for Rivers and Harbors and the Chief of Engineers. The first cost of the project is equal to $1,023,000, of which the Corps of Engineers pays $807,500, the Coast Guard $5,000 for aids to navigation, and local interests $211,000. The local contribution is in the form of land, easements, and rights of way. The annual maintenance expense is estimated to be $15,000, of which $14,500 is to be paid by the Engineers and the balance by the Coast Guard.

Table 29. Benefits and costs of four plans for Columbia Slough, Oregon

	Plan 1	Plan 2	Plan 3	Plan 4
Benefit				
direct	96,800	87,400	72,300	32,400
indirect	10,000	8,700	6,500	1,500
Total	106,800	96,100	78,800	33,800
Estimated annual cost*	217,000	122,000	56,000	36,000
Benefit-cost ratio	0.5	0.8	1.4	0.9

* Annual cost assumes economic life of 50 years and interest of 3 percent on federal investment, slightly more on other investment.

This analysis does not present a strong case for undertaking this project. First, indirect benefits from the enhancement of property value represent double counting; the value of sites which have access to more favorable transportation methods is merely a capitalization of the lower charges on water transport, and these benefits are fully measured by the direct benefits. If indirect benefits are subtracted, the benefit-cost ratio falls to 1.29, which, according to the principles discussed in Chapter III, is hardly sufficient to justify the use of resources in this investment. If federal project costs were used as a denominator instead of all project costs, the ratio would be slightly higher, equal to 1.31, which still shows the project to be of a marginal character at best.

4. *A Large Navigation Project: The St. Lawrence Seaway*

In the next few years a significant percentage of the total federal investment in navigation will be in the St. Lawrence Seaway. The total cost of the navigation aspects of this multi-purpose project will be in excess of $400,000,000.

The project is untypical in many ways. It is international in scope, and consequently was considered in Congress by the committees on foreign affairs. It is to be administered by a government corporation, responsible to the President, instead of being run by the Corps of Engineers, though the Corps will be in charge of its construction. Perhaps most important of all, the project is to be self-financing, with sufficient revenue to be raised through tolls to repay the entire cost of the project in fifty years or less.

Despite these elements which limit the applicability of the lessons of the example for other projects, we shall discuss the economic analyses which supported it because the project is such an important part of the whole program, and because many of the difficulties attendant on the analysis of such a vast undertaking will occur with any other navigation project of similar scope.

The basic analyses of recent years have been carried out by the Department of Commerce rather than by the Corps of Engineers. A large study of the impact of the waterway and of its feasibility was published in 1941,[31] but the analyses which entered into the final decision were carried out in 1947 and 1948. They were introduced as supplementary documents to the testimony of General Pick, Chief of Engineers, before the House Committee of Public Works in 1949,[32] and were the basis of testimony by the same officer in 1951 and by his deputy in 1953.

The analysis of 1947 is concerned with the traffic in the four bulk commodities which are expected to provide most of the tonnage on the Seaway. The most important is iron ore, to be shipped from the newly found deposits in Labrador to the centers

[31] U.S. Department of Commerce, *The St. Lawrence Survey* (1941).
[32] *Hearings on the Great Lakes–St. Lawrence Basin Project, Committee on Public Works* (House, 81 Cong., 2 sess.), "Domestic Transportation— an Economic Appraisal of the St. Lawrence Seaway Project, Aug.–Nov., 1947," pp. 29–74; also "Potential Traffic on the St. Lawrence Seaway" (prepared by the Transportation Division of the Office of Domestic Commerce, U.S. Department of Commerce, Dec. 1948), pp. 75–94.

of steel making in Pennsylvania, Ohio, and elsewhere in the Midwest via the Seaway and the Great Lakes system. The approaching end of good ore from the Mesabi range is forecast, and all the substitute sources are examined in turn. The cost of using low-grade ore and the cost of ores from overseas, including Venezuela and Liberia, are estimated and compared with the cost of mining and shipping ore from Labrador. The study finds that the latter has a substantial cost advantage. In order to estimate the annual tonnage, a long-run output is assumed for the steel industry, based on industry plans and including some growth in the early years; remaining reserves in the Mesabi range are calculated, and the total usable ore in Labrador is estimated. From these figures an overall total tonnage of ore shipments is predicted for the entire life of the project and an annual estimate is derived. The total for all years can be estimated more accurately than the figure for a typical year, since the total ore reserves can be derived from geological studies, while the annual rate is contingent on many factors, including the growth rate of the industry and general economic conditions. With iron-ore shipments expected to be about half of the total tonnage of the river, a fairly firm estimate for this total goes a long way toward predicting the overall feasibility of the navigation project. A range of 30 to 37½ million tons a year is projected.[33]

Another important bulk commodity which can be expected to move over the waterway is grain. The main route for most Canadian and much American wheat consists of Great Lakes shipments to the rail terminal at Buffalo. The Seaway can be expected to divert most of the overseas exports now passing through Buffalo. An estimate for this traffic is derived from figures of grain exports transhipped at Buffalo. A range of 6½ to 11½ million tons is projected, the uncertainty stemming from the possibility of railway rate adaptation and shifts in trade patterns.

A substantial tonnage can also be expected from coal, which now moves by rail from mines in the United States to the province

[33] Industry spokesmen supported this view. See the testimony of G. M. Humphrey, then president of Iron Ore Company of Canada, chief promoters of Labrador ore. Mr. Humphrey, subsequently Secretary of the Treasury, gave a very detailed presentation of expected ore traffic. *Hearings...Great Lakes–St. Lawrence*, pp. 233–264.

of Quebec. Movement by water would be much cheaper, and is expected to be 4 million tons.

Finally, the possibilities of petroleum shipments are investigated. The study of 1947 does not predict any tonnage from this source, though it mentions it as a good possibility. The traffic would only develop if refineries in the Great Lakes area were forced to use imported oil due to exhaustion of oil fields in the central United States. There was also some doubt that the capacity of the Seaway, particularly of the Welland Canal, would be adequate to handle oil traffic, which presumably would be marginal traffic compared to the other commodities.

Table 30. Possible range of toll charges and revenues on the
St. Lawrence seaway—1947 study

Commodity	Estimated annual tonnage (millions)	Toll charge per ton	Total revenue (in million dollars)
Ore	30 –37½	$0.50	15.000–18.750
Grain	6½–11½	0.25–0.35	1.625– 4.025
Coal	4	0.25–0.35	1.000– 1.400
Ballast	19½–22	0.15	3.300– 2.925
Total			20.925–27.100

Source: *Hearings . . . Gt. Lakes–St. Lawrence*, p. 75.

The purpose of this study was not to estimate the benefits of the Seaway, but to see if tolls could be imposed on an adequate volume of traffic to repay the cost of the project. Thus it was necessary to derive an appropriate set of tolls for these commodities, tolls which presumably were limited by the rates that would be charged by competitive means of transport. Since actual revenues were to be estimated, the possibility of competitive rate cuts had to be considered in setting the toll rates. Table 30 summarizes the findings of the study.

The study of 1948 added an estimate of 11.3 million tons of possible general cargo. This estimate was derived from a sample of railroad waybills, from which it was computed what share of our exports through the Atlantic ports originated in the seven Great Lakes states. It divided these exports into groups and estimated what share could be diverted to direct shipments overseas via ports on the Great Lakes, subtracting one third to allow for the four winter months when the route will be closed.

Table 31. Possible range of toll charges and revenues on the St. Lawrence seaway—1948 study

Commodity	Tonnage (millions)	Toll charge per ton (dollars)	Total revenue (dollars)	
			minimum	maximum
Iron ore	30–37.5	0.50	15,000,000–18,750,000	
Grain	6.5–11.5	0.25–0.35	1,625,000– 4,025,000	
Coal	4	0.25–0.35	1,000,000– 1,400,000	
Petroleum	6–20	0.25	1,500,000– 5,000,000	
Agriculture machinery	0.048	1.25	60,000–	60,000
Autos and parts	0.640	1.25	800,000–	800,000
Iron and steel	1.371	1.25	1,713,750– 1,713,750	
Office appliances	0.007	1.25	8,750–	8,750
Wheat flour	0.555	0.50	277,500–	277,500
Industrial chemicals	0.013	1.25	16,250–	16,250
Coffee	0.245	1.25	306,250–	306,250
Sugar	0.963	1.25	1,203,750– 1,203,750	
Oil seeds	0.125	1.25	156,250–	156,250
Wool	0.006	1.25	7,500–	7,500
Newsprint	0.121	1.25	151,250–	151,250
Manganese and other ores and metals	0.240	0.50	120,000–	120,000
Copper	0.034	1.25	42,500–	42,500
Nitrogen fertilizer	0.025	1.25	31,250–	31,250
Residual general cargo traffic	6.885	1.25	8,606,250– 8,606,250	
Ballast shipping	25.5–42.	0.15	3,825,000– 6,300,000	
Total			36,451,250–48,976,250	

Source: *Hearings . . . Great Lakes–St. Lawrence*, p. 94.

It did not include any allowance for new traffic, working entirely from the sample of waybills. Nevertheless, the amount of diversion assumed seems excessive especially since the winter interruption compels continued existence of all the trading facilities and institutions in the traditional ports.

To calculate the transportation savings as a basis for computing possible toll charges, actual rail rates were not used at all. Instead, out-of-pocket cost estimates were used, thus assuming from the start that the railway rate structure would be revolutionized to meet the waterway competition. The costs estimated in 1939 by the Bureau of Investigation and Research, a temporary agency concerned with transportation problems, were increased by 50 percent to allow for cost increases. It was estimated that

Table 32.   Three estimates of tonnage on the St. Lawrence Seaway

Source	Tonnage in millions
Canadian Department of Trade and Commerce	44.5
Great Lakes–St. Lawrence Association	45.7
(a group promoting the Seaway)	
U.S. Department of Commerce	64.5–83.5

Source: *Hearings on the St. Lawrence Seaway*, p. 46.

the total revenue that could be collected would lie in the range of $36.5 to $49 million, with tolls set sufficiently low to provide an incentive for shippers to change their routes. Table 31 summarizes these estimates.

In the hearings of 1953,[34] Walter Williams, undersecretary of Commerce, mentioned three estimates of the total expected tonnage, listed in Table 32. But he stressed particularly that a minimum of traffic was assured to yield the necessary revenue. He contended that there was an assured base load of 20 million tons of ore plus 10 million tons that now move over the existing 14-foot waterway on the Canadian side.[35] Thus he showed that

[34] *Hearings on the St. Lawrence Seaway* before a subcommittee of the Committee on Foreign Relations, U.S. Senate, 83 Cong., 1 sess.
[35] *Hearings on the St. Lawrence Seaway*, p. 475.

there was little question of the financial success of the waterway, since the revenues assured from these movements would be adequate by themselves.

General Pick, Chief of the Corps of Engineers, provided a benefit-cost analysis of the project, based on the figures of the Department of Commerce. He estimated costs, benefits, and revenues, shown in Table 33.[36]

Table 33. Revenues, benefits and cost of St. Lawrence Seaway

Total first cost:	$827,359,000
Allocation to power:	446,152,000
Net first cost of navigation	381,207,000
Interest during construction	34,308,000
Total investment, navigation	415,515,000
Interest and amortization*	16,163,000
Annual operation and maintenance expenditure	4,250,000
Annual cost	20,413,000
Annual benefit	60,000,000
Benefit-cost ratio	2.94
Possible revenue	36,500,000
Revenue-cost ratio	1.79

Source: *Hearings on the St. Lawrence Seaway*, p. 476.

* Calculated with interest of 3 percent and amortization over 50 years.

The costs of the project were derived from the project plans; the revenues were based on the more conservative value of the range projected by the Department of Commerce. No explanation was offered for the benefit figure, except that it was derived by the staff of the Chief of Engineers from the most conservative of the traffic estimates of the Department of Commerce. Benefits exceed revenues by 55 percent; to some extent this difference can be explained by the fact that the toll rates which were suggested

[36] These figures all apply to the St. Lawrence portion of the project; another sizable project must be undertaken on the Great Lakes to derive full use of the Seaway, and Lake ports will have to be improved to accommodate the new traffic.

were not the maximum rates which could be charged; they were designed to provide an incentive to shift traffic, yet still yield an adequate return, so that the actual transportation savings may be somewhat higher than the estimates of expected revenue. Perhaps the Engineers used actual transportation charges rather than the rail cost estimates used by the Department of Commerce; or perhaps the Engineers simply desired to convey the general magnitude of the benefits, both direct and indirect, without any kind of detailed estimate. In the latter event, the ratio should not have been quoted to two decimal places.

The general picture which emerges from our cursory survey of the analyses submitted to Congress is this: there were a number of different estimates of expected traffic, all well above the needed volume. The official study, which indicated the uncertainty surrounding any figure by means of a wide range of estimates, and the verbal presentation by the spokesman of the administration conveyed the fact that it was the iron-ore traffic which was the backbone of the justification of the project, and showed that this traffic was very likely to develop. It appeared to be recognized by all concerned that the effects of a project of such a magnitude were not predictable, and that nothing more was possible than to indicate some of the main sources of traffic and the possible magnitudes. There was a good deal of discussion in the hearings of some of the figures, but in the end, one could only conclude that much human judgment was involved, and each congressman could choose to accept or reject the judgment of those who supported the Seaway.

One cannot expect as complete an airing of the economic issues of smaller projects, because the time of the Congress and of top officials is too valuable to be diverted into extensive hearings for every small undertaking. Nevertheless, the Congress could be given more of the data and of the assumptions about the economics of smaller projects. The very concise summaries of expected transportation savings published in the project reports do not convey much of an idea about the issues on which the success or failure of the project may turn. The judgment is exercised by the Corps of Engineers; the Congress has little basis on which to evaluate the reliability of the Corps' judgment.

Finally, the self-liquidating nature of the project forced the

Department of Commerce to tackle the problem of competitive rate cuts by railroads. It was shown that it is possible to use direct estimates of the out-of-pocket cost of hauling commodities as a base line for calculating transportation savings rather than existing railway rate structure. This supports the practicality of the proposals outlined above for estimating navigation benefits from railway cost data instead of from rail rates.

5. *The Benefits of Harbor Improvement*

The problems of evaluating the economic worth of harbor-improvement projects are very similar to those met on inland waterways, and the approach of the Corps of Engineers is very much the same.[37] The responsibilities of the federal government are usually limited to providing and maintaining adequate channels for ports and protecting them by means of breakwaters and jetties. Measurable benefits are usually limited to the savings of shippers. Since there is no real alternative to harbors, there is very little question about the proper allocation of traffic among systems.

The nature of these benefits can perhaps be seen most clearly by looking at two examples. The first of these is a project for the port of Lynn, Massachusetts.[38] Local interests requested an improvement of the approaching channel and an expansion of a turning basin which would permit the use of the port by coal-carrying vessels of 10,000 tons. Vessels of such size had become standard along the Atlantic coast for the delivery of coal, and the local power company estimated that there would be a saving of 45¢ a ton if the large modern vessels could deliver coal directly to their plant. The company also contended that any saving would be passed on to the community since its rates were based on a cost formula which would definitely lead to a rate reduction. A benefit-cost ratio of 15.3 results from these savings on coal shipments. Obviously, such a project should be undertaken, and it was recommended by the Corps of Engineers.

To cite a project of more dubious worth, let us examine the

[37] *Annual Report of Chief of Engineers* (1951), p. 301.
[38] *Report on Lynn Harbor, Massachusetts*, House Doc. 568, 81 Cong., 2 sess.

Channel Port Royal to Beaufort, South Carolina,[39] which was to provide access to the sea from Beaufort, and thus open up the possibility of a development of a port there. A traffic survey was made to see how large the potential use of the new harbor would be, and it was concluded, after examining three alternative plans of improvement, that the most favorable one would yield a benefit-cost ratio of 1.20 on an expenditure of $700,000. The project was recommended for construction. One company was expected to supply half the traffic, the Plywoods-Plastics Corporation, which expected to ship in logs for hardwood veneers from South America, and to export plywoods and plastics through the port. No cash contribution by local interests was required by the Engineers, though it is within their power to insist on such contributions if the benefits are extremely concentrated among the beneficiaries. The Bureau of the Budget, in its review of the project, stated that the traffic expected from the one company would probably not develop because exchange-rate changes had made export possibilities unlikely. The project has not been constructed.

The Corps of Engineers also has a program of improvement of small-boat harbors for recreational purposes. It subjects such projects to uniform evaluations of recreational benefits in monetary terms.[40] The benefit is taken as equal to the net return which would be earned on the boats which use the harbor if they were all operated for hire. To calculate this net return it is necessary to estimate the value of the boats and to compute the rate of return which is earned on capital in the "boats-for-hire" business in the region. This rate varies from 6 percent to 15 percent for different areas. An improvement may permit more intensive use of existing boats and it may attract new boats to the harbor; both of these are considered. Sometimes, damage from storms is also prevented by the improvement, and this, too, is a benefit.

The above benefit measurements may contain some merit as criteria, since they will favor projects with high expected usage and will favor those areas where the rate of return on boats for

---

[39] *Report on Channel Port Royal to Beaufort, S.C.*, House Doc. 469, 81 Cong., 2 sess.

[40] *Annual Report of Chief of Engineers* (1951), pp. 302–304.

hire is high, indicating relatively high popular demand. But the actual figures for benefits have very little meaning, and need bear little relation to the real benefits. The income equivalent of the boats would be a measure of benefit if the project eliminated the need for boats. Since the boats must also be supplied, only the profit or its equivalent which is in excess of the rate of profit that could be earned elsewhere under similar condition of risk is a true net benefit. If 6 percent is an appropriate rate for capital in such uses, only the return above 6 percent can be considered a benefit.

But it must be remembered that recreational benefits are largely intangible, and that the satisfactions of the people are well in excess of the cost of the boats. Since projects must be compared for purposes of selection for construction, some measures must be used, measures which should reflect, at the least, the expected use of the harbor. And in a crude way, the present procedure accomplishes this aim, though it would be more informative and more helpful to reviewing agencies and especially to the Congress if the criteria were not obscured by being forced into the benefit-cost framework. A statement of intensity of use in terms of number of people, number of boats, and length of season would convey more useful information.

B. FINANCIAL ANALYSIS

6. *Should There be User Charges on the Waterways?*

It has been the traditional policy of the United States to impose no charges on the use of its waterways. The Rivers and Harbors Act of 1884 formalized this tradition, and no exceptions to it have been authorized except for the recent legislation for the St. Lawrence Seaway. Charges on that project, strictly speaking, are not a violation of the principle, since it is an international rather than an inland waterway. But the railroads have always contended that the absence of tolls leads to a diversion of traffic to the waterways which is uneconomical and simply due to the presence of a subsidy on water transportation.

Whether charges should be imposed or not is primarily a

political question.[41]   The main effect of imposing tolls is distributive; especially on old waterways it is perhaps best considered to be the imposition of a tax, increasing the public revenue and reducing the prosperity of those whose fortunes are linked to the waterways.   But there are some matters of economic analysis which should not be overlooked in dealing with the issue.

First, the complete absence of tolls makes for an inefficient division of traffic between railways and waterways.   Ideally, each commodity should be hauled by that system which can do so at least social cost, that is, for which the long-run out-of-pocket (or marginal) costs are the least.   In order to achieve this division of traffic the rates faced by shippers should reflect marginal costs. Profit-maximizing shippers will then select the system with lowest social costs or, in the event of significant differences in the quality of service, will decide whether the better service is worth the extra cost.

The marginal cost of waterways will usually be a relatively small percentage of average cost since the waterway has to be made navigable and maintained in safe condition to permit any vessel to use it;[42] the addition of any increment of traffic would lead to relatively little extra expense.   However, there are two important exceptions.   First, where a waterway is used to capacity, the marginal cost should include not only the expense incurred by the waterway but also the cost of the increase in congestion caused by the vessel, or, where the capacity limitation is absolute, the value of the service to others which must be foregone.   From this point of view, an ideal toll would rise as congestion rises, would be lowered after the bottleneck is broken, and would then start to rise again.   Second, where a waterway is used by vessels of different size and depth, the marginal cost of providing a channel adequate for the largest vessels may be large and they should be charged accordingly.

[41] The most thorough exploration of this issue can be found in Board of Investigation and Research, *Public Aids to Transportation*, House Doc. 159, 79 Cong., 1 sess.   Also see "User Charges on the Waterways of the United States," by J. H. Frederick, in Commission on Organization of the Executive Branch of the Government, *Task Force Report on Water Resources and Power* (June 1955), vol. III, pp. 1299–1316.

[42] The marginal cost of operating a vessel is substantial, of course. But this cost is reflected in the rates charged by barge lines and would have no direct bearing on tolls imposed for the use of the waterway.

A charge greater than marginal cost prevents the waterway from rendering an optimum amount of service to the nation since higher tolls will discourage some traffic from the waterways even though the value of the service may exceed the social costs that would be incurred. On the other hand, rail rates are not based on marginal costs, as we saw earlier, but must embody sufficient gaps above marginal costs to cover the common costs of the railroad. If waterway tolls were to equal marginal costs, while rail rates were closer to average costs, some traffic would continue to be attracted to the waterways which could be carried more economically by rail, for marginal cost pricing on one alternative does not lead to an efficient allocation of resources if other alternatives are priced by different principles.

For the sake of symmetrical treatment, railroad interests have argued that waterways should also be made to operate on a self-sustaining basis. But there are three significant limitations on the validity of this argument. First, at the time the basic railroad facilities were established, they were also the recipients of large subsidies.[43] Second, their present financial capital structure no longer corresponds to the original investment costs, so that the present rate structure need not produce revenue for all historical overhead, but only for some portions. Finally, and most importantly, there is a big quantitative difference in the cost structures of the two systems. Only about 25 percent or so of railroad costs are constant as volume changes, while 80 percent or more of the waterway cost does not increase with volume in cases where capacity is not fully utilized. Thus the average deviation of railway rates from the out-of-pocket cost of hauling various commodities is much smaller than the deviation for waterways, were they to adopt the principle that revenues must be sufficient to cover all their costs. Should we desire to have the prices of the two systems exceed marginal costs by the same percentage, tolls on waterways should cover no more than 25 percent or so of the total costs where there is excess capacity in the waterway.[44] In the case of the St. Lawrence project or the

[43] For a summary of these subsidies, see *Public Aids to Transportation*, pp. 105–187.

[44] The figure is derived as follows: with marginal costs on railways equal to 80 percent of average costs, rail rates are 1.25 times marginal cost. If waterway marginal cost is 20 percent of average cost, tolls

impending reconstruction of the Ohio system, instances where present traffic is straining capacity, tolls should be considerably higher from this point of view.

There are other strong economic arguments in favor of some user charges on waterways, foremost among which is the fact that the collection of tolls assures that only those projects which really hold the promise of substantial transportation savings will be promoted by local interests and will be considered justified by the Corps of Engineers and the Congress. Benefit-cost analysis is a partial substitute for the test of revenue collection, and with sufficiently tightly defined concepts, it presents the possibility of an alternative test of economic worth. But it is inevitable that those who have an interest in the promotion of waterways will sometimes tend to overestimate the likely benefits of a project. And this is especially true in the absence of effective detailed review of the analyses by disinterested persons either in the executive branch or in the Congress. The reality of the toll, and the easy check which it provides both on the worth of the project and on the projections which justified it, much diminishes the possibility of wasteful overexpansion of the waterway system.

If tolls are to be imposed it would be necessary to set the rates not on the basis of the traffic of the early years, but in such a way that the proper amount of revenue is yielded over the economic life of the project. Typically, growth of traffic takes place slowly. Loading facilities must be provided, shippers must become aware of the new opportunities, and the pattern of location of new plants will only be adapted gradually. Thus the revenue should be small in the early years. In the case of old waterways, revenues should only be sufficient to cover operating and maintenance costs, for the investment is a sunk cost which cannot be diminished by any present action of the government. Tolls would lead not only to underutilization of existing capacity but to dislocations for existing barge lines and for the shippers who have set up their operations on the assumption of free use of the waterways.

---

should be 1.25 times this amount, or 25 percent of average cost. This principle would be valid if the demand for the two services together is completely inelastic.

CHAPTER VII

Irrigation

THE current irrigation program of the federal government began with the passage of the Reclamation Act of 1902, which authorized the Bureau of Reclamation to build irrigation projects.[1] The act set up the Reclamation Fund, which provided revenue from sale of public lands for this purpose; it also required that settlers on the projects must sign contracts to repay construction costs in ten annual payments, and it set down a very basic principle of the program that largely governs to this day, that no settler is to be permitted to receive irrigation water for more than 160 acres.[2] Most of the other principles have been modified in subsequent legislation. Funds are now also provided out of general appropriations as well as from specific sources, such as revenues from the sale of electric power. Agreements to repay construction costs are no longer signed by individual settlers but by irrigation districts, governmental entities which have been given the power of taxation over a project's beneficiaries. The repayment period has gradually been extended from ten years to forty years and need not begin until a development period of ten years has passed. The program is confined to the seventeen Western states and to Alaska.

[1] Two excellent volumes have appeared recently which deal with the irrigation program. A. R. Golzé, *Reclamation in the United States* (1952), is an extremely detailed account; R. E. Huffman, *Irrigation Development and Public Water Policy* (1953), is more concerned with the major issues of policy. For a highly critical discussion of the program, see R. Moley, *What Price Federal Reclamation?* (1955).

[2] Huffman, *Irrigation Development and Public Water Policy*, p. 25. In the case of the Columbia Basin project the acreage limitation is adapted to the very intensive agriculture of the area; a 160 acre farm would be more than a family-size farm. There are also some loopholes in the law; for example, different members of the same family can own 160 acres and operate them jointly.

Irrigation

A typical irrigation project must pass through many planning stages before it becomes a reality. The Secretary of the Interior and the Congress have the power to initiate surveys to be undertaken by the Bureau of Reclamation and to see if a project is feasible from the point of view of engineering and of reimbursement. Unless Congress waives the requirement, a project can be authorized only if it can be shown that the total cost of all reimbursable purposes can be repaid during the repayment period. If the project passes both feasibility tests, the Secretary has the power to authorize it,[3] though in recent years Congressional authorization has been used exclusively. In addition, the Bureau of Reclamation analyzes the economics of the project by means of a benefit-cost analysis. Projects are generally not recommended for authorization unless benefits exceed costs.

Construction cannot be started until the water rights for the project have been secured from the state governments and until the Congress has appropriated the funds. The choice of settlers on the project is determined by lot in public drawings, with veterans having preference. Once a project is completed and the development of its potential acreage is well advanced, the Bureau of Reclamation will turn over the management and maintenance of the facilities to the irrigation district.[4] The Bureau continues to collect payments under its contract with the district until the total is equal to the share of construction costs which was to be repaid by irrigation. Sixty projects or portions of projects had been transferred to water-user organizations by June 1952 out of a total of fifty-four completed and eighty-three partially completed projects.[5]

Table 34, giving figures of acreage and annual crop values, gives some indication of the size and growth of the program. It is

[3] The President's Water Resources Policy Commission, vol. III, *Water Resources Law*, p. 201.

[4] Projects built under section 9e of the Reclamation Act are based on water-user contracts under which the Bureau retains the water rights and merely sells water service. Such projects remain under the control of the Bureau even after the repayment period is past. For the disadvantages of this form of contract, see S. V. Ciriacy-Wantrup, "Cost Allocation in Relation to Western Water Policies," *Journal of Farm Economics* (February 1954), pp. 108–129.

[5] Department of the Interior, Bureau of Reclamation, *50 Years of Reclamation* (1952), p. 5.

interesting to note that reclamation was carried on by the federal government on a large scale for a number of decades before the Great Depression. It must also be stressed that there was much irrigation by private organizations prior to the federal program, and that even today the acreage of the federal projects is only about one quarter of the irrigated land in the seventeen Western states.[6] The importance of the federal program in relation to the nation's agriculture is indicated by the fact that the irrigated

Table 34. Irrigated acreage and total crop value for selected years

Year	Irrigated acreage	Total crop value
		(dollars)
1910	473,423	12,974,639
1915	856,778	18,164,452
1920	2,205,420	113,677,420
1925	2,339,470	131,264,730
1930	2,790,856	119,661,820
1935	2,935,616	106,781,294
1940	3,391,070	117,788,677
1945	4,162,588	435,184,395
1950	5,077,186	578,237,709
1952	5,955,750	935,679,755
1954	6,125,766	865,025,682

Source: Secretary of the Interior, *Annual Report*, 1955, p. 50.

acreage is ½ percent of the total land in agricultural use, and that the resultant crop value is 2.8 percent of the total agricultural output for the country.[7] The composition of this output is indicated in Table 35.

Table 36 gives the appropriations which Congress made available for all of the work of the Bureau of Reclamation, including its construction of hydroelectric power capacity and its other purposes, while Table 37 shows the federal investment in irrigation and the multipurpose projects of the Bureau.

[6] The 1950 Census of Agriculture gives figures for total irrigated land; cited in Golzé, *Reclamation in the United States*, p. 42.

[7] National total is given in the *Survey of Current Business*, biennial edition, 1953.

Table 35. Crops on federal reclamation projects, 1949

Products	Percent of total revenue		Products	Percent of total revenue	
Cereals		13.1	Vegetables and		26.3
Barley	4.6		Truck		
Corn	0.9		Beans	3.5	
Oats	1.3		Onions	1.2	
Rye	0.0		Potatoes, white	8.8	
Wheat	5.2		Potatoes, sweet	0.1	
Other	1.1		Truck	11.6	
			Gardens	1.1	
Seed		5.7	Fruits and nuts		10.1
Alfalfa	0.8		Apples	2.3	
Clover	1.9		Peaches	0.7	
Other	3.0		Pears	0.6	
			Prunes	0.1	
			Citrus fruits	1.0	
			Small fruits	4.9	
			Miscellaneous	0.5	
Hay and forage		18.5	Miscellaneous		23.4
Alfalfa hay	12.0		Sugar beets	4.9	
Other hay	0.8		Cotton, lint	15.0	
Corn fodder	0.4		Cotton, seed	1.7	
Other forage	0.6		Other crops	1.8	
Beet tops	0.2				
Pasture	4.5				
Other revenues, including payments by government	2.9				
	100.0				

Source: Golzé, *Reclamation in the United States* (1952), p. 43.

Though the future trend of appropriations cannot be predicted, it appears that the program will continue on a large scale. Under the Democratic administration the Commissioner of Reclamation estimated in 1952 that completion of the program then projected would call for average expenditures of $301,662,000 a year for the period 1953–1959.[8] Actual appropriations have

[8] Department of Interior, Bureau of Reclamation, *The Reclamation Program*, 1953–1959 (1952), p. v.

Table 36. Appropriations for Bureau of Reclamation, 1902–1957
(in millions of dollars)

1902–1910*	6	1943	94
1911–1920*	11	1944	47
1921–1930*	14	1945	42
1931	10	1946	128
1932	32	1947	122
1933	16	1948	149
1934	115	1949	272
1935	35	1950	367
1936	43	1951	278
1937	43	1952	242
1938	82	1953	215
1939	47	1954	148
1940	84	1955	168
1941	81	1956	183
1942	105	1957†	221
		Total	3,677

Source: Secretary of the Interior, *Annual Report*, 1955, p. 70; and *Budget of the United States Government*, 1956, 1957.

* Average per year.
† Budget request.

Table 37. Cost of plant, property, and equipment as of June 30, 1955

Completed works	
Irrigation	$779,557,805
Electric	574,671,487
Municipal water supply	14,041,384
Flood control	13,319,716
Multipurpose	987,186,637
Construction in progress	285,583,593
Other physical property	20,746,915
Total	2,675,107,537

Source: Secretary of the Interior, *Annual Report*, 1955, p. 72.

been smaller, less than $200,000,000 in recent years. The study of 1952 claimed that there are further development opportunities in these states which would involve about five times as much acreage as has already been developed.

Irrigation

A. ECONOMIC ANALYSIS

1. *Present Practice: Direct Irrigation Benefits*

The supply of water to a number of farms is the actual service rendered by the federal government when it constructs an irrigation project. It might therefore be expected that the benefit of this operation would be measured by the prices which the farmers would be willing to pay for the supply of the water. But there are strong reasons which preclude so simple a measure; if farmers had to pay as much for the water as it was worth in terms of additional output, there would be no incentive for them to bother moving to the project or to engage in the long and backbreaking task of bringing the irrigable acreage into intensive cultivation. In addition, it is not generally practicable to sell the water by the acre foot or even year by year; rather, the beneficiaries must sign long-term contracts to meet the total obligations for the project before construction is started. Thus, a direct measure of the economic worth of the water supply could not be predicated on actual revenues, but rather on a hypothetical computation of the maximum amounts which farmers would be willing to pay if they were perfectly rational entrepreneurs. This amount is taken to be equal to the expected change in the income of the irrigator families.

There are three categories of direct farm benefits:[9]

(1) the increase in "family living," including the home-grown products consumed by the family, the higher level of other perquisites such as the farm dwelling, and the increase of the cash allowance for family living expenditures;

(2) the increase in cash income after the deduction of all production expenses, including a charge for depreciation and interest on the farm investment, and the deduction of the increase in the cash living allowance; this figure is equal to the repayment capacity of the project and is used for checking its financial feasibility;

(3) an allowance for accumulation of owner equity in the farm investment, equal to 1 percent a year.

At the conceptual level, the first and second categories of direct benefits measure precisely the benefit, or extra income, which

[9] Department of the Interior, Bureau of Reclamation, *Reclamation Manual*, vol. XIII, *Benefits and Costs*, March 1952, par. 2.2.1.

accrues to the irrigators. The third category is justified by a peculiarity of accounting. An amortization charge of 1 percent is included among the associated costs of the farms; this charge is not a genuine cost but represents the acquisition of ownership by the farm families; the allowance for accumulation of equity simply offsets the erroneous inclusion of both amortization and depreciation among costs.

The basic data for these computations are drawn from farm-budget studies which have been undertaken by the Bureau. These studies show output, production expense, and family living expense figures for farms of different types. For any given project it can be determined what kinds of farms are likely to be developed and in what numbers; these figures can be combined with the budget studies and price estimates[10] to derive an aggregate analysis for the entire farming operation on the project.

Table 38 shows a model computation of direct benefits based on these concepts, which is presented in the official *Manual* of the Bureau. Lines 1 to 9 summarize some of the physical and gross income and production data. Line 10 shows the first category of direct benefits, the increase in the family living allowance. It is based on an allowance of $2,250 per family, reflecting the goods and services consumed on the farm (lines 6 and 7), plus an allowance for cash requirements for outside purchases; this figure will vary from one project to another. The direct benefits from this category are derived by subtracting a family living allowance of $1,000 per family, which, it is assumed, each family would have received if it had not settled on the project. There are 90 new families on the project of the example, so that $90,000 must be subtracted from the living allowance earned on the project site. The figure of $1,000 is generally used as the basic family allowance that would be earned by the settlers without the project, which implies that they are assumed to come from very poor farm land. This assumption can be defended even if the settlers come from land that yields somewhat more, since their departure makes room for some other farm family to take their place, and so on. It is the family allowance on the land which is marginal in the area within which there is

---

[10] For a discussion of the prices used in the analysis see Chapter III, Section 12.

Table 38. Derivation of direct farm benefits from project-wide
totals of farm budget data
(annual values under full development)

Item	With irrigation	Without irrigation	Difference	Direct farm benefit
1. Type of farm	Irrigated farm	Dry farms and grazing		
2. Number of farms	100	10	(90)	
3. Acres per farm	160	1,600		
4. Irrigable acres	16,000	16,000		
5. Farm products sold	$1,350,000	$100,000	$1,250,000	
6. Products consumed in home	$50,000	$3,000	$47,000	
7. Rental value of dwelling	$25,000	$2,000	$23,000	
8. Gross farm income	$1,425,000	$105,000	$1,320,000	
9. Production expenses	$900,000	$60,000	$840,000	
10. Family living allowance	$225,000	$22,500	$202,500	$112,500
11. Payment capacity	$300,000	$22,500	$277,500	$277,500
12. Farm investment	$4,000,000	$400,000	$3,600,000	$36,000
13. Total direct farm benefit				$426,000

Source: Department of the Interior, *Reclamation Manual,* 2.2.3.

substantial family mobility that is of relevance. But it must be remembered that the kind of people who are willing to undertake the backbreaking task of developing new irrigated land, and who are willing to take the risk on the substantial investments which are required, are not typical farmers; they are usually in the healthiest age groups, in their twenties or thirties, and are among the most venturesome in the farm population. Their alternative earnings are probably a good deal more than $1,000.[11] The computation also makes no allowance for the cost of moving the family to the project, a cost composed of the money charges actually incurred by the family to move themselves and their belongings, plus the intangible psychic costs of settling in a new and uncertain environment.

The second category of direct benefits, line 11, corresponds to the remaining increase in net cash income, the share not needed for the living allowance and therefore available for the repayment charges. Thus the two categories are equal to the total net change in farmers' income before water charges. The third category, line 12, is based on the accumulation of owner equity, and is equal to 1 percent of the added investment. Total direct benefit is the sum of these three categories.

Of course, much the largest question about the validity of the direct benefits is raised by the federal farm support program. To some extent, the present price projections make some allowance for this factor by postulating a fall in price of 20 percent for the major commodities which are in surplus and under federal support. This is not an adequate adjustment, of course, since the direct benefit of crops that end up in storage is zero, the resources being used up contributing nothing to real national income. Or to look at the matter more broadly, is it reasonable to add to the country's arable acreage at high cost, when the total capacity of agriculture is obviously too great, with the excess a heavy burden to the federal treasury?

The Department of Interior has attempted to answer this charge in a statement submitted by Fred A. Seaton, Secretary of the Interior, to the Joint Economic Committee of the Congress (printed in *Federal Expenditure Policy for Economic Growth and Stability*, "Federal Expenditures and Programs for the Develop-

[11] I owe this point to D. Gale Johnson.

ment of Natural Resources," Joint Committee Print, 85 Cong., 1 sess., pp. 645–656, November 1957). Its defense runs along two lines; first, the irrigation program is considered to be justified by long-run trends in the economy, including the growing population, rising consumption per capita, and the removal of good acreage from agricultural uses because of the growth of cities and highways. Second, it is contended that the contribution of the irrigation program to the surpluses is very small because of the nature of the crops grown and because of their geographic dispersal. Neither of these defenses is adequate. As for the first, in the short run there is clearly a surplus of agricultural land, and even if our present long-run projections say that the situation will be reversed, there is little point in committing resources now to cope with this problematical contingency.

To illustrate the second contention, the Bureau of Reclamation has prepared figures which show that its projects grow no more than 0.4 percent of total corn production, 2.0 percent of wheat, 2.8 percent of rice, 5.8 percent of cotton, and no tobacco. These are the major crops under price supports. On the other hand, the projects grow a large percentage of the fruits, nuts, and vegetables, which on the whole are not supported. Assuming that a proportionate share of the output of each crop in each state grown on projects ends up in storage, the annual support cost is on the order of 40 million dollars, given the physical output figures submitted by the Bureau.

This is a small figure in relation to the agricultural program, less than 2 percent. Compared to the reclamation program, it looms considerably larger, however, adding at least 25 percent to the annual cost of the program. More important, however, the figure vastly understates the support cost. It assumes that if, say, 10 percent of a crop in a state ends up in storage, 10 percent of that crop grown on irrigation projects in that state also can be considered to be purchases by the federal program. But the output on irrigated land should really be considered incremental for the country as a whole. If a crop is in surplus, all of the extra output caused by irrigation must be considered to add to the surplus, not just a proportionate share. Computing the support cost on this basis would yield a figure about four times as large, or about equal to the direct annual appropriation for irrigation.

2. *Present Practice: Indirect Irrigation Benefits*

Indirect irrigation benefits, which have also been known as secondary benefits, have been the subject of a great deal of controversy in recent years. The Subcommittee on Benefits and Costs has not been able to get agreement on the use of this category of benefits.[12] The Presidential Advisory Committee on Water Resources Policy has recommended that benefit-cost ratios should be computed on the basis of direct, or primary, benefits alone, though any agency is permitted to submit figures for secondary benefits as "supplementary material." The Committee permits use of secondary benefits for project justification where resources are otherwise unemployed but argues that they should not be confused with primary benefits. The report of the Committee is only advisory, however, and it remains to be seen to what extent actual agency practice will be modified. At the same time, there has been considerable pressure in Congress to continue the use of secondary benefits.

Essentially, indirect benefits are designed to reflect the impact of the project on the rest of the economy. The methods of computing these benefits have been changed a number of times, but they have always rested on certain assumptions and principles. In order to be able to come to an evaluation, we shall describe the procedures that were in use in recent years and shall then discuss them from the points of view of the present study.

Table 39, reproduced from the Bureau *Manual*, gives an example of the computation of indirect benefits. It can be seen that the entire analysis is carried out on the "with and without" principle. The indirect benefits are divided into three categories. Category A is designed to measure the profits earned on commodities of the projects which are sold locally.[13] The figure is derived by simply multiplying the total local sales by 5 percent, which approximates the average profits earned on sales by local distributors. Category B measures the profit expected to accrue

[12] In January 1952 the Federal Inter-Agency River Basin Committee, Subcommittee on Benefits and Costs, issued its *Revised Statement on Secondary Benefits* which suggested procedures that would have confined their use to cases where there were idle resources or underutilized capacity. However, the Department of Interior issued a minority statement recommending continuance of the practices it then applied.

[13] *Reclamation Manual*, Department of the Interior, vol. XIII, 2.2.4.

Irrigation

Table 39. Derivation of indirect irrigation benefits from summary of farm budgets for entire project

(annual values under full development)

Item	With irrigation	Without irrigation	Difference	Factor	Indirect benefit
1. Type of farm	Irrigated farms	Dry farms and grazing			
2. Number of farms	100	10	(90)		
3. Acres per farm	160	1,600			
4. Irrigable acres	16,000	16,000			
5.	*Sales to local wholesale and retail business*				
6. Fruit and vegetables	$50,000	—	$50,000	5	$2,500
7. Hay and forage	300,000	$10,000	290,000	5	14,500
8. Subtotal, Benefit A	$350,000	$10,000	$340,000		$17,000
9.	*Sales for local and nonlocal processing, marketing, etc.*				
10. Grain	$25,000	$50,000	− $25,000	48	− $12,000
11. Fruit and vegetables	25,000	—	25,000	24	6,000
12. Sugar beets	250,000	—	250,000	26	65,000
13. Seed crops	10,000	—	10,000	10	1,000
14. Dry beans	10,000	—	10,000	23	2,300
15. Soybeans	5,000	—	5,000	30	1,500
16. Livestock (meat)	550,000	25,000	525,000	11	57,750
17. Wool	75,000	5,000	70,000	78	54,600
18. Dairy products	25,000	5,000	20,000	7	1,400
19. Poultry products	25,000	5,000	20,000	6	1,200
20. Subtotal, Benefit B	$1,000,000	$90,000	$910,000		$178,750
21.	*Purchases for family living and production expenses*				
22. Direct farm benefit			$112,500		
23. Less increased perquisites			− 70,000		
24. Increased purchases for family living			$42,500		
25. Increased farm production expenses			840,000		
26. Subtotal, Benefit C			$882,500	18	$158,850
27. Total Indirect Benefits A, B, and C					$354,600

Source: Department of the Interior, *Reclamation Manual*, 2.2.6.

to "all other enterprises between the farmer and the final consumer, from handling, processing, and marketing...." In order to facilitate the analyses of specific projects, the Bureau has derived statistically a set of indirect-benefit factors; each factor represents the ratio of total profits in later processing to the value of the commodity at the farm. By multiplying the list of output quantities by the respective indirect-benefit factors, the total extra profit is approximated. These two categories of benefits have been called the "stemming" benefits.[14]

Category C represents the "profits of all enterprises from supplying goods and services for the increase in farm purchases for family living and production expenses, usually called the induced benefits." In other words, it is the profit earned on the purchases made by the project. The profit rate has been computed to be an average of 18 percent for all farm purchases, and this figure is multiplied by the sum of the production expenses and the purchases for family living. In addition to the three categories included in Table 39 indirect benefits are also expected to accrue from the rise in residential land values in towns near the project. To get an annual figure, a rate of return of 4 percent is applied to the rise in residential real-estate values. This figure measures the induced benefit of additional rental services.

The procedures outlined above were submitted by the Bureau to an independent panel of three distinguished consultants, Professors J. M. Clark, E. L. Grant, and M. M. Kelso,[15] who made a number of criticisms, but who endorsed the general approach. After examining the alternative, abandonment of measuring secondary benefit and inclusion of relevant statistical facts in project reports, they conclude,

> We see force in this view [that the evaluation of offproject effects be left to the judgment of higher authorities]; but we recognize also that the pressure for rules of thumb is strong, and the advantages of more definite uniformity great. We

[14] Besides the indirect benefit factors which are listed in Table 5, three others were estimated: cotton, 83 percent; oil crops, 30 percent; and rice, 13 percent.

[15] Department of the Interior, *Report of Panel of Consultants on Secondary or Indirect Benefits of Water-Use Projects to Michael W. Straus, Commissioner*, Bureau of Reclamation, June 26, 1952.

therefore propose continued use of formulas, regarded as rules of thumb, and altered from present Bureau practices, for "stemming" and "induced" benefits; but for some elements we propose that they be left to the exercise of judgment, without attempting quantitative measurement.[16]

As a rule of thumb the consultants question these procedures on the grounds that the factors vary too much among commodities, ranging from 6 to 83 percent, with those commodities which appear to have the firmest demand, such as fresh fruits and vegetables, and dairy, meat, and poultry products, having low factors, while cotton and wool, for which there is little need, have the highest factors.[17] They also recommend that the benefit-cost ratio be expressed in a way that makes clear what portion of benefits are indirect,[18] and that separate ratios be given for separable segments of projects. With regard to stemming and induced benefits, they find that present procedures involve double counting. They reason as follows: to increase national income, both the supply and the demand of commodities must be increased, the first to prevent higher monetary demand from merely raising prices, and the latter to prevent higher output without a corresponding increase of monetary demand to take the goods off the market. They conclude, therefore, that either one or the other should be counted, but not both for any period of time.

The consultants interpret induced benefits to be those originating in the fuller utilization of underemployed resources and labor; stemming benefits are assumed to be caused primarily by increasing the productivity of resources. They conclude that induced benefits should be granted during the period of construction, with the amount related to general employment conditions, and that stemming benefits be credited during operation, the amount to be much reduced below present practice. They also propose that an indirect benefit factor be applied to project costs, to indicate what indirect benefits would have been generated

[16] *Report of Panel...to Straus*, p. 12.
[17] *Report of Panel...to Straus*, pp. 13, 19–21, 42. Monopolistic processing industries with high profits will also tend to be favored, an anomalous result.
[18] This recommendation has been followed in recent reports.

if the resources had been used elsewhere. If the factor applied to project costs were as great as the average of the other indirect benefit factors of a project, this recommendation alone would be sufficient to eliminate justification of projects through the use of indirect benefits, for any project with direct benefits smaller than direct costs would have more foregone indirect benefits on the cost side than positive indirect benefits from its outputs. Indirect benefits could only magnify the difference between a project's benefit-cost ratio and a ratio of 1.0; they could never push the project above or below the justification point.

Before we turn to a critique of the use of indirect benefits, one important distinction must be made.[19] Benefits accruing locally or in the region are different from national benefits. Economic activity generated by a project will lead to an increase in wages, profits, and other incomes in the proximity. To some extent these increases will be offset by decreases elsewhere, but this is irrelevant from the local or regional point of view. Conversely, some of the benefits may accrue outside the area. In the following two sections we shall take up both the national and regional points of view.

3. *Indirect Benefits from a National Point of View*

The impact of a project on the rest of the national economy depends very much on the state of the economy at the time. Let us first examine induced benefits, which are assumed to be the benefits caused by the monetary payments which spring from the project.

In a time of depression, when the national output is far below capacity and there are idle resources diffused through the economy, induced benefits from the construction of a project are very real and important. The income payments which are made are respent by the recipients for the purchase of goods and services, setting

[19] This distinction is stressed by H. E. Selby, "Indirect Benefits from Irrigation Development," *Journal of Land and Public Utility Economics* (February 1944), pp. 45–51. For a somewhat different discussion of indirect irrigation benefits, but which reaches conclusions broadly similar to those of the present study, see J. Margolis, "Secondary Benefits, External Economies, and the Justification of Public Investment," *Review of Economics and Statistics* (August 1957), pp. 284–291.

off a long chain of impulses, putting idle men and resources back to work. This is the range of effects which is analyzed by the Kahn–Keynes theory of the multiplier effects of public works.[20] The appropriate induced benefit factor is the multiplier, which can be estimated from a knowledge of the marginal propensity to consume in the economy. If national average figures are considered too crude, a better multiplier can be approximated by estimating the marginal propensities to spend of the groups which will receive most of the income payments, and calculating a multisector multiplier as outlined by J. S. Chipman.[21]

Induced effects from the operation of projects are likely to be either very small or nonexistent during a depression. Since commodities are in oversupply, the money payments received for the project's output and respent by the farmers are likely to displace income payments to other farmers. If the commodity is sold in a free market, the extra supply will lower the price, and in view of the low elasticities of demand for farm products, may lower the total income received by farmers.[22] If there are government price-support programs, the extra supply will simply mean an increase of government purchases of surpluses. This will lead to an increase of income payments and does open the doors to multiplier effects, but the effects are due to the increase in the government deficit caused by the price-support program. There are other ways that are far more desirable by which the deficit can be increased, which do not take the roundabout route of building irrigation projects, with farmers working to grow crops in order to be able to sell them to the government which will put them in storage. Tax cuts or useful public expenditures are preferable ways of having the government increase personal income. We therefore conclude that the operation of projects does not create induced benefits in depression other than the

---

[20] See R. F. Kahn, "Home Investment and Unemployment," *Economic Journal* (1931), pp. 173–198; and J. M. Keynes, *The General Theory of Employment, Interest and Money*, chap. 10.

[21] J. S. Chipman, *The Theory of Intersectoral Money Flows and Income Formation* (1952); also see J. M. Clark, *The Economics of Planning Public Works* (1935), pp. 80–104, where a discussion of the specific multiplier values and of the time lags involved can be found.

[22] There may be induced benefits from an increase in operation and maintenance expenses, but they are a small part of total cost.

effect of the price-support program, but that the construction of projects does induce substantial amounts.[23]

In times of inflation, when the total monetary demand for commodities exceeds the supply of goods, thus forcing a rise of prices, the induced effects are reversed. Project construction adds fuel to the inflation by bidding up prices and pumping more money into income streams, while project operation has relatively small induced effects, since the additions to expenditures made by farmers are largely offset by the increased output streams of commodities.

In times of economic balance, when there is high employment and a relatively stable price level, induced effects are likely to disappear. With the pattern of money flows and the production of commodities in harmony, the construction of a project should have no induced effects, especially if the government's revenue policy is linked to its expenditures, which of course include the project.[24] And the operation of the project again merely adds to both the income and the output streams.

The picture is quite different for the stemming benefits, which are defined to originate in the processing stages of production and which therefore must be confined to the period of operation of the project. In times of depression, the extra profits earned in processing commodities for the market must be nil or negative, since similar profits for processors of alternative sources of supply have been displaced to some extent and since the price drop caused by the increase in supply and the low elasticities of demand will reduce the total profits of all processors. If the farm output is sold to the government as part of a price-support program, usually no processing actually takes place, precluding stemming benefits altogether. Should the government buy processed commodities at fixed prices, there would be an increase of processing profits, but an increase at the government's expense.

[23] This conclusion is also reached, for essentially similar reason, by the consultants. See *Report of Panel...to Straus*, pp. 13, 18–20.

[24] The balanced budget multiplier will not apply in a state of continued economic balance because the federal fiscal and monetary policies, if run to preserve the balance, will contain a correction for the inflationary effects of an increase of the level of a balanced budget. This does not require an understanding of the intricacies of the requisite correction; the policies need only be run on the basis of compensating for any departures from balance, whatever the cause.

While there may be the induced benefit of an increase in the government deficit, there is no stemming benefit which raises real national income since the commodity ends up in storage.

In times of inflation, open or suppressed, when there is a genuine shortage of goods, stemming benefits become possible. Particularly if there is a shortage of the outputs of a project, stemming benefits in processing are likely where the increase of output makes possible an increase of processing. The magnitude of the benefits will depend on the nature of the shortage. If it is very severe, so that the commodity can be assumed to be rationed, all of the profits in processing can be taken as a measure of stemming benefits, not only because they are made possible by the existence of the project's output, but also because that profit will be a reflection of the state of demand; it will represent the economic value of the processed goods minus the cost of other inputs, which must be assumed not to be in short supply.[25] But it should be noted that the shortage of the project outputs must take the form of some sort of interference in the market, such as rationing, for otherwise it would express itself in higher prices at the farm, and would be reflected completely in the primary benefits.

When there is economic balance, stemming benefits become possible only if some extraordinary assumptions are made in the analysis. If the premise of mobility is denied, so that it can be assumed that none of the factors of production would be put to a useful purpose in another location, and if there are pockets of unemployment in the area, then the output of the project may create processing opportunities and earning possibilities for resources that would otherwise be idle. These possibilities are the source of stemming benefits. In our earlier discussion of this premise we pointed out that in a capitalist system, in which the movement of resources into their proper places is accomplished through the existence of differentials in reward, policies cannot be predicated on a general denial of mobility. Policies which reduce mobility, such as removal of the differentials which are to induce movement, destroy the foundations on which the viability of the system rests.

[25] If other inputs are also in very short supply, only a portion of the profits can be credited to the project.

209

Like all policy criteria, the premise of mobility must be applied with moderation. There are situations where mobility is simply impossible; if processing facilities already exist in an area, are not used up to optimal capacity for reasons such as depletion of the soil, and cannot be moved because of excessive transportation costs, then the premise can legitimately be denied. This is likely to be particularly significant for projects which provide supplementary irrigation in areas in which the agricultural economy has been declining because of falling supplies of water. We saw another example in the case of flood control, where we assumed that movement of productive facilities could not be expected in anticipation of rare floods, and where we thus justified the existence of indirect benefits. There are other instances where the mobility of people cannot be assumed, perhaps because of specific ethnic or sociological obstacles.

Stemming benefits can also occur where output prices are not set competitively and the processors are able to earn monopoly profits. Since the markets for most agricultural commodities are competitive, this will be a rare but not an impossible case. For example, sugar-beet processors are likely to have some monopoly power in dealing with their suppliers,[26] since transportation costs are so important that the beets cannot be shipped far for processing. Yet the optimal size of processing capacity is so large that it will not pay a second processor to move into an area to compete. Thus the processor may be able to set a price that does not reflect the full value of the beets.

But any exceptional instance must be warranted by circumstances that are peculiar to the case. We definitely reject the idea that all irrigation projects involve circumstances which permit denial of the premise in order to justify the use of indirect benefit factors on all its outputs even in times of economic balance.

Economies of scale in associated enterprises may also give rise to stemming benefits. Fuller use of transportation facilities is the most important instance likely to be found where a project is located in a previously undeveloped area. Following the reasoning of our transportation analysis in Chapter VI, stemming benefits from this source will equal the difference between the

[26] I owe this point and the example to Dr. J. V. Krutilla.

210

total transportation charges for the project's inputs and outputs and the long-run incremental costs incurred by the transport system. The quantitative significance will depend on the magnitude of transportation charges in relation to the values of the commodities and the difference between marginal costs and transportation rates.

Physical interdependence among economic units is another possible source of stemming benefits. An irrigation project involves such interdependence; the management of the water at the reservoir, in canals, and in irrigation ditches requires full recognition of these physical relationships. But the measurement of primary benefits and of costs already presupposes that these problems have been solved, that is, that the water is released and distributed according to a reasonable plan, and so no further benefits can be anticipated from this source. To claim benefits under this heading, it would need to be shown that the water supply of persons not on the project is improved.

The appeal of the idea of stemming benefits is very strong. Anyone can quickly discover that processors do earn substantial profits on the commodities produced by projects, and it seems only natural that these benefits accruing to others be computed and included in the benefit-cost ratio. The premise of mobility leads to rejection of this line of thought because it implies that neither the processors nor their capital[27] would be unemployed if the project did not exist. Perhaps they would be absorbed in a similar business somewhere else, or perhaps entirely different industries would offer alternative opportunities where they would earn an equal return. In times of economic balance it must be assumed that the alternatives do exist.

In summary, we conclude that stemming benefits are very unlikely in depression, are a possibility during inflation if the specific commodities are in particularly short supply, and can only be granted for periods of economic balance in those instances where the premise of mobility can be denied because of extraordinary circumstances. The routine calculation of stemming benefits, therefore, is not warranted.

[27] I mention both the entrepreneurs and their capital because the accountant's profit figures which are used to compute stemming benefits include both a return on capital and the reward for entrepreneurship.

Induced benefits, on the other hand, are largely confined to the construction of the project. They are large in times of depression, nonexistent in times of economic balance, and negative during inflation.[28]

But the basic assumption of benefit-cost analysis is that the investment in natural resources is made in a framework of economic stability and of steady growth. The increased need for resources and the justification of the entire program in the minds of the public are predicated on the future growth of the system. The entire economic analysis and the financial analysis as well rest on the absence of wide departures from economic balance. Especially in view of the long interval between the time the project reports are drawn up and the time the project is built, it has been found wise to assume neither inflation nor depression. With benefits expected to be reaped over an extraordinarily long period, usually fifty years or more, it has been felt impossible to make more specific assumptions.[29]

Yet a condition of economic balance is the state of affairs in which both induced and stemming benefits are nil or very small. It can therefore only be concluded that the use of indirect benefits in benefit-cost analysis must be confined to cases where it can be shown that there are unemployed and immobile resources or that there is underutilized capacity in associated economic activities.

4. *Indirect Benefits from a Regional Point of View*

In evaluating the use of indirect benefits, we must first decide whether benefit-cost analysis is to take a national, a regional, or a local point of view. Throughout the present study we have assumed that it is the national interest which the analysis is to maximize; we shall continue to assume that decision making in

[28] This is not to say that the calculation of induced benefits is the best way to adjust decisions on public investments for variations in general economic conditions. It was contended earlier (Chapter III) that the nature of the decision process prohibits dealing with this variable within the benefit-cost analysis.

[29] See Subcommittee on Benefits and Costs, *Proposed Practices...*, p. 2; and Department of the Interior, *Reclamation Manual*, vol. XIII, par. 1.2.9.

this area is best served by using the benefit-cost analysis to measure the change in real national income.

Yet in the case of the irrigation program, as in some other resource fields, regional development is an important policy objective and is perhaps the main rationale of the program. It is certainly true that both induced and stemming benefits accrue within the region. The money spent in the construction of the project at least in part contributes to local wages and profits. The addition of a large new economic enterprise will lead to the development both of processing capacity and of service industries which are complementary to the project; the increase in purchasing power of the settlers will also trigger the development of other businesses to supply them with the consumer goods they will wish to purchase. The generated activities will induce still further enterprises, and so on. A project is an addition to the economic base, producing a superstructure of service activities. In order to indicate the expected development of the local or regional economy, it may be worth while to present information along these lines, and, from the regional or local point of view, some of these effects may properly be called indirect benefits.

A methodology for measuring these indirect benefits has recently been devised by M. E. Marts,[30] who studied a town which was based almost exclusively on the services it performed for an irrigation project. He derived a ratio of direct benefits to indirect benefits, using the increase in net farm income as a measure of the former and the increase in the total of labor, business, and property income for the latter. The estimates for farm income were derived from budget studies; business income was estimated from an analysis of actual business records in the town; wage income was estimated from official payroll data; while property income was estimated from an analysis of state income figures, separating farm property income from the rest. Marts found that indirect benefits generated locally by the operation of the project were 1.27 times as large as the direct benefits. Several studies of other projects have been undertaken using Marts' method, with the resultant indirect benefit factors ranging from

---

[30] M. E. Marts, *An Experiment in the Measurement of the Indirect Benefits of Irrigation—Payette, Idaho*, prepared for Region 1, Bureau of Reclamation, U.S. Department of Interior, Boise, Idaho, June 1950.

1.12 to 1.74.[31] Projects suitable for the most intensive agriculture appeared to produce the most indirect benefits.[32]

The recommendation of the Presidential Advisory Committee on Water Resources Policy,[33] permitting submission of indirect benefit data as supplemental information or as a basis for local cost sharing, but keeping them out of the benefit-cost ratio, is well designed to make use of the kind of indirect benefits measured by this method. They can be clearly labelled to be local or regional rather than national. They will convey the general magnitude of the developmental effects of a project, and at the same time will tend to make more of the local beneficiaries subject to taxation for financing.

Yet even this limited application of indirect benefits is subject to abuse. If the indirect local benefits are listed as if they were a net addition to direct benefits, the impression is created that the true benefits are the sum of the two categories. It must be made clear that in times of economic balance most of the local indirect benefits represent diversion of economic development from one region to another; there will be indirect benefits outside the region "without" the project. Systematic application of the "with and without" principle would require that the indirect benefits foregone elsewhere should also be listed.

5. *Present Practice: Public Benefits*

Besides direct and indirect benefits, a third group, public benefits, is evaluated and expressed in monetary terms. This group contains five effects of projects that are considered advantageous, and for which it was felt that meaningful monetary equivalent values could be estimated.

[31] The findings of these studies are summarized in M. E. Marts, "Use of Indirect Benefit Analysis in Establishing Repayment Responsibility for Irrigation Projects," *Economic Geography* (April 1956), pp. 132–138.

[32] For an alternative statistical approach, using input-output analysis, see W. Isard, and R. E. Kuenne, "The Impact of Steel upon the Greater New York–Philadelphia Industrial Region," *Review of Economics and Statistics* (November 1953), pp. 289–301. Also see J. V. Krutilla, "Criteria for Evaluating Regional Development Programs," *American Economic Review* (May 1955), pp. 120–132, for a comparison of techniques.

[33] The President's Advisory Committee on Water Resources Policy, *Water Resources Policy*, p. 27.

The first category consists of settlement opportunities. A benefit of $1,000 per family is credited to a project for every opportunity to establish a family farm. This figure is quite arbitrary, though it just equals the family allowance that is considered the alternative income which the family would have received in the absence of the project. The combination of the two practices is equivalent to the assumption that the income of the family without the project would be zero, which is, of course, contrary to the facts.

This benefit must be explained in terms of the intrinsic worth of the creation of opportunities for family farms, and must be valued in terms of the advantages of independent farm life. To attach a price tag of $1,000 to the social value of farm ownership implies a very precise value judgment, which should not be made by an administrative agency and which should not be obscured by being buried in the benefit-cost analysis. This judgment should be made by the Congress and the President. To present the benefits of settlement opportunities in a way that is useful to reviewing groups, it is only necessary to state the number of opportunities created by a project. This figure is also subject to verification once the project is functioning.

Employment opportunities are another category of public benefit. These benefits are computed on the assumption of high employment and steady growth, so that they are not an attempt to adjust the estimates for fluctuations in national income. Employment opportunity benefits are confined to the increase in income of laborers who might otherwise be seasonally unemployed, and to the wages paid to persons not regularly in the labor force, such as housewives and school children who earn extra money during harvesting and canning. The benefit is conditional on the absence of alternative employment opportunities and is measured by the total income paid to such people. The lack of possible mobility for the labor in question must also be shown.[34]

The economic nature of these benefits is closely akin to primary benefits, since income payments of this sort are the same as the income earned by the farm family from its work on the project. There is only one difference: while it can be assumed that the farmer would be working with or without the project, and the

[34] *Reclamation Manual,* par. 2.2.11.

215

benefit to him can be entirely measured by the change in his income, the alternative for the people in question here is not work without pay, but leisure without pay. To find out the economic benefit of giving them the opportunity to work, one would have to discover how much they value the alternative of staying home. The experiment which would have to be performed is the following: through test situations, one would have to find out the minimum pay which would induce each person to enter the labor force. The benefit is the difference between the actual pay and the minimum pay which would induce them to give up their leisure. Such experiments are impractical; but it is clear that the present measure of total income payments overstates the benefit, and some factor less than one, such as one half or two thirds, should be applied to the total extra income to derive the benefit from new employment opportunities.

The creation of new investment opportunities is another listed public benefit.[35] If an area offers no investment opportunities to local owners of investment funds, a benefit is claimed for the interest payments made on the farm investment. The benefits can only be claimed if it can be demonstrated that there are no alternatives in sight during the project's life. They may not exceed 1½ percent on the farm investment, since the borrowing rate is assumed to be 4 percent and there is always the alternative of purchasing government bonds at a yield of 2½ percent.

These benefits are hard to justify, not only because it is difficult to show the absence of investment alternatives for fifty years or more, but also because the loans to farmers at 4 percent are much more risky than investment in government bonds at 2½ percent. There must be compensation for the considerable risk bearing done by the lenders, and it is not clear that the differential of 1½ percent is more than adequate for this purpose.

Benefits are also claimed for improving community facilities and services. They consist of the extra governmental services made possible by the extra taxes paid by the farms due to the income produced by them. The amounts of such benefits are determined from tax data found in farm-budget studies, by estimating the increase in real and personal property taxes.[36]

[35] *Reclamation Manual*, par. 2.2.12.
[36] *Reclamation Manual*, par. 2.2.13.

Since new farms and new people require increases in government services, and since it is not clear that the extra taxes equal or exceed the extra "social overhead" supplied by local governments, benefits of this kind are questionable.

The extra services can be classified into production services and consumption services. Police protection, fire protection, roads, and so forth, are, to some extent, genuine costs of production, and the taxes paid for them are costs, not benefits. Schools and parks may be considered closer to consumption. Just like any other consumption goods which the farmer purchases out of his income, their benefit is already included in the direct benefit, the increase of farm income, if computed before tax payments.

This is not to say that the level and quality of government services does not rise when a marginal farm area is brought to thriving prosperity. But this rise is one of the effects of raising the incomes of poor people. It is a byproduct of every project and inclusion of tax estimates among the benefits is neither a legitimate part of the economic justification of a project, nor does it shed any light on its merits relative to other projects.

Finally, public benefits may be claimed for stabilization of local and regional economy.[37] The economies of areas subject to unpredictable drought are stabilized by the presence of an irrigation project because the project receives its water supply from storage dams which can meet the project's needs under all conditions except severe and prolonged droughts, and even in that case a project can expect some part of its requirements. Thus the uncertainties of economic life are reduced for the people in the area. The benefits of this type are arbitrarily set at 5 percent of direct benefits except in areas where stabilization is desperately needed, where twice as much benefit is allowed.

These benefits are analogous to the benefits from flood control which are described as "enhancement of the security of the people," and which the Army Engineers include among intangible benefits. Their method of dealing with benefits of this kind is more appropriate, since there is no rational basis for calculating a monetary equivalent. Estimates for the value of this benefit, as seen by the beneficiaries, could be derived from experiments.

[37] *Reclamation Manual,* par. 2.2.14.

If people were given the opportunity to buy insurance against these fluctuations of income, it would be possible to discover how much they would be willing to pay for the security against these hazards. Such experiments are not practical as part of the planning process of every project, though just one experiment in a typical area would provide some basis for monetary evaluation. In the absence of such experiments, these benefits should be included among the intangible benefits of the project. Their nature can be fully conveyed to the Congress by including a brief history of drought conditions in the general description of the area as part of the intangible analysis.

There is also serious question whether irrigation really reduces the riskiness of income in every case. The physical hazards attributable to an irregular supply of water are reduced, of course, but this reduction may be more than offset by an increase in economic risks. Irrigated agriculture is usually production for the market and income from it will depend on price fluctuations. Where irrigators abandon production for home use or switch to cash crops suffering from particularly severe market instability, the benefit in this category may be negative.

6. *Water is a Scarce Resource*

The measurement of benefits and costs by means of market prices presupposes that all the goods used in a project are bought at market prices which reflect the value of the opportunities which are foregone. For irrigation projects, the most important input, the water taken out of rivers, has no market price. Yet irrigation constitutes 52 percent of the total water use in the United States. Since it is a consumptive use, that is, little of the water is returned to the streams, while most industrial uses are not consumptive uses, perhaps as much as 80 percent of the total water consumption is for irrigation.[38] In the Western states, where rainfall is light and where most irrigation takes place, 92 percent of all water withdrawals are by irrigators, 3 percent by industry, and 5 percent by domestic users.

There is no need to summarize here the complexities of Western water law. It is sufficient to point out that the arid states operate

[38] Estimates from President's Materials Policy Commission, *Resources for Freedom*, vol. V, pp. 84–90.

at least in part under the "doctrine of appropriation," under which the right to the use of some portion of stream flow is granted to anyone who will put the water to a beneficial use. The right is granted to the first qualified applicant, who keeps it as long as he uses it.

Irrigators have preëmpted most of the water rights in some portions of the West. Yet the lack of water may prove one of the biggest blocks to industrialization, since any new industry which needs large quantities of water, such as steam electric power, steel, petroleum refining, or chemicals, will be seriously hampered. The water laws of most Western states accord priority to irrigation, which precludes the development of these industries and which helps to keep the areas predominantly agricultural.[39] For example, a study made for the President's Materials Policy Commission points out that the oil-shale reserves in the Colorado area may be kept from being developed because the refineries must be near the deposits and there may not be any water supply because it is committed to irrigation.[40] Yet industrial uses of water yield a much higher economic return than irrigation, which is the least intensive of the major uses of water.

Because water has no market price and because one cannot foresee the value of the opportunities for industry which are being lost by appropriating the water rights for a specific irrigation project, the real cost of the water cannot be included in the benefit-cost analysis. But some other way must be found to assure that there will be no large economic losses from this source. One way of carrying out the principle set down by the President's Materials Policy Commission that "highest economic use must be made of scarce supplies [of water]"[41] would be to include an analysis of the economics of water of an area in each project report, so that reviewing authorities and the Congress would be able to exercise their judgment with regard to the relative merits of irrigation versus industrialization where such a choice impends. Such an

---

[39] *Resources for Freedom,* p. 87. Increasing the marketability of water may help to alleviate this problem. For an exploration of this issue, see the forthcoming study by J. De Haven and J. Hirshleifer of the RAND Corporation.

[40] President's Materials Policy Commission, *Resources for Freedom,* p. 78.

[41] *Resources for Freedom,* vol. I, p. 55 (italics theirs).

analysis should include figures on the total water supply and its current uses and on the potential which remains for new purposes. It should also give some indication about the possibilities of industrialization in terms of the resources of the area, and should estimate how much water the new industries might need.

A separate analysis of one input is an awkward device. But as long as the water laws determine use by priorities rather than by economic value, one cannot overlook the possibility of lost opportunities for lack of water.

Project reports already contain studies of the water resources of the area. But the purpose of these studies is usually to demonstrate the availability of the flow required to meet the needs of the project, or to show how increased storage capacity increases the total supply. It would be a simple matter to go one step further by comparing these data with other potential uses.

7. *Benefits and Costs of Chief Joseph Dam Project, Washington*

Let us now examine briefly the benefit-cost analyses of two projects, one of which brings new acreage under irrigation, while the other provides supplementary water for existing acreage. The first project is the Chief Joseph Dam project in the State of Washington,[42] one segment of which was included in the budget for 1956. It would receive water and pumping power from Chief Joseph Dam, a dam, which, when complete, will be one of the largest hydroelectric projects in the world. The ultimate development of the project would irrigate 75,000 acres at a cost of $33,000,000, but only three of the ten separable divisions were proposed for immediate construction and were analyzed in detail in the project report. To be irrigated would be 8,700 acres, of which 5,300 would be expected to be devoted to apples. Much the largest share of the benefits of the project would come from apple growing.

The direct benefits were estimated from a series of budget studies of typical farms that would be expected to develop on the project site. Two kinds of apple farms were studied, one of which we shall discuss here for purposes of illustration.

A typical farm of this sort would consist of 25 acres and would

---

[42] *Report on Chief Joseph Dam Project*, House Doc. 374, 83 Cong., 2 sess.

Irrigation

require a private investment of $31,000.[43] Since apple orchards take seven to eight years before they yield substantial crops, a ten-year development period is assumed. The gross income of the farm is estimated to be $12,535,[44] with annual expenses, including interest on investment, equal to $7,651. Of the remaining $4,884, which represent net income, $1,000 are deducted as the alternative income of the family, and the rest is direct benefit. For the project as a whole Table 40 summarizes the farm-budget studies. Indirect benefits were claimed of both the stemming and the induced variety. Public benefits for settlement opportunities were claimed at the rate of $1,000 for each regular farm plus $200 per part-time farm; a public benefit from improved community facilities equal to the extra local property taxes was also claimed.

Table 40. Direct benefits of Chief Joseph Dam project

Increased gross farm income	$2,402,800
Less increased farm operating cost	1,457,500
Less interest on increased farm investment	268,300
Less alternative family income	191,000
Total direct benefit on new land	$486,000
Savings on water cost of existing acreage	22,600
Total direct benefit	$508,600

Source: *Report on Chief Joseph Dam Project*, House Doc. 374, p. 83.

Table 41 gives the benefit-cost analysis of the project. The analysis reveals that it is justified. To be sure, most of the indirect benefits of $1.56 per $1.00 of direct benefit are impossible to justify from a national point of view and the $0.50 of public benefits per $1.00 of direct benefits are largely unacceptable for reasons outlined above; but there remain direct benefits of $1.94 per $1.00 of cost, which is sufficient justification for the project and would give it high priority compared to other projects.

[43] The Department of Agriculture commented on the project that special credit facilities would have to be provided to make it possible for irrigation settlers to make so large an investment for so long a period. *Report of Chief Joseph Dam Project*, p. vi, p. 75.
[44] *Report on Chief Joseph Dam Project*, p. 76.

221

Table 41. Benefits and costs of Chief Joseph Dam project,
initial development

Benefits		
Direct benefits		$508,600
Indirect benefits		
stemming	$494,400	
induced	300,000	
Total		$794,400
Public benefits		
Increased settlement opportunities	$191,000	
Improved community facilities	61,000	
Total		$252,000
Total irrigation benefits		$1,555,000
Adjusted for development lag: 88.5		
percent (10 years, discounted at 2½ percent)		$1,376,200
Loss of fish and wildlife		$400
Net annual benefits		$1,375,800
Costs		
Net federal investment		$5,624,000
Annual investment cost		153,600
(2½ percent, 100 years)		
Operation, maintenance, replacement		
and water pumping charge		77,700
Total annual cost		$231,300
Benefit-cost ratio		5.95
Direct benefit to cost ratio		1.94

Source: *Report on Chief Joseph Dam Project*, pp. 85–86. The report
does not give the ratio of direct benefits to cost.

It might also be noted that the federal subsidy which is granted
through the absence of interest charges and through other devices
discussed in section 12 below, is about $22,000 per farm.[45] This
is an extremely large amount of money to be spent for the benefit
of one family. While the justice or propriety of such a subsidy
is beyond the scope of the present discussion, the simple fact
should be made known to all who participate in the decision
process and to the general public.

[45] Assuming all the land to be in non-Indian hands.

8. Benefits and Costs of the Frying Pan–Arkansas project, Colorado[46]

Much of the irrigation work of recent years provides supplementary water for existing irrigated acreage. A project of this type is the Frying Pan–Arkansas project, a large, multipurpose project which is to provide power, irrigation water, municipal water supply, and flood control in the upper Arkansas River Basin. The President included the project in his budget requests for 1956 and 1957, but so far Congress has not voted any money. The waters of the Arkansas River are overappropriated, so that there is inadequate water for land now under irrigation. The supply of water is to be improved by building a 50-mile system of canals and tunnels to collect water from Hunter Creek and Frying Pan River, two tributaries of the Colorado River, to divert the water across the Continental Divide into the Arkansas–Mississippi system; total storage capacity is to be increased by extending two existing reservoirs and building two new ones.[47] The area from which the water is to be diverted is virtually uninhabited; the beneficiary area contains about 400,000 people who make a living from farming, processing, tourism, mining, and some heavy industry. There is much good farm land, on which about 150,000 of the people live, the productivity of which is constrained by the inadequate water supply. There is a clear demand for power and for municipal water; and there has been considerable flood damage, two thirds of which would be averted by the project.

The decreed diversion rights to the waters of the Arkansas River are about ten times as large as the average flow.[48] The storage capacity of the reservoirs which had been constructed to correct this condition is being diminished by sedimentation and has become inadequate for current needs. The water rights on the Colorado River have been divided among the states and Mexico by a series of compacts. The rights to the water to be diverted from the Colorado watershed across the mountains into the Arkansas would come entirely out of the share assigned to

[46] *Report on Frying Pan–Arkansas Project*, House Doc. 187, 83 Cong., 1 sess.
[47] *Report on Frying Pan–Arkansas Project*, p. 12.
[48] *Report on Frying Pan–Arkansas Project*, pp. 31, 81–90.

the State of Colorado within which the project lies; the project water rights will be inferior to all existing rights on the originating side of the Continental Divide and to any transmountain rights which have been granted previously. As part of the project, a reservoir is to be built on the western slope of the mountains which will increase the total water available to the Colorado River system by a sufficient amount to permit the project to appropriate rights for the diversion which is planned. It is estimated that Colorado's total share of the Colorado River will be 3,855,000 acre feet. The present consumptive use plus estimated future use by authorized irrigation projects in the state are estimated to be 2,030,000 acre feet,[49] leaving 1,825,000 acre feet for other uses in the state. The project would divert about 200,000 acre feet, including 15,000 acre feet for municipal water supply, which represents 11 percent of the remaining Colorado River water rights of the state. The report gives no hint of the possible needs for industrial purposes, such as the development of the oil-shale deposits.

The construction of the project, including both the transmountain diversion and the improved storage on the Arkansas River, would provide more adequate water supply to existing irrigated acreage. No new farms would be created, nor need there be much local channel work. The physical effect of the project would be to increase the total flow of water on the Arkansas River and to provide additional regulation over the seasons.

The benefit-cost analysis is based on budget studies for four typical farms: (1) intensive general agriculture with truck crops; (2) intensive general agriculture; (3) extensive agriculture, and (4) mountain-valley agriculture. Each of the four farm budgets shows the yield per acre, the number of acres to be devoted to various commodities, and the resultant quantities of outputs that can be expected with and without the project. Values for the original detailed analysis of 1950 were derived by applying prices based on the average for 1939–1944; the project-report revision of 1953 used the prices recommended by the Subcommittee on Benefits and Costs. Production expenses were also estimated in order to compute the direct benefits for the typical farms. With

[49] Including 440,000 acre feet set aside for future obligations under existing compacts as reservoir capacity declines through siltation.

the number of farms of each type known, the total direct benefits could be derived for the project. Indirect benefits were calculated by applying the official indirect benefit factors to output in order to derive the stemming benefits, and to farm expenditure for the induced benefits. No public benefits were claimed. Table 42 summarizes the detailed analysis of 1950.

The revision of 1953 resulted in a drop of the direct benefit ratio to 0.73 because construction costs rose by 25 percent while direct benefits rose only 7 percent. On the other hand, indirect benefits were boosted by 50 percent, which left the ratio of all benefits to costs unchanged.

On the basis of our analysis of indirect benefits as a method of project justification we can only conclude that the project does

Table 42. Benefits and costs of irrigation Frying Pan–Arkansas
project, 1950

Benefits		
Annual increase gross farm income		$2,368,200
Annual increase in farm costs		
Farm investment cost	$9,800	
Farm operation cost	1,293,600	
Total associated costs		$1,303,400
Annual direct benefit to farmers		$1,064,800
Annual direct benefit to others (interest and wages)		436,500
Total direct annual benefit		$1,501,300
Indirect annual benefit		
From farm expenditures (induced)		$361,300
From processing and marketing (stemming)		1,476,200
Total indirect annual benefit		$1,837,500
Total annual benefits		$3,338,800
Costs		
Allocated irrigation investment		$59,930,000
Annual investment cost		1,636,800
(interest at $2\frac{1}{2}$ percent, economic life of 100 years)		
Annual operation, maintenance and replacement cost		76,080
Total annual costs		$1,712,880
Benefit-cost ratio		1.95
Direct benefit to cost ratio		0.88

Source: *Report on Frying Pan–Arkansas Project*, House Doc. 187, pp. 34–35, 102.

not possess economic soundness. With an assumed economic life of one hundred years and an interest rate of $2\frac{1}{2}$ percent, two very liberal figures, the direct benefits are expected to be only 73 percent of the cost under the revised analysis.[50] There will be some genuine indirect benefits from a national point of view, in this case, because it represents a "rescue operation." There are large sunk investments of resources that are not used to their full potential because of the decline of agriculture induced by the inadequate water supply and there are probably other resources the productivity of which would rise if the agricultural economy in the area were to resume its development. It is unfortunate that present indirect benefit measures give no clue to the magnitudes of these benefits. But, to justify the project, these indirect benefits would have to be about equal to the direct benefits, which is unlikely. There also remains the unanswered question of the adequacy of the state's future water supply for the development of the oil-shale deposits and for other possible industrialization.

B. FINANCIAL ANALYSIS

9. *Subsidies in Irrigation*

Federal irrigation projects are usually only authorized if it can be shown that the total revenues which can be collected exceed the total costs, except for the costs allocated to navigation, flood control, or other nonreimbursable purposes.[51] The requirement does not mean that each reimbursable purpose must be financed out of funds received in payment for that purpose; it applies only to the sum of revenues versus total reimbursable costs. Irrigation revenues must be collected in forty annual payments which need not start till a development period of ten years has passed.[52]

[50] This analysis has assumed that cost is allocated correctly. It is based on a cost allocation under the method of alternative justifiable expenditure, which is a good method, but which can penalize excessive benefit estimates. If only direct benefits were used, the cost allocation to irrigation might have been smaller and the benefit-cost ratio slightly more favorable.

[51] *Water Resources Law,* The President's Water Resources Policy Commission, pp. 195, 202–212.

[52] Many projects have been granted much longer periods of payment, up to two hundred years in some cases. See Moley, *What Price Federal Reclamation?,* p. 38; and U.S. Congress, House Committee on Interior and Insular Affairs, *Construction Costs and Repayment on Federal Reclamation Projects,* Committee Print, September 1952, p. 18.

Irrigation

There are a number of reasons which make it impossible for irrigation revenues to be sufficient to meet the cost of irrigation on most federal projects of recent years. At first glance one might expect that if the benefits exceeded the costs, it should be possible to raise revenues equal to costs, but it is quite obvious that the collection of revenue from those who reap public or indirect benefits would require a form of collection other than the contractual payments of water users. Even direct benefits, which measure the increase in income of the settlers, do not provide a measure of revenue potential since it is impossible to charge a price for water which would leave the incomes of irrigators unchanged. Since one of the main objectives of the program is the creation of new family-farm opportunities and of a new life for relatively poor farmers, payments for irrigation water must be sufficiently low to leave them significantly better off. In accordance with these objectives, the irrigation benefits are spread over many families, each of whom is to enjoy an increase in its standard of living. If we suppose that a typical family's income is raised from $1,000 to $4,000 before water charges, payments of more than $2,000 are hardly possible, which would produce revenues equal to only two thirds of direct benefit.

The Bureau of Reclamation computes the repayment capacity of a project by subtracting a family living allowance for every family from the net income of the project. This allowance, which varies from project to project, but which has frequently been set equal to $2,250, is based on the cost of a certain standard of living. In the example of Table 38, direct benefits of $426,000 produce a repayment capacity of $277,500, 65 percent of direct benefits.

With the somewhat contradictory objectives of full repayment and of raising living standards for the people on the project, a number of devices have been invented which make it possible to justify projects despite these obstacles. All of these devices are some form of subsidy to irrigation and reduce the amount of repayment which the settlers have to meet.

The original Reclamation Act of 1902 embodied provision for the most important of the subsidies now in use.[53] It called for

[53] For a historical account of repayment requirements and subsidies see Commission on Organization of the Executive Branch of the Govern-

the repayment of all costs, but did not consider interest to be a cost. This means that the total of the repayments is equal to the money cost, or one fortieth of the total a year. In fact, there is an interest cost to the country of course—at the least equal to the government bond rate and probably equal to twice that figure, as we saw in Chapter IV. On a typical irrigation project, with a development period of ten years and repayment in forty annual installments, the resultant subsidy can easily be estimated. The actual payment under present procedures will be $2\frac{1}{2}$ percent of the investment, which will total 100 percent after forty years. If the project were to pay its own interest cost at a rate of $2\frac{1}{2}$ percent, including interest during the development period and on the unamortized balance, it would have to pay a total of 5.1 percent for interest and amortization. Thus the payments of the settlers for the investment in the project would double. In terms of present values, if the forty actual payments of $2\frac{1}{2}$ percent were discounted to the period of construction, they would be worth 49 percent of the actual construction cost. Thus this one element alone leads to a subsidy of half the cost, paid by the nation's taxpayers for the benefit of the irrigation settlers, even if they meet their repayment schedules, and assuming only a minimal interest rate.

But the subsidy from the taxpayer is often much larger, though the form is more obscure and misleading. There is a group of subsidies to irrigation, which, at first glance, appears to be paid by the beneficiaries of other purposes, but which in fact is still paid by the taxpayer. Until 1952, these subsidies took the following form: the price of power was set on the basis of cost, including the cost of interest at 3 percent plus repayment over fifty years; but the interest component of the resultant revenues was considered to be helping to repay the construction cost of

ment, *Task Force Report on Water Resources and Power,* vol. II, *Report of the Task Group on Reclamation and Water Supply* (June 1955), especially pp. 669–671. Also see "Application of the Interest Component of Power Revenue from Reclamation Projects under the Solicitor's Opinion and the Collbran Formula," by C. D. Curran, in *Task Force Report on Water Resources and Power,* vol. III, pp. 1205–1214. For an economic analysis of the pricing principles implicit in the present system of charges based on repayment capacity, see J. Margolis, "Welfare Criteria, Pricing and Decentralization of a Public Service," *Quarterly Journal of Economics* (August 1957), pp. 448–463.

irrigation. This practice was considered justified by interpreting the provisions of the Reclamation Act of 1902, which freed irrigation projects from interest payments, in such a way that the power features were also part of the irrigation project. The resultant subsidy is quite large; on a typical project, with power investment equal to the irrigation investment, the interest component of the charge for the investment is 49 percent of the total charge for capital; and if all of it is applied to aid in repayment of an irrigation investment that is not charged interest, it is almost adequate to repay the entire irrigation investment. In fact, power was never assigned more of the irrigation cost than the excess above computed repayment capacity; but for the sixteen projects which include both power and irrigation, $512 million out of the expected power revenues of $1,032 million were assigned to the repayment of irrigation costs as of January 1, 1947, which is 50 percent of all power revenues.[54] The formula suggests that it is power revenues which help repay the irrigation cost. In fact, power users pay rates which are designed to do no more than return the power investment with interest; the rates do not include any charge for irrigation repayment. By crediting irrigation with the interest component of power revenues, the total revenues to be received by the Treasury are diminished and this portion of the cost of irrigation is shifted to the general taxpayer.

In 1952, the "interest component formula" was replaced by a new device which appears to answer some of the objections raised against its predecessor, though it is essentially very similar. It was first applied to the Collbran, Colorado, project[55] and is known as the "Collbran formula." It provides for repayment of all power costs including interest at 3 percent and of the costs of industrial and municipal water supply with interest at the prevailing long-term government bond rate. After these purposes have completed their own repayment, the further revenues that they will produce will be applied toward repaying that part of irrigation cost which is beyond the repayment ability of the settlers. The formula limits the repayment period of water supply to fifty years, the same as the usual practice for power. Thus,

[54] U.S. Bureau of Reclamation, *How Reclamation Pays* (1947), p. 111.
[55] A statement can be found in *Report on Collbran Reclamation Project, Colorado*, Senate Report 1719, 82 Cong., 2 sess.

for the first fifty years of the project's life, no payments are made for irrigation above those of which the settlers are capable. From the sixth decade on, power and water supply will turn over all their revenues, except for small operating expenses, to repay irrigation.

Once again, the impression is created that power will aid irrigation, and that the project as a whole is self-financing. In fact, it is still the taxpayer who can be expected to pay most of the subsidy, the magnitude of which will be little changed. The reasons are not far to seek; in the first place, the size of the total subsidy to irrigation will remain the same since the irrigation payments are still determined by repayment capacity, and nothing else. Second, the subsidy from the failure to charge interest on the irrigation investment is much compounded. If part of the irrigation cost is not repaid for fifty to one hundred years, the interest charge which has been shifted to the taxpayer becomes very large. For every dollar sunk into irrigation which is repaid without interest after seventy-five years, the taxpayer must make interest payments of 2½¢ a year for seventy-five years. The present worth of these payments is 84¢, leaving only 16¢ which could be shifted to other purposes. Whether it will be shifted cannot be discovered for fifty years, but there is good reason to doubt it, for it presupposes that it will be possible to set power rates and rates on water supply in the remote future which will be adequate for this purpose. In the case of power, the rapid rate of technological progress which is driving down the costs of power from alternative sources, which is bringing atomic energy toward competitive levels, and which may make solar energy an economic source, makes lower rates probable. A period of fifty years, which is the basis for repayment of the power investment, is already a very optimistic assumption about the competitive position of hydroelectric power based on current design; to stretch the assumption to apply for eighty or a hundred years is absurd. If it turns out to be impossible to charge the necessary power rates in the first and second decades of the twenty-first century, the government will surely lower the rates toward operating costs, and if that proves impossible, it will abandon the power installations altogether. As for municipal water supply, technological progress which would present cheap alternative sources is not as clearly in sight, though controlled rain making would be a step in this direction. The revenues from this source are of a smaller order of magnitude than of power, and it could shoulder no more than a small part of the remaining irrigation cost, even if the users, who are largely municipalities, do not balk at the payments when the time comes. Thus, there will be little choice but to write off any unamortized irrigation investment as a government loss, unless the contracts with the water users are changed to incorporate a provision extending the period of payments. And even this possibility involves some strong assumptions about the technological progress in agriculture.

Table 43. Summary of cost and repayment of irrigation investment, Frying Pan–Arkansas project, using "interest component formula" (ignoring interest)

Allocated cost	$59,930,000	
Repayment by water users, 40 years		$10,881,600
From power revenue, 40 years		35,478,000
From municipal water revenue, 40 years		13,570,400
		$59,930,000

Source: *Report on Frying Pan–Arkansas Project*, pp. 13, 34.

Let us contrast the effect of the two formulas. The "interest component formula" results in payment of all irrigation cost above repayment capacity by the taxpayer. The "Collbran formula" results in payment of at least 80 percent of the excess above repayment capacity by the taxpayer, with the remainder paid by power and water supply in the unlikely event that technological progress has not precluded sufficiently high power and water rates for the first decades of the next century.

The effect of the two formulas can be seen from a study of the financial features of the project discussed earlier, the Frying Pan–Arkansas project, which was first planned with the old formula but was revised to conform to the "Collbran formula" by the Republican administration. Table 43 summarizes the repayment plan as outlined in 1951.

To show the actual costs, Table 44 gives the division of the burden on the assumption that the Treasury pays interest of

$2\frac{1}{2}$ percent and that this cost should be included. The table gives the present values of the series of future payments to be made by the irrigators, and the present value of the extra $\frac{1}{2}$ percent above average Treasury borrowing cost to be paid by the power users. The table does not include the rest of the interest component on power nor any of the 2-percent interest component collected on municipal water supply, since these revenues must

Table 44. Cost, present value of revenues to be collected to repay irrigation investment, and federal subsidy on irrigation features of Frying Pan–Arkansas project

(interest component formula)

		percent
Construction cost	$59,930,000	
Payments of irrigators ($272,040 annually for 40 years)	6,838,057	11.4
Interest premium on power revenues (estimated to be $150,000 a year for 40 years)	4,254,300	7.1
Federal subsidy through absence of interest charge on irrigation and diversion of interest component on power and municipal water supply	48,837,643	81.5
	$59,930,000	100.0

The table is computed by discounting the series of payments at $2\frac{1}{2}$ percent to the present. The estimate for the annual value of the extra $\frac{1}{2}$ percent on the power investment is derived by assuming that all of the power facilities are amortized over 50 years and by calculating the difference in the annual interest and amortization charge at the two rates. The federal subsidy is the remainder of the irrigation construction cost.

be set aside for the payment of interest on the investments for those purposes.

The repayment provisions under the Collbran formula, as proposed by the Department of Interior in 1953, are summarized in Table 45. There is still no interest charge on the irrigation investment; irrigators are expected to pay $622,000 a year for sixty-nine years. All the net power revenues from the fifty-third to the sixty-ninth year are applied to irrigation, as well as the revenue from water supply in the sixty-second to the sixty-ninth year. The rates on the latter two purposes are based on full repayment including interest of 2½ percent in fifty-three years for power and in sixty-three years for water supply.

Table 45. Summary of cost and repayment of irrigation, Frying Pan–Arkansas project, using Collbran formula (ignoring interest)

Construction cost, irrigation	$75,128,000	
Repayment by water users in 69 years		$42,918,000
By power revenues in years 53–69		25,472,000
By water supply revenues in years 63–68		6,738,000
		$75,128,000

Source: *Report on Frying Pan–Arkansas Project*, p. 8.

Table 46. Cost, present value of revenues to be collected to repay irrigation investment and federal subsidy to irrigation features of Frying Pan–Arkansas project

(Collbran formula)

		Percent
Construction cost (including interest during construction) $78,271,000		
Payments by irrigators	$20,352,028	26.0
Payments from power revenues	5,678,351	7.3
Payments from water supply revenues	1,311,627	1.7
Federal subsidy through failure to charge interest	50,928,994	65.0
	$78,271,000	100.0

The table has been computed by discounting at 2½ percent the set of payments stated in the project report, *Report on Frying Pan–Arkansas Project*, p. 8.

Table 46 shows the actual distribution of the cost, including interest at 2½ percent, discounting all payments to the present. It can be seen from the table that the federal subsidy will be between 65 and 74 percent, depending on the fulfillment of the revenue expectations on power and water supply in the sixth and seventh decade of the project. This contrasts with a federal subsidy of 81 percent under the interest component formula.

But the small reduction in the subsidy was purchased at the price of extending the repayment period by thirty years.

The federal subsidy to irrigation under the two formulas is little influenced by the use of power revenues because the basic rates for power are unaffected at least during the first fifty years of the project. The President's Advisory Committee on Water Resources Policy recommends that excess power revenues be used to repay irrigation if the power is sold within the same area.[56] The Committee sees such excess revenues as a method of taxing indirect beneficiaries. This intention is carried out if power rates are set above power costs from the beginning. In the case of the Upper Colorado River Storage project, authorized in 1956, power rates were set in this manner and so one can legitimately speak of power revenues helping to repay irrigation costs. Table 47 summarizes the repayment analysis and recomputes it, including an interest cost charged at $2\frac{1}{2}$ percent. It can be seen that irrigators will pay only 5.4 percent of the irrigation cost if they can meet their contractual charges and that the rest of the cost is divided about evenly between power users who pay rates above power cost and taxpayers who must meet the interest subsidy.

A closely related device for subsidy is the basin account, which has been widely advocated for projects in the Columbia Basin, though not yet written into law, and which has been interpreted to apply to water-resource activities in the Missouri Basin.[57] This device would merge the finances of all projects in the basin. Not only would it make the formulas discussed above apply to the power and irrigation of a project, but it would make it possible to subsidize irrigation anywhere in the basin through diversion of power revenues from any power project in the same basin. It is clear that the basin account multiplies the possibilities of the hidden subsidies which are paid by the tax-payer, besides opening the door to subsidies from strong purposes to weak and from good projects to bad.

Finally, the cost allocation procedures which are used to assign the costs of common facilities to the different purposes have served to reduce the total cost of irrigation. Because of the complexity

[56] The President's Advisory Committee on Water Resources Policy, *Water Resources Policy*, pp. 31–32.
[57] Huffman, *Irrigation Development and Public Water Policy*, p. 174.

and importance of the cost-allocation problem we shall treat it separately;[58] in the present connection, let it only be pointed out that the "priority of use method" which the Bureau of Reclamation has applied widely in the past but which has now been eliminated, is particularly suitable for lightening the burden on irrigation. Under this method, different purposes are assigned priorities of

Table 47. Summary of repayment analysis of irrigation investment of Colorado River storage project

Source	Total payments ignoring interest (in millions)	Present value of total payments* (in millions)	Percent distribution of total payments including interest
Payments of irrigators†	36.6	15.2	5.4
Contribution from power revenues‡	246.2	139.7	49.4
Contribution of taxpayers	—	127.9	45.2
Total	282.8	282.8	100.0

Source: *Report on Colorado River Storage Project*, House Report 1087, 84 Cong., 1 sess. Our analysis assumes that the cost allocation is correct.

* We assume an interest rate of $2\frac{1}{2}$ percent.
† Assumes equal annual payments for 50 years after a development period of 10 years. No specific development period has been authorized as yet, but 10 years is the usual figure.
‡ Assumes equal payments for 50 years. Since actual power revenues will build up gradually, the contribution from power is overstated slightly.

use, and the first purpose is allocated all costs necessary for its operation as long as costs do not exceed benefits. The second purpose need only bear the cost of the additional facilities needed, and so on for the third. If a nonreimbursable purpose is assigned

[58] See Chapter IX.

priority, total repayment is minimized; if irrigation is the top priority purpose, total repayment is reduced by putting most of the common costs on an interest-free basis.

All of these devices interfere with sound formation of public policy. They mislead the public and the Congress into thinking that the projects as a whole are self-supporting. By their technical obscurity they hide both the size and the source of the subsidy. They make it impossible for the public and the Congress to see the financial issues clearly, and they prevent a judgment on the question whether irrigation projects are worth the subsidies which they entail.

It would be desirable to change irrigation law to correspond to the actual conditions of project finance. Congress might appropriate funds to build a project, to indicate what share of the cost is to be repaid by irrigators, what share is to be financed out of power revenues, and, finally, what share is to be a subsidy out of general revenues. If the present laws are accepted to be beyond change, the issue could still be made to emerge in its true proportions if the financial analysis of each project report would include figures which indicate the size and the source of the various studies. Such figures might be computed and presented in the manner of Tables 46 and 47.

CHAPTER VIII

Electric Power

FEDERAL production of electric power has been the subject of violent controversy for the last twenty years. Public power originated as a by-product of multipurpose water-resource projects, and it generally remains a secondary purpose of projects which, at least in principle, are undertaken primarily to provide flood control, irrigation, or other public services. There are some single-purpose hydroelectric projects, but they are part of multipurpose programs.

Most of the controversy has been ideological. The proponents of public power contend that it represents a check on private-power monopolies and that it can act as a stimulus for the development of relatively poor and backward regions; its opponents view it as a socialistic threat by vast bureaucracies to our free-enterprise system.

The present study is not concerned with the ideological features of this controversy. It is sufficient for us to assume that the federal government will continue to promote flood control and irrigation, partly by building dams. Since the production of power is frequently a very economical by-product of dams, it can be assumed that the opportunities to generate power will continue to be developed, and while it may be possible to contract with private enterprises to develop the power potential, the evaluation of the economic worth of the power features of multipurpose projects will remain a necessary task of planning and reviewing agencies.

Public power has grown rapidly since the mid-thirties, when it represented less than 1 percent[1] of the industry. By 1955, the capacity of federal power facilities was 16-million kilowatts,

[1] Twentieth Century Fund, *Electric Power and Government Policy* (1948), p. 495.

15 percent of the nation's total. This capacity has largely been constructed by three agencies: the Tennessee Valley Authority, the Bureau of Reclamation, and the Corps of Engineers. Table 48 gives the share of each agency.

Table 48. Power capacity constructed by federal agencies to June 30, 1955

Constructing agency	Nameplate capacity in kw
Bureau of Reclamation*	4,854,550
Corps of Engineers†	3,299,200
TVA‡	7,809,985
Total	15,963,735

* *Annual Report of Secretary of Interior*, 1955, p. 59.
† *Annual Report of Chief of Engineers*, 1954, p. 12.
‡ TVA, *Financial Statements for the Fiscal Year Ended June 30, 1955*, p. 25. Includes 4,307,250 kw of steam capacity.

Special marketing agencies have been set up to sell some of this power. The Corps of Engineers markets none of the power generated at its projects, but turns it over to marketing agencies in the Department of the Interior. The Southwestern Power Administration and Southeastern Power Administration were set up in order to sell the output of Corps of Engineer projects in those two regions, and the Bonneville Power Administration sells the power of all federal projects, built by both the Engineers and the Bureau of Reclamation in the Pacific Northwest. The Bureau of Reclamation sells its own power in all other regions as well as the rapidly expanding output of the Corps of Engineers' projects in the Missouri Basin. The TVA markets all of the power it generates. Table 49 shows the shares of the marketing agencies.

Public-power capacity will continue to grow in the next few years, though its relative share in the national total is likely to fall. The TVA expected to add another 4.5-billion kilowatts by 1956,[2] most of which is steam power destined for the Atomic Energy

[2] Tennessee Valley Authority, *Power Operations* (1953), p. 6.

Commission. The Bureau of Reclamation expected to add 560-million kilowatts by 1957, with the new starts in the Colorado River Storage project assuring subsequent additions to capacity. The Corps of Engineers has projects under construction which will yield more than 5 million kilowatts, including three large dams in the Missouri Basin,[3] bringing the total capacity of Corps projects to 8.5 million kilowatts by the end of 1958.

Table 49. Power marketing agencies and their share of public
power during fiscal year 1955
(million kwh)

Bonneville Power Administration*	21,823
Bureau of Reclamation*	10,455
Southwestern Power Administration*	778
Southeastern Power Administration*	2,121
TVA†	41,389
Total	76,566

* *Annual Report of Secretary of Interior*, 1955, p. 4.
† TVA, *Financial Statement, 1955*, p. 11.

A. Economic Analysis

1. *Power Benefits: The Alternative-Cost Principle*

The standards for evaluating the economic worth of the power features of water-resource development projects have been much improved in recent years. Two agencies have been responsible for the economic analyses, the Bureau of Reclamation for its own projects, and the Federal Power Commission for the projects of the Corps of Engineers.[4]

Until October 1952, the Bureau of Reclamation evaluated power

[3] *Annual Report of the Chief of Engineers* (1951), p. 70.
[4] We shall not be concerned with the criteria of the TVA which does not use benefit-cost analysis in its planning. Since this agency is the only producer of power in its area, it must meet the needs of its area at the existing rate structure, or else raise rates. So far, the policy has been to meet the expanding demand while keeping rate levels constant by continually searching for the most economical ways of expanding capacity. Though the good hydroelectric power sites have all been used, the high rate of technological progress in steam power has permitted the agency to expand capacity without running into substantially increasing costs, and the rate structure has remained low. Under these policies, the problem of project evaluation becomes largely an engineering question.

benefits with concepts similar to those applied to irrigation. Direct power benefits were equal to actual expected revenues to be collected by the Bureau. Indirect benefits included cost savings of private utilities that retailed the power, a share of the profit of private retailers, a share of the profits of industrial and commercial power users, and savings in energy costs of ultimate consumers. But in 1952 the Bureau changed its procedures completely, perhaps in response to the critique of its panel of consultants on indirect benefits,[5] the recommendations of which have been followed in large part. The new procedures measure benefit by the cost of power from the most economical alternative source.[6]

The Federal Power Commission has used this principle for many years and has not included indirect benefits in its computations. But it has not used the same interest and tax charges in calculating the cost of private alternative as it has applied to the cost of federal power,[7] thus biasing the comparison in favor of public power and overstating benefits.

Usually the alternatives do not supply exactly the same kind of power. Steam plants are generally located in closer proximity to the markets, reducing transmission costs. Steam power is also immune to limitations on output caused by inadequate stream flow in times of drought. On the other hand, hydro power requires less reserve capacity and is more flexible. To make the alternatives comparable, the cost of steam power is corrected for its lower transmission losses and a flat allowance of 5 to 10 percent is sometimes granted to the hydro project.[8]

In what sense is alternative cost a measure of benefit? At first

---

of comparing costs of different project plans in a manner quite analogous to private practice. The only important difference comes in the use of interest rates; where private utilities use private borrowing rates to determine their capital intensity, the TVA uses a rate close to the long-term government bond rate. It might be added that this rate was used even at a time when the rate structure could be based on even lower interest charges.

[5] *Report of Panel...to Straus*, Department of the Interior, pp. 46–61.

[6] *Reclamation Manual*, Department of the Interior, vol. XIII, revision of October 1952.

[7] Federal Inter-Agency River Basin Committee, Subcommittee on Benefits and Costs, *Measurement Aspects of Benefit-Cost Analysis*, pp. 67–82.

[8] *Measurement Aspects of Benefit-Cost Analysis*, pp. 76–81.

glance it would appear that the value of electric energy would be equal to its market price. But since the rate structure is kept in check by regulatory agencies which endeavor to limit the rate of return on capital to a "fair" value, the actual rates are lower than the rates which utilities could charge. On the other hand, the fact that each power company has a natural and legal monopoly in its own market area enables it to develop a discriminatory rate structure which would be impossible under conditions of competition. Thus, there are two opposing influences which make power rates differ from the rates that would prevail under competition; they are raised by the monopoly position of the companies, and they are lowered by the actions of regulatory commissions.

If electric power were produced under conditions of constant cost, it could be assumed that the regulated price of power is equal to its average and marginal costs, so that the cost of adding to alternative private capacity is equal to the true benefit of power. Under these conditions, alternative cost per unit would equal price, and thus would equal benefit. But this assumption is not valid empirically. Costs are not constant but are decreasing, and so discriminatory pricing must be used to cover total costs. The actual pattern of discrimination is determined by historical precedent, by convenience, and by the traditions of the industry and the regulatory agencies. The amount of power that is sold under this rate structure need not be equal to the amount that would be sold if all marginal demands were met by offers to provide the power at the present marginal power cost. The high rate of technological progress, which continuously lowers the marginal cost of power capacity below old historical costs, suggests that the rates which are faced by the persons with marginal demands in ordinary times will be higher than actual current marginal costs. On the other hand, the recent years of inflation have made historical costs fall far short of replacement costs, tending to make the rate structure so low that the rates on marginal uses fall short of current marginal costs. It is not clear which of the two factors is more important. It can only be concluded that the present rate structure does not assure that amount of power capacity and output that would result from a perfect allocation of resources, and that the direction of the error remains unknown.

We cannot hope to resolve this problem within the context of evaluating public-power projects; it is a proper task for regulatory agencies. We can only endeavor to ascertain whether the growth of power output, be it at the right rate or not, is being accomplished in the most efficient manner, using the least amount of the nation's resources. The alternative cost principle assists in achieving this objective, for if benefits are limited by the cost of the cheapest alternative, a benefit-cost ratio greater than one can only occur if the cost of the project is smaller than the cost of the alternative. The degree to which the ratio exceeds unity indicates the relative advantage of the project over its alternative.

The use of alternative cost as a measure of benefit does not imply that all projects with benefit-cost ratios greater than one should be undertaken. In Chapter III it was shown that as long as the availability of federal funds acts as a constraint on the water-resource development program, those projects which have the highest ratios should be chosen, and that separable segments of projects should be included only if their ratio was greater than the prevailing marginal ratio. As long as there are alternative uses for the federal funds, even pure cost-saving investments cannot be carried out to the extent that would be appropriate in the absence of the financial constraint.

Since the alternative-cost principle is designed to determine the most efficient way of expanding power capacity, that is, at least cost of the nation's resources, it is important that the value of the resources that would be needed for each of the alternatives be measured with the same set of prices. The use of different prices would mean that the resources which are used up in the alternatives would not be valued with the same yardstick, and that the final cost estimates used to determine their relative merits would not be comparable from the nation's point of view.

Among the prices that must be applied uniformly to all alternatives is the rate of interest, the price for the use of capital. Although private steam plants are financed at a higher interest rate than public hydroelectric projects, the difference in the interest rates is partly due to the fact that government bonds do not reflect the riskiness of power projects. Uniformity of treatment must also extend to the taxes, which are included among costs. If the costs of the public project are estimated with a different set of taxes than the alternative steam plant, the cost of the alternative is overestimated, for the extra taxes do not represent real costs in terms of resources.

Table 50. Fixed charges on power at the busbar used by Federal Power Commission up to 1953, and fixed charges that would apply to public steam plant

Item	Public hydro project* (percent)	Private steam alternative* (percent)	Public steam project† (percent)
Interest	2.50	5.0	2.50
Amortization (2½ percent sinking fund basis 50 years for hydro, 30 years for steam)	1.03	—	2.28
Interim replacements	0.90	—	—
Depreciation (30 years— 5 percent sinking fund basis)	—	1.50	—
Insurance (allowance "in lieu of insurance" on public project)	0.12	0.30	0.30
State and local taxes (allowance "in lieu" on public project)	1.40	1.75	1.75
Federal taxes	—	1.00	—
	5.95	9.55	6.83

* Source: Federal Inter-Agency River Basin Committee, Subcommittee on Benefits and Costs, *Measurement Aspects of Benefit-Cost Practices*, pp. 78–80.
† Computed by the author.

Table 50 illustrates this point. It shows the practice for computing fixed charges which was followed by the Federal Power Commission up to 1953.[9]

The difference between the private-steam costs that were actually used and the public-steam costs that would have been consistent with the practice applied to the public hydro project, was quite substantial, 2.72 percent, which is more than a third of the public fixed cost. A difference of 1.72 percent is due to the

[9] U.S. Bureau of the Budget, *Circular A–47*, called for use of consistent tax and interest rates at that time.

higher interest rate which is used to determine both the interest cost and the depreciation or amortization charge. The other 1 percent is due to the inclusion of federal taxes in private costs. The rate of the capital charge for steam capacity is generally higher than for hydro capacity because of the shorter economic life of the plant and the equipment.

Since the capital cost is typically about one half of the total annual cost for steam, and since the operating costs are the same for public or for private alternatives, the total alternative cost was overstated by about 14 percent.[10] Thus the alternative cost which was the measure of benefit of public projects was overstated by about 14 percent. The inconsistent procedure was used in the years when the gigantic projects in the Missouri Basin as well as some of the projects in the Pacific Northwest were planned, so that the errors which resulted in the estimation of power benefits were large and widespread.

Since 1953 there has been a trend toward more consistent standards for measuring alternative costs. In the case of federal taxes, all agencies now include an item, "taxes foregone," as a cost of federal power development.[11] This practice is equivalent to evaluating both alternatives with private standards for taxation, which is desirable from the point of view of the federal government because it includes the decline in taxes among federal costs and thus makes the benefit-cost analysis indicate the total impact on the expenditure-revenue position of the government.

No similar consistency of practice has been adopted for depreciation or amortization, where the period of amortization on public projects may exceed the private period of depreciation, and where the sinking-fund method implicit in public practice calls for lower depreciation allowances than the methods of straight-line, declining balance or sum of the year-digits used by private utilities. The choice of this allowance is a technical question which, from the social point of view, bears no relation to the ownership of the project. If there is disagreement between

[10] The overstatement is $\frac{2.72 \text{ percent}}{9.55 \text{ percent}}$ times one half, or 14 percent.

[11] W. Whipple, Jr., "Principles of Federal Hydro-Electric Power Development," *Proceedings, American Society of Civil Engineers 81* (July 1955), Paper No. 739, p. 7.

private and public practice, either the government should adopt private standards, or regulatory agencies should reëxamine the depreciation practices of private power companies. In the next section we shall indicate why the present public standards are too liberal.

The treatment of interest rates also remains unsymmetrical, with a rate of $2\frac{1}{2}$ to 3 percent on the public alternative and with a higher rate in the private case.[12] Consistency could be achieved by adopting private standards for the public project or public rates for the private alternative. Since the public rate of interest presumably is a better reflection of the collective judgment about the intertemporal allocation of output, reflecting perhaps a more conservationist philosophy,[13] the best application of the alternative-cost principle requires use of the public rate of interest for measuring the cost of the private alternative.

The alternative cost principle is only applied if it is clearly established that the increased amount of power can be sold at the going rate structure. If some portion of the extra output can only be sold at a lower price, it does not yield a benefit as great as the alternative cost, since it would not have been purchased at the price which would have been necessary. The benefit from such sales can be derived from the revenues which could be collected.

2. *Power Benefits and Technological Progress*

In computing the alternative costs for the estimation of power benefits, actual current prices are used. Thus the benefit is equal to the present cost of constructing additional steam capacity. This benefit is an annual benefit which is assumed to recur in equal amount in every year of the economic life of the project. In the absence of technological progress the cost of the alternative would remain constant, and so the benefit would continue undiminished. But when the reality of technological change is recognized and introduced into the analysis, the alternative cost of later years becomes smaller and the benefits are impaired. The

[12] The Presidential Advisory Committee on Water Resources Policy recommended that the same interest rates should be used in comparing private and public alternatives, though for purposes of the benefit-cost ratio the federal rate is to be applied. *Water Resources Policy*, Dec. 22, 1955, p. 27.

[13] See Chapter IV for a fuller discussion of this issue.

past rate of technological progress in the generation of power can be seen from the fact that the average residential power rate fell 70 percent from 1925 to 1950, or 3 percent a year.[14]

It cannot be expected that the downward trend of costs will be halted in the future. In 1952, it still took 1.1 pounds of coal to generate an average kilowatt hour while the most modern, large steam plants required only 0.8 pounds[15] per kilowatt hour. We cannot predict the future price of coal, to be sure, but the decline in its demand and the increasing mechanization of mining of recent years makes a rise in its price unlikely, unless it is raised artificially by the imposition of tariffs on competing fuels. Other costs, especially the cost of generating equipment, can also not be expected to rise, since the greater complexity of high-pressure, high-temperature equipment is gradually offset by the rising productivity in the equipment industry.

Other alternatives than steam must also be considered. If the present rate of progress on generation of power from nuclear sources continues, atomic energy will become competitive with steam power long before the economic lives of projects are over. This will cut the cost of alternative power in the later years and will reduce the corresponding benefit. Solar energy may also be a reality before the fifty or more years assumed for the economic life of projects have passed.

In order to measure the bias inherent in the present procedure, we must study the typical life cycle of the alternative equipment. New steam capacity during its first decades is utilized as part of the basic capacity, operated all the time. As time passes, and as other, more efficient, equipment is added, it is used less and less, finally being relegated to the stand-by reserve capacity. After thirty or forty years, it may be scrapped.

As long as the alternative equipment would be part of the basic capacity, the alternative cost which the public project prevents is equal to the cost of generating power on the alternative equipment. For the sake of illustration, let us assume that the equipment is used fully for twenty years. As the use of the equipment gradu-

[14] The President's Materials Policy Commission, *Resources for Freedom*, vol. 1, p. 117.
[15] Tennessee Valley Authority, *Facts about TVA Operations*, p. 14, Pamphlet, TVA, Knoxville, Tenn.

ally declines, the alternative cost of power becomes a mixture of the cost of using the original equipment and the cost with later equipment. The proportions in this mixture change as less of the power is generated by old equipment and more by later equipment. Finally, when the original equipment is retired, the alternative cost is measured by the cost of the equipment which has been used as a replacement. In the case of the projects of the Bureau of Reclamation, where the economic life has been assumed to be as long as a hundred years, the second equipment cycle is followed by at least one more cycle, reducing the alternative cost still further.

An arithmetic example will indicate the magnitude of the overstatement of benefits. Let us assume that equipment is used fully for twenty years, scrapped after thirty years, and taken out of service by 10 percent each year during its last decade. Let us also assume that the productivity of alternative equipment, whether it be better coal-burning installations or atomic furnaces, rises by 3 percent a year, a figure corresponding to historical experience. Finally, let it be assumed that an interest rate of 3 percent is used in the analysis. For the first twenty years, the benefit will be the same under the assumptions of our example as it is with constant technology. During the third decade, a difference in the two estimates begins to emerge, ever widening thereafter. The present value of all benefits over an economic life of fifty years is 16 percent smaller on our assumptions than it would be under present procedures, a figure which is derived by discounting the benefit of all years to the present at an interest rate of 3 percent. With an economic life of a hundred years and a second replacement cycle for the alternative equipment, the divergence in the benefit estimates rises to 26 percent.

The forecasting of technological change is extremely difficult and our assumption of 3 percent per year may not be accurate. Nevertheless, we can be certain that there will continue to be cost-cutting improvements in the generation of power, and since the present procedures assume no progress at all, they bias the benefit estimates upward. As part of the estimation of the benefits of large projects, there should be consideration of the possible future alternatives, and the findings of such study should be reflected in the benefit-cost analysis. In the absence of detailed studies, remote benefits based on current alternative costs should be reduced by some percentage. Our arithmetic example suggests that a good rule of thumb would be to multiply the present benefit estimates of projects with economic lives of fifty years by 0.84, and projects with lives of one hundred years by 0.74.

3. *Power Benefits Downstream*

If a dam is built to provide storage capacity in order to change the stream-flow patterns of a river, it will generally affect the power output of any dams which are downstream from it. Where water is stored at the end of a wet season in order to increase the stream flow during the dry season, it will increase the power output not only at the dam behind which it is stored, but at all other dams through which it subsequently passes. These benefits have long been recognized. The Federal Water Power Act specifies that the Federal Power Commission be empowered to impose payments on downstream beneficiaries which must be made to private or public agencies that undertake an upstream improvement.[16]

The evaluation of these benefits is extremely difficult, since the operation of all downstream installations will be improved and the effect on the more remote dams will depend not only on the upstream addition, but also on the manner in which the operations of other dams are modified. The Federal Power Commission estimates the total effect on the entire river basin without attempting to assign the effects to different dams, since the total for the whole river can be estimated more reliably than for particular installations. The output of the new project is subtracted from the total increase to derive the downstream benefit. The Federal Power Commission does not use this estimate in the determination of payments by downstream beneficiaries, but confines it to the benefit-cost analysis.[17]

4. *The Power-Market Survey*

Before any project is built, the need for additional power in an area must be established. The Federal Power Commission has

---

[16] Federal Water Power Act of 1920, Section 10 (f).
[17] Federal Inter-Agency River Basin Committee, Subcommittee on Benefits and Costs, *Measurement Aspects of Benefit-Cost Analysis*, p. 81.

made market-power surveys for most of the regions in the United States and has supplied the surveys for all projects of the Corps of Engineers outside the Northwest. The Bureau of Reclamation and some of the marketing agencies in the Department of the Interior have made surveys of their own, but the Federal Power Commission reviews the surveys of other agencies.

The typical survey contains extensive descriptions of the physical, demographic, and economic characteristics of the region. The economic activities of each locality and the resultant needs for electric power are analyzed and compared with the available capacity of the local electric power companies. The history of the economic development and particularly of the past growth of the electric load are studied and are projected over the coming decade. The resulting forecasts of the supply and demand of electric power are used both by private companies and by government agencies to help establish the rate at which power capacity must be expanded.

While there is a general methodology of power-market surveys, with great stress on detailed examination of local power needs and on piecemeal projections, each survey is adapted to the particular characteristics of the area and to the purposes for which it is undertaken. Therefore, we shall illustrate the problems which are encountered by examining some specific investigations, the surveys that were used for the benefit-cost analyses of the most recent stages of the development plan for the Columbia River Basin.

5. *Phase C–2 in the Development of Hydroelectric Power in the Pacific Northwest: the Power-Market Surveys*

In 1948 the Bonneville Power Administration, in coöperation with the Corps of Engineers and the Bureau of Reclamation, undertook an examination of the remaining hydroelectric power potential of the Columbia River and its tributaries. Phase A of power development in the Northwest was defined as all projects which were already in operation, while Phase B was defined as all projects which were under construction or which had been authorized by Congress.[18] After looking over the remaining

---

[18] *Report on Columbia River and Tributaries*, House Doc. 531, 81 Cong., 2 sess., Vol. 8, App. O, *Power Generation and Transmission*, p. 4052.

opportunities, the agencies recommended another set of projects for authorization, which are defined as Phase C–2,[19] and outlined two more stages for later development, Phases D and E.

The power-market survey undertaken by the Bonneville Power Administration (BPA) was published as part of the project report. BPA examined the demands for power of ten different groups, and projected their power needs on the basis of specific, detailed assumptions about general economic conditions and impending technological changes. The total projected demand for the year 1960 is almost three times as great as the actual demand for 1947, an amount large enough to justify vast federal investment in further power facilities.

Table 51. Power demand projections for 1960 by BPA and FPC (in million watt-hours)

Item	BPA maximum	BPA minimum	BPA adopted	FPC	FPC as percent of BPA adopted
Domestic and farm	9,389	9,389	9,389	8,966	96
Commercial	7,082	7,082	7,082	3,766	53
Industrial aluminum	34,000	24,000	29,300	11,700	40
other	17,400	11,629	16,465	10,434	63
Irrigation	2,234	2,234	2,234	2,558	114
Miscellaneous	993	993	993	763	77
Total use	71,098	55,327	65,463	38,187	58
Losses	9,954	7,746	9,165	5,824	64
Total energy requirement	81,052	63,073	74,628	44,011	59
Peak demand (in mega-watts)	12,393	10,020	11,535	7,185	62
Load factor	74.7	71.9	73.9	65.1	

Source: *Report on Columbia River and Tributaries*, House Doc. 531, Vol. 8, Appendix S, *Review Report Prepared by the F.P.C. for the Corps of Engineers*, p. 4314.

[19] Phase C-2 was substituted for Phase C when local opposition to one of the projects, Paradise Dam, necessitated replacing that project with another, Libby Dam.

As part of its review report the Federal Power Commission made an independent survey and Table 51 summarizes the findings of the two studies. It is readily apparent that the two estimates differ widely, though both are high enough to justify considerable expansion of capacity. The FPC made an analysis of the causes of the differences. It found that the very large discrepancy in commercial demand was due to three causes: first, the FPC defined the category differently, thereby starting with a past load which was 17 percent smaller. Second, although both studies used the same projection of population growth, the FPC projected a growth of 50 percent in the number of commercial establishments from 1940 to 1960, while the BPA expected the number to be double. BPA also expected the load per establishment to double, while the FPC expected it to grow by 75 percent. Since these deviations are multiplicative, the total estimate of the FPC is little more than half the estimate of BPA.[20]

The enormous difference in the expected power demand from the aluminum industry is partly due to different assumptions about the power program in the Northwest. BPA assumed that the needed power would be provided, and that a market survey which was to determine the need for the program could not assume that the program would be rejected. The FPC felt that it was already clear at the time of the survey that the expansion could not come in time to attract the industry's expansion to the Northwest in the first half of the 1950's, and that only the growth of the industry after 1955 could be considered. On these grounds, and in view of the close competition which power generated from natural gas in the Southwest could offer, the FPC anticipated that 55 percent of all the new aluminum capacity of the country would locate in the Northwest, while the BPA estimates ranged from 73 to 94 percent. There was also wide divergence in their projections of the national growth of the aluminum industry, with the FPC expecting it to reach 1.2 million tons by 1960, and the BPA estimating a range of 1.7 to 2.7 million tons. The national growth so far tends to support

[20] FPC's definitional basis is 83 percent of that of BPA; it anticipates 75 percent of the growth in customers that BPA expects, and a load per customer which is 87 percent of the BPA figure. Multiplying these percentages, we get the total of 53 percent.

the BPA; total aluminum capacity had reached 1.5 million tons by the end of 1954. Only 48 percent of the new facilities located in the Northwest,[21] but the Northwest power shortage is part of the explanation. The rest of the new capacity was located in the Gulf area, using power from natural gas. The rise in natural gas prices precludes much further expansion in that area, but an agreement to import large quantities of aluminum from Canada plus other capacity located near cheap coal probably will remove the necessity of much further domestic expansion. Nevertheless, if more cheap hydroelectric power had been available, it would have found a market.

The difference in the estimates for other industrial demands springs largely from two sources; the FPC doubted that there would be much expansion of magnesium refining or much development of rayon manufacture in the area. While these industries did not expand in the area, the power shortage was surely a contributory cause.

We cannot pass judgment on these projections since the end of the period is not at hand and since, in fact, the capacity has not been expanded to meet the possibility of all needs. But the importance of review of market projections by a nonoperating agency has been demonstrated. Where the surveys are made by agencies other than the FPC, the Commission can act as an effective check. If there is disagreement, which is to be expected in long-range projection, reviewing authorities in the administration and in the Congress will be given an opportunity to examine two different sets of assumptions and the resultant projections, and can evaluate them, using their own judgment. Whether the FPC exercises equal caution when it is the sole source of information for a region is hard to discover; perhaps some other agency should review its reports.

6. *Benefits of Phase C-2*

We turn to the method of estimating the benefits anticipated from Phase C-2 of the power program in the Columbia Basin. Since the power to be generated will become part of the Northwest power pool, a common source of supply to meet all demands in the area, a figure for the average value of a kilowatt hour of

[21] I owe these figures and their explanation to Dr. Franklin V. Walker.

additional power in 1960 was derived. This value was found to be equal to 4.46 mills. The total benefit of the entire plan is equal to the expected annual power output in kilowatt hours times 4.46 mills. The average figure is also used in estimating the benefit of individual projects.

To derive the average benefit, the total demand was divided into three classes: (1) electroprocess industries, (2) normal-load growth of private utilities in the absence of further federal projects; and (3) growth in excess of normal because of low federal rates. The proportion in which total sales fall into each of the classes was then estimated.

The share going to electroprocess industries, of which aluminum represents the largest part, is projected to be 55 percent. This figure represents a compromise between the findings of the BPA market survey, which implied a share of 65 percent of the additional power, and the share available to this class if it is limited by the amount of capacity that can actually be expected to be built by 1960. The benefit figure was computed as follows: in 1939, the local charge for power for this purpose was 2.2 mills, while alternatives elsewhere had costs of about 3.5 mills. The costs of the alternatives have risen about 40 percent in the interim, which implies that the Northwest would keep its relative advantage if its charge also rose 40 percent. Raising the rate of 1939 by 40 percent yields the figure of 3.1 mills.

The benefit for the normal-load growth in the area is measured by the alternative cost of private power, estimates of which were provided by the FPC. This cost is computed by deriving the optimum combination of steam and hydro expansion of capacity, that is, 20 percent steam, 80 percent hydro, and estimating present costs.[22] For the hydro capacity, it is assumed that it could be expanded at costs equal to the original costs multiplied by construction-cost indices; costs of further steam capacity were computed directly. Private costs, including private taxes and interest rates, were used in the computation, resulting in a cost of 6.86 mills.

The benefit to the third class of demand, the growth in the load which was stimulated by the low federal rates, was estimated by

[22] In this context, private power also includes some power generated by municipalities.

taking an average of the first two rates, which assumes that the demand curve is a straight line between the two rates; in the absence of more detailed analysis, this is as reasonable an assumption as any other. A rate of 5.09 mills results. The division of the load between the latter two classes was made by examining the growth between 1939 and 1947 and estimating how much of this growth would have occurred if the rates of private utilities had continued to prevail. Table 52 shows how the composite figure of 4.46 mills was derived.

Table 52. Computation of power benefit of phase C–2, Columbia River Basin

Class of demand	Percent of sales	Rate of benefit	Weighted amounts
1. Direct sales to electro-process industries	55	3.10	1.71
2. Nonfederal utilities: normal load growth	26	6.86	1.78
3. Nonfederal utilities: load growth in excess of normal	19	5.09	0.97
Average rate of benefits (in mills)			4.46

Source: *Report on Columbia River*, Appendix O, *Power Generation and Transmission*, p. 4116.

The theory behind this analysis is not the alternative-cost principle. Instead, an attempt is made to estimate benefit from the revenues which people are willing to pay. Since the demand of class 1 and class 3, representing 74 percent of the demand, would not have developed in the region under private rates, local alternative cost could not be used as a measure.

The alternative-cost principle could have been applied from a national point of view and would have had certain advantages. It would have required that the cost of producing aluminum elsewhere be estimated, using the same interest and tax standards for both alternatives. At the time the analysis was made, power from natural gas in the Southwest was the most economic alternative. In valuing the power to be used for aluminum, the alternative cost of the power in the Southwest was considered to determine the ceiling on the rates that could be charged. But it was the actual cost, including the taxes and interest rates to be paid by a private company in the Southwest, that was used in the analysis, which corresponds to an alternative-cost computation in which the public alternative cost has lower interest and tax charges than the private alternative. Thus the analysis did not assure that the most efficient alternative would actually be selected for meeting the need for power for aluminum.

If the same standards are used, the revenue approach of the study of the BPA should yield the same answer as alternative-cost calculations, for the willingness to pay is circumscribed by the cost of alternatives; in the event that the alternative cost is too high for some classes of demand, revenue provides the measure for benefit under both methods. But in the case of electro-process industries, the alternative-cost principle needs to be extended beyond the geographic limits of the region.

7. Benefits of Individual Projects of Phase C–2

The benefit-cost ratio of the entire program proposed for Phase C–2 is 1.26, $162,549,000 of annual benefits at an annual cost of $129,179,000.[23] In order to show the merit of each project in the program, individual benefit-cost ratios were developed by assigning specific shares of the total benefits. The procedure which was used was rather complicated. Because of its profound effect on the ratios of individual projects we shall, at least, outline it briefly.

Part of the program consists of completing the installation of generating equipment at projects which were part of Phase B. Benefit estimates had been prepared for this work at the time they were originally proposed. Benefits equal to the original estimates were assigned to the old projects, leaving the incremental benefits of the new projects of Phase C–2. Projects of two kinds were proposed: run-of-the-river power dams downstream and storage dams upstream, the objective being to store the water seasonally far up the river, permitting it to pass through as many dams as

[23] *Report on Columbia River and Tributaries*, House Doc. 531, App. O, p. 4123.

possible during the dry, or "critical flow," season. To derive the benefits of the dams, benefits equal to the cost of the transmission system were subtracted from the remaining total for Phase C–2. Each dam was assigned benefits equal to its "prime capability," which is defined to be the amount of power it would generate if it were the only project to be added to Phase B. Because of the high efficiency of the combination of storage and of old and new run-of-the-river dams, substantial benefits still remain to be assigned, and these are distributed as follows: each dam is assigned benefits equal to the cost of the extra generating equipment which is needed; the rest is distributed equally between the dam where the power is actually generated and the storage dams which help to make it possible. The division among storage dams is in accordance with their contribution to the increase of stream flow during the critical flow period. The resultant division of benefits is shown in Table 53.

Table 53. Power benefits and costs of projects in phase C–2
(000 omitted)

Dam	Benefits	Costs	Benefit-cost ratio
Glacier View	$ 7,773	$ 4,609	1.84
Libby	19,830	11,139	1.95
Albeni Falls	4,430	1,683	2.65
Priest Rapids*	18,520	17,517	1.22
Hell's Canyon	19,877	16,532	1.31
John Day*	24,581	18,357	1.21
The Dalles*	16,382	13,997	1.25

Source: *Report on Columbia River*, Appendix O, p. 4125.
* Run-of-the-river dams.

These rule-of-thumb methods of assigning benefits to projects serve no useful purpose since they cannot relate to any economic decision. Yet they may well confuse the true economic merit of various projects; they produce a ranking of projects which bears no relation to any possible order of construction and they justify projects even though their incremental benefit-cost ratios may fall short of 1.0. In planning a river-basin program, an optimal combination of projects must be derived, which requires computation of incremental benefit-cost ratios for each project considered as an addition to alternative groupings of other projects. At the appropriation stage, when specific projects must be chosen as the next step in a sequence of development, incremental benefit-cost ratios can again serve a useful purpose by showing the merit of each addition to the system. If the original combination of projects was selected correctly, the incremental benefit-cost ratios derived at the time of appropriation will be favorable.

B. FINANCIAL ANALYSIS

8. *The Determination of Power Rates*

All power generated at federal projects is considered reimbursable; rates are set in such a way that the total revenue over a specified number of years is sufficient to cover all costs, including interest. On projects of the Corps of Engineers, rates are set by the Secretary of Interior which will return all costs over fifty years with interest rate of 3 percent. Projects of the Bureau of Reclamation generally use the same standards,[24] except that an interest rate of $2\frac{1}{2}$ percent has been used in the last few years.[25]

The marketing of federal power differs from private practice in two ways. First, public bodies and coöperatives are given preference over private utilities in acquiring the limited quantity of low-cost federal power;[26] the objectives of Congress in specifying this priority are not primarily economic. Second, the rate structure of important federal projects, including the TVA and the power program in the Northwest, is based on the "postage stamp"

[24] President's Water Resources Policy Commission, *Water Resources Law*, p. 295.
[25] For example, the *Report on Colorado River Storage Project*, House Doc. 364, 83 Cong., 2 sess., p. 49; and *Report on Frying Pan–Arkansas Project*, p. 9.
[26] For a detailed discussion, see "The Preference Clause in Federal Electric Power Development and Distribution," by J. B. O'Brien, Jr., in Commission on Organization of the Executive Branch of the Government, *Task Force Report on Water Resources and Power* (June 1955), vol. III, pp. 1107–1150. For an unsympathetic view of federal power pricing policies, see *Report of the Task Force on Power Generation and Distribution*, vol. II, pp. 294–298.

principle, which means that the same rate is charged anywhere on the transmission line network. Private utilities usually base industrial rates as well as commercial and residential rates on the cost of transmitting the power to the specific locality. The "postage stamp" principle results in a greater total transmission cost, since private firms will not consider the transmission costs when locating new plants. From the point of view of economic efficiency, it would be sounder to make each firm bear its own transmission costs. But in this era of atomic warfare, the greater dispersion of industry which results from the use of the principle may be sufficient justification for incurring the higher transmission costs. And in the case of the largest users, power contracts do reflect transmission costs, of course.

In the evaluation of projects, the decline of federal tax revenues because of public development is now considered among the costs. The actual power rates are still based on costs without federal taxes, making public power cheaper because of the more favorable tax treatment. Private utilities have objected violently to this practice.

We shall pass no judgment on this matter. There is no doubt that the absence of federal taxes represents a subsidy to the consumers of public power and thus represents a redistribution of income. It also leads to a demand for public projects motivated by the desire for this subsidy, but this is probably offset by the intensive propaganda campaign against any kind of public power regardless of the merits of any specific project. Also, Congress may wish to use cheap public power as a means of regional development. And as long as priority for public power is given to "preference" customers rather than to those willing to pay the highest price, financial feasibility may require that some sort of subsidy be given to compensate for the loss of potential revenue. If Congress chooses to use public power to accomplish specific social objectives, the rates must reflect this desire. Whether the resultant subsidy is good or bad in anyone's judgment depends upon his acceptance or rejection of these political values.

CHAPTER IX

The Allocation of Joint Costs

EVER since the federal government started building multipurpose projects, one of the most persistent problems has been the allocation of joint costs to the several purposes which are served. A typical multipurpose project will include a dam which is used to form a reservoir, the storage capacity of which will be used to provide flood control, stream-flow regulation for navigation, seasonal or annual carry-over of water for irrigation, as well as long- and short-term storage for hydroelectric power. Some of the costs, such as expenditures for electric generating equipment or for irrigation pumping facilities, can be assigned to one of the purposes, but much of the investment, especially the dam and reservoir, is necessary for each purpose. Even when specific portions of the storage space behind a dam are assigned to the different purposes,[1] the storage cost cannot be assigned unambiguously because the cost of any one layer of storage space depends on the existence of the layers above and below it.

The problem of cost allocation has often been a political issue because the cost of public power depends upon the allocation method. Opponents of public power have often charged that public power is cheap because less than a fair share of joint costs is allocated to it.

The TVA, which has built many large multipurpose projects since the 1930's, has been accused of this charge from its beginning. After some years of dispute, M. G. Glaeser, a noted independent expert, was appointed in 1937 to develop an acceptable method. He proposed the procedure which has been in use in the TVA

[1] There are three common methods of reservoir operation: the first calls for assignment of layers of storage space to each purpose; the second uses the same space for different purposes, depending on the season, rainfall, and other conditions; the third assigns priorities to some purposes, leaving the others whatever space is left over.

ever since, and which has now been adopted by the other agencies as well.[2] In 1946, the Federal Power Commission made an independent study of the TVA's methods and found no cause to object.

As other agencies, especially the Bureau of Reclamation and the Corps of Engineers, started to build multipurpose projects, they were also forced to embrace one or another of the allocation methods. Unlike the TVA, these agencies did not commit themselves to the use of one method, but applied different ones at different times and places.

It has long been recognized that it would be desirable for all agencies to use the same methods; consistency among projects would assure that there would be less favoritism toward the beneficiaries of any one purpose, since any one method will not be particularly advantageous to one purpose under all circumstances. One of the most important fruits of the Inter-Agency River Basin Committee has been an agreement by the Bureau of Reclamation and the Corps of Engineers[3] to use the same method.[4] The agencies agreed to use the method proposed by the Subcommittee on Benefits and Costs,[5] the method of separable costs–remaining benefits, widely known as the "green book" method, wherever practical.[6]

In this chapter we shall briefly examine the major methods and the principles which determined them. We shall also show the relation of cost allocation to the benefit-cost analysis.

1. *Why Allocate Costs?*

A private firm which produces under conditions of joint cost need not allocate the joint costs at all. In principle, if it wishes

[2] A full discussion of the methods which the TVA considered and their history can be found in J. S. Ransmeier, *The Tennessee Valley Authority* (1942).

[3] The TVA did not participate in the agreement, but its allocation method is the same as the method to which the other agencies agreed.

[4] *Cost Allocation*, mimeographed, No. 57981–2 (Washington: March 1954). No issuing office given.

[5] Subcommittee on Benefits and Costs, *Proposed Practices...*, pp. 53–56.

[6] The statement also approved a variant, the method of alternative justifiable expenditure, if the requisite data are not available, and of proportionate use of capacity where it is "consistent with the basis of project formulation and authorization." See Section 3 below.

to maximize profits, it need only compute the marginal revenues of different numbers of bundles of the joint outputs from the separate demand curves, and compare them with the marginal costs of the bundles. Where the marginal cost of a bundle of joint outputs is equal to its marginal revenue, the profit of the firm is maximized.[7] If the firm bases its investment, price, or output decision on any rule-of-thumb cost allocations, it is not maximizing profits.[8]

This reasoning does not apply to public multipurpose projects for two reasons. First, some of the purposes are not reimbursable, their costs being financed out of general tax revenue. In order to determine the cost which is reimbursable and to test the financial feasibility of the project, the total reimbursable cost must somehow be computed. Second, while public enterprises in these fields do not endeavor to maximize profits, according to the Reclamation Act of 1902 and according to other laws and administrative regulations, rates on reimbursable purposes must be set in such a way that the total reimbursable cost is collected during the project's life. Since the rules require that total revenue equals total cost, average prices must be equal to average costs, and average costs cannot be discovered without an allocation of the joint costs between reimbursable and nonreimbursable purposes.

It will be recalled from our earlier discussion of the financing of the different purposes that navigation and flood control are nonreimbursable. Recreation, a by-product of some multipurpose projects, is in the same category, leaving only irrigation, power, and water supply subject to the reimbursability requirement. According to the Reclamation Act of 1902, the requirement

---

[7] This assumes the conventional conditions about the firm, including increasing cost for bundles, perfect information, and so forth.

[8] There is one exceptional case. In oligopolistic industries where full-cost pricing is consonant with long-run profit maximization, costs have to be allocated to derive a cost for each product on which the markup can be based. Regulated industries also pose instances where joint costs must be allocated. To simplify decision making, firms may sometimes find it convenient to allocate modest amounts of overhead which do not increase with small additions to output or with additions of minor product lines, but which do increase after several small additions. For a fuller discussion, see J. A. Beckett, "A Study of the Principles of Allocating Joint Costs," *Accounting Review* (1951), pp. 327–333.

does not apply to each purpose individually but to the sum of reimbursable purposes, that is, power revenues plus irrigation water charges plus water supply charges must equal the total allocated cost of the three purposes. In fact, the charges imposed on irrigators are based on the repayment capacity, which is derived from estimates of net revenues of irrigated farms before water charges after subtraction of the "family cash living allowance." Thus charges on irrigation are based on the ability to pay, and not on cost. Whatever part of the irrigation investment cannot be paid through water charges is largely paid by the taxpayer through diversion of power revenues and through other devices. Thus, of the six purposes mentioned, only the rates on electric power and water supply are based on allocations. And in some important instances, power and water rates have been set before costs were allocated, which left the formal cost allocations no more than an interesting, though pointless, exercise in accounting.[9]

2. Cost Allocation and the Benefit-Cost Analysis

It is important to stress that cost allocation and benefit-cost analysis have very little in common. Allocation is an essential part of the financial analysis of projects, while benefit-cost analysis is the main component of the economic analysis. Since, by their very nature, cost allocations must be arbitrary, the introduction of their results into the benefit-cost analysis only serves to obscure the essentials of the economics of a project.

The results of the cost allocation can enter into the benefit-cost analysis in the following way: after allocated costs have been computed, benefit-cost ratios are given for each purpose. Such ratios are meaningless; the allocated costs are arbitrary numbers and the ratios do not correspond to possible decisions since, in fact, one purpose could not be undertaken at the allocated cost.

[9] For a proposal to set prices at levels that market conditions allow, abolishing cost allocations altogether, see S. V. Ciriacy-Wantrup, "Cost Allocation in Relation to Western Water Policies," *Journal of Farm Economics* (February 1954), pp. 108–129. This view is also expressed in K. Gertel, "Recent Suggestions for Cost-Allocation of Multiple-Purpose Projects in the Light of the Public Interest," *Journal of Farm Economics* (February 1951), pp. 130–134. Ransmeier, *The Tennessee Valley Authority*, also concludes that cost allocation is not a meaningful procedure for setting prices.

The only choices which are open to the government are whether to do the project at all and whether to include all of the purposes. Benefit-cost ratios which would assist in these choices would be based on total costs and benefits for the over-all decision, and on benefits and separable costs of each purpose. Thus cost allocation can and ought to be confined to the financial analysis.

3. Some Methods of Allocation

Several methods of allocation have received attention and use in recent years.[10] The first step in all methods is to separate those costs which are only incurred for one purpose, such as the cost of irrigation ditches and power-generating equipment, from the truly joint costs, though not all methods define joint costs in the same way. Once they have been isolated, the allocation method is applied to the joint costs.

All of the methods to be discussed allocate joint costs to different purposes in proportion to numbers computed for each purpose, which we shall call the allocation base. Each method defines a different allocation base, and thus results in allocating joint costs in different proportions.

The method which has been recommended by the Engineers' Joint Council, an association of professional engineering societies, is the method of proportionate use of capacity.[11] It determines the allocation base from engineering data by determining how much of the capacity of an installation is needed for each purpose; joint costs are allocated in proportion to the required capacity. The main difficulty of the method is the ambiguity of the concept of capacity of multipurpose projects. Where storage space is assigned, it can be specified in terms of the acre feet of space of each purpose, but where the same space is assigned to different purposes depending on the season, capacity is not defined so clearly. Further, power capacity depends not only on storage

[10] There are numerous other methods which we shall not discuss. Some of them are analyzed in Ransmeier, *The Tennessee Valley Authority.*

[11] Engineers' Joint Council, *Principles of a National Water Policy* (July 1951), p. 193; and *Tentative Report of Committee on Cost Allocation for Multiple Purpose Water Projects,* and *Appendix,* a committee of the American Society of Civil Engineers, July 1948. This method would correspond to a benefit method if the value of a physical unit of capacity were the same for all purposes.

space but also on head, the vertical difference in the water levels above and below a dam. To be sure, arbitrary rules can be devised to define capacity for each particular problem,[12] but as the set of rules which must be specified becomes more and more complex, it becomes more susceptible to manipulation and less subject to intelligent public judgment.

The method of priority of use has been used widely in the past, particularly by the Bureau of Reclamation, but it has now been abandoned. It assigns highest priority to one purpose, usually irrigation in the case of projects of the Bureau, second priority to another purpose, and so on. The purpose with highest priority bears all the joint costs that must be incurred to produce it, while the others need only bear their incremental costs. As a result, the purpose with highest priority has a very large share of the costs allocated to it. If it is a nonreimbursable purpose, taxpayers bear the brunt of the allocation. Where irrigation was given highest priority, the total repayment requirements for the reimbursable purposes were lowered by making most of the joint investment repayable without interest. It is clear that this method is a powerful device for shifting the cost to the taxpayer.

A method which has always had much appeal to students of the problem but which has never been used in pure form is the benefit method. Benefits are the allocation base, implying that joint costs are allocated in proportion to benefits. The costs which can be attributed to each purpose are first subtracted from the respective benefit, leaving the remaining benefits as the allocation base. The method has never found wide application because the procedures for estimating benefits have never been sufficiently conservative or consistent to permit the use of the figures in so immediately concrete a manner. For example, allocations to irrigation would have been extremely large because of the extensive use of indirect and public benefits.

It should also be added that the benefit method can only be used as long as benefits are not derived from the actual prices to be charged, for if that were the case, the result would be circular reasoning. Prices would have to be known to estimate benefits and benefits would have to be known for the allocation

[12] This is done with great ingenuity in *Appendix*, American Society of Civil Engineers.

264

of costs which determines prices. In fact, we have seen that the benefits of none of the purposes are derived directly from revenues, except for some portions of power benefits on projects which are very large in relation to their markets. In those cases, the benefit method could not be used. On the other hand, if power benefits are derived from power revenues and if power rates are set at levels determined by the market, there is no need to allocate costs at all; with irrigation payments based on ability to pay and with power rates set by the market there are no further prices to be set.[13]

The other two methods we shall discuss are variants of the benefit method. The first is the method of alternative justifiable expenditure, which makes the allocation base equal to the lesser of two numbers, (1) the benefit of the purpose or (2) the cost of providing a single-purpose alternative project, each net of the direct costs of the purpose. This method was used widely by the Corps of Engineers before the recent interagency agreement. It requires the estimation of the costs of single-purpose alternatives, which is usually done not on a project-by-project basis but for entire programs. For example, the navigation alternative may be a series of low dams; the power alternative may call for a small number of high dams; flood control may be provided by a series of levees, and irrigation by upstream storage reservoirs. Each system is computed as if it were the only system on the river, and its cost is the allocation base provided it exceeds benefits. If the single-purpose alternative is not justified, benefits become the allocation base for that purpose.

The method of separable costs–remaining benefits has been adopted by the two major agencies as the method generally to be followed. It is identical with the previous method except in one respect: the method of alternative justifiable expenditure calls for subtracting the direct costs of each purpose from benefit or from the cost of the alternative to derive the allocation base, where

---

[13] If water supply is also one of the purposes, its price must also be determined. Since there is no market for it, the recipient localities can either be charged the cost they would have to incur in the absence of the project or be charged on the basis of cost with the project. If the latter method of determining the charge is used, costs must be allocated to derive a cost figure, again precluding the use of the benefit method unless benefits are determined independent of revenues.

direct cost is the cost of those items which clearly are used only for one purpose. The present method subtracts separable costs instead, where these are defined to be the difference of the cost of the entire project and the cost of the same project without that purpose. An example will make the difference clear: the direct cost of navigation of a project may be the cost of building and operating the locks; the separable cost is the cost of building and operating the locks minus the cost of extending the dam across the space to be filled by the navigation lock. Separable cost is the true incremental cost of the purpose; the resultant joint cost is the total cost minus the sum of the separable costs.

From a theoretical point of view, separable cost is a better concept than direct cost because it measures the actual extra cost which has to be incurred for a purpose. The remaining joint cost is also a truer measure of those costs which are independent of the inclusion of any purpose. Thus, even though the method of separable costs–remaining benefits involves some extra hypothetical engineering calculations, it is preferable conceptually to the method of alternative justifiable expenditure.

4. *Principles of Cost Allocation*

Various principles could govern the choice of allocation method. One principle which has played a substantial role in the past is minimization of the cost to beneficiaries. Since either the beneficiaries or the taxpayers pay costs, this principle is equivalent to maximizing the cost to taxpayers. Local interests have this principle closest to their hearts and exert pressure on the agencies to reduce the charges on themselves. The competition among agencies makes these local pressures more effective.[14]

This principle can find expression in a number of ways. First, that method of cost allocation can be selected which allocates the largest share to the nonreimbursable purposes, such as flood control and navigation. Once that group of allocations is maximized, it is to the advantage of local interests to allocate as much as possible to irrigation, since the investment allocated to that purpose need only be repaid without interest. Since the pay-

---

[14] For an example, see A. Maass, "The King's River Project," reprinted in H. A. Stein, ed., *Public Administration and Policy Development: A Casebook* (1952), pp. 533–572.

ments of irrigators are not determined by the cost allocated to them, the amount allocated is a matter of indifference to them. Power users, on the other hand, need pay less if the share allocated to power, and thereby the total cost which is reimbursable with interest, is diminished.

The most effective countermeasure to reduce the influence of this principle has been taken by the adoption of a common method by all agencies. Any one method will favor one purpose on one project and hurt it on another as long as the same method has to be applied everywhere. Random chance will to some extent determine whether the beneficiaries of reimbursable purposes pay much or little. The possibility of systematically selecting the method most favorable to local interests is eliminated.[15]

The principle behind the method of proportionate use of capacity appears to be a desire for equity in the physical sense; let each purpose pay in accordance with the amount of use it makes of the common facilities. Whether fairness should be judged by a physical measure of use is an ethical question; it certainly is a standard used widely in pricing other economic goods. But there is one great disadvantage to the principle and its resultant methods: it can lead to wrong investment decisions. According to economic principle, the investment (or separable cost) for a specific purpose should be undertaken if the benefits sufficiently exceed the costs and if the project as a whole is worth undertaking. The allocated cost of each purpose derived from a proportionate use of capacity will be greater than the separable cost, regardless of the distribution of benefits among purposes. In the event that one purpose produces benefits which are barely greater than the amount needed to justify inclusion of the purpose in the project on the basis of separable cost, the method of proportionate use of capacity may make the allocated cost of the purpose so large that it will be excluded from the project plan. Thus purposes may be excluded when they are justified. This problem does not arise, of course, if allocated costs are kept strictly separate from the economic analysis.

[15] This is not to say that there do not remain controversial technical details of cost allocations which can raise or lower local costs. Each method is open to interpretation in application, and administrative decisions can still reduce the charges to any group.

On grounds of pure economic theory, another principle has been suggested. It calls for minimizing the distortions in the price structure which inevitably result from the requirement that total revenues equal the total cost of reimbursable purposes rather than that price equals marginal cost.[16] If the assumptions about economic welfare which are fundamental to the benefit-cost analysis are applied to cost allocation, including the assumption that benefits are weighted equally "to whomsoever they may accrue," then the joint costs should be covered by higher rates on those outputs for which the demand is inelastic.[17] For these are the commodities that will be bought in little diminished quantity despite the fact that their prices exceed their marginal cost. In the limiting case, with demand completely inelastic, the joint cost is financed by a lump-sum tax, with no distorting effects whatsoever. In the general case, the joint costs should be allocated in inverse proportion to the elasticities of demand of the outputs of the different purposes.

This method is extremely difficult to apply in practice. Not only are the elasticities of demand for the reimbursable purposes unknown, but the relevant elasticities for the nonreimbursable purposes would also have to be estimated. Since these purposes are primarily financed out of general taxation, it would not be the elasticities of demand for the product or service which would determine the magnitude of the losses from distortive effects, but the nature of the impact of marginal tax rates. In theory it would be possible to construct a distortive measure for the tax impact which would be comparable to the elasticities of demand of reimbursable outputs; but as a statistical problem it is a task well beyond the present frontier of knowledge.

Finally, there is the principle which is most widely accepted at this time and which is the rationale for methods both of the alternative justifiable expenditure and of the separable costs–remaining benefit, the principle of sharing the saving from joint

---

[16] A. S. Manne, "Multiple-Purpose Enterprises—Criteria for Pricing," *Economica* (August 1952), pp. 322–336; M. Fleming, "Optimal Production with Fixed Profits," *Economica* (August 1953), pp. 215–236; and M. Boiteux, "Sur la gestion des Monopoles Publics astreints à l'équilibre budgétaire," *Econometrica* (January 1956), pp. 22–40.

[17] This assumes that marginal-cost pricing is ruled out because it does not produce enough revenues to cover total reimbursable costs.

production equitably. The cost of providing for several purposes separately is greater than if they are combined into one multipurpose project; let the joint costs be distributed in accordance with the saving that is made for each purpose. The purpose which would be most expensive to provide in an alternative way will bear the biggest part of joint costs. If the alternative would not be justified, the idea of a cost saving is not applicable, and the benefits of the purpose replace the alternative cost in the allocation base.

This principle seems as equitable as any other; if we hold no particular brief for the beneficiaries of any single purpose, the present principle, while arbitrary, has an appeal of fairness.

5. *Is the Method of Separable Costs–Remaining Benefits Acceptable?*

An allocation method must pass one economic test: does it interfere with the derivation of correct investment and output decisions?

Turning first to investment decisions, the justification of a project as a whole is never influenced by cost allocation because total benefits and total costs are unaffected. Decisions about the inclusion of any one purpose can be affected by the allocation, though they should not be, if benefit-cost ratios based on allocated cost are computed for each purpose and the cost allocation is too high. But the method of separable costs–remaining benefits will never lead to such misallocations. For if the benefit is so low that it barely exceeds the separable costs, the method will not allocate any further costs to this purpose. Thus the economic criterion is preserved: as long as the benefits of a purpose exceed the separable costs, the benefit-cost ratio for that purpose, even if based on allocated costs, will be favorable.[18]

---

[18] According to our analysis in Chapter III, the benefit-cost ratio of marginal projects or project segments should be at least 1.3. For multipurpose projects this means that purposes should be included as long as their benefits exceed the separable costs in the ratio of 1.3. Following this rule, the present allocation method could lead to the exclusion of purposes which are justified, for the benefit-cost ratio based on allocated cost might be between 1.0 and 1.3, yet might be based on substantial allocations of joint costs. In this instance the allocation would push the purpose below the point of justification.

The allocation method could easily be adapted to our rule, however. At present the allocation base is computed by subtracting separable costs

As for output decisions, power is the only output which could be influenced by cost allocations because it is the only one which is sold at rates directly derived from allocated costs. Among the reimbursable purposes, irrigation charges are based on the repayment capacity of a project; the pricing of municipal water is also usually relatively independent of allocated costs. The supply of output is determined by the investment decisions; it is only through the effect of prices on demand that cost allocations can determine output, and it is only the price of power which will generally be modified.

Generally, a correct allocation of resources would require that power be sold to marginal purchasers at rates equal to marginal costs, which in the case of multipurpose projects correspond closely to separable costs. Cost allocations will raise rates above separable costs. But this departure from marginal-cost pricing is a desirable offset to other deviations from the marginal-cost principle in the power field. In the regions in which public power is concentrated, actual rate structures reflect the average allocated costs of old and new installations rather than present marginal cost. Because of cost increases due to inflation and because of the declining quality of the remaining hydroelectric power sites, these average costs are below current marginal costs and so the rates are too low. Cost allocations raise these rates and thus help to offset the larger error in output caused by the use of average historical cost pricing. If we draw our comparison with private-power rates in the economy, a similar argument holds. Because of the differences in tax and interest rates, public power is relatively cheaper than the differences in real cost would suggest. The cost allocations move the public rates closer to real cost relationships.

We see, therefore, that the method of separable costs–remaining benefits does not exercise a disturbing influence on investment or on output decisions under present procedures. If the proposals of Chapter III with regard to justification of projects were

---

from benefits (or from alternative justifiable cost) to derive the allocation base. Our decision rule would require that the separable costs be multiplied by 1.3 before subtracting them. With this modification, the investment decision would never be made incorrectly due to the above allocation method.

adopted, the method could easily be modified to make it consistent with this point of view.

6. *Incremental or Total Cost Allocations?*

One important point of procedure in the method has not been settled as yet. It has not been made clear how it is to be applied to later additions of projects to a program. Should an independent allocation be made for the project or for the group of projects, or should the entire program be reallocated? The TVA has used the second form; if a new project is added, the cost of single-purpose programs with similar total outputs is computed to determine the allocation base. Because it is the benefit of the entire program that is compared with single-purpose alternative programs, the alternative cost has always proved smaller than the benefit and has become the allocation base; except for one instance, the alternative expenditure has been the allocation base for every project of the TVA. There is one anomalous result of this procedure: the proportions in which joint costs are allocated on subsequent projects tend to remain constant. For example, if a project is added which primarily produces power benefits, the change in the allocated costs includes an increase in the allocated costs of all purposes. An arithmetic example will make this clear: suppose that the total joint cost of a program is raised from $180,000 to $200,000 through the addition of a power project; suppose that the old allocation had divided the joint cost equally among three purposes, that is, $60,000 each; suppose that each of the old alternatives cost $100,000, and that the cost of the new power alternative is $120,000. The new allocated cost of power will be ($120,000/320,000)($200,000), or $75,000, and of each of the other purposes ($100,000/320,000)($200,000), or $62,500. Thus $2,500 of the cost of the additional power is allocated to each of the other two purposes. In fact, a project that only produces power will be considered a separable cost, but as soon as there is some benefit to another purpose all joint costs become subject to this allocation technique.

Even though there are no absolute standards for allocation procedures, it can well be argued that the above result is undesirable. It would be more fitting to allocate the cost of an incremental addition to a program in accordance with the increases

271

in the alternative costs or the increases in benefit, whichever is smaller. Under the latter method, purposes that receive no benefit from a project can receive no allocated costs. To be sure, it is technically difficult to compute single-purpose alternatives at every stage of a program, and so projects must be grouped together for cost allocation. But there is no need to keep all projects, even if they are constructed decades apart, in the same group. At the least, the joint costs of major phases of a long-run program should be allocated on an incremental basis.

CHAPTER X
Conclusion

HAVING surveyed the benefit-cost procedures in four major fields of water-resource development, we can come to certain general conclusions about the present and the potential usefulness of the technique. Ideally, benefit-cost analysis would permit us (1) to rank projects in the same field, (2) to compare projects in different fields, and (3) to determine the proper expenditure levels for each of the federal programs. In fact, present procedures fall considerably short of these objectives, and while perfection in decision making involving projects that have economic lives of more than half a century is impossible, conceptual inconsistencies in current practice keep the contribution of benefit-cost analysis far short of what it might be. A benefit-cost ratio of 1.0 does not mean that a project will actually produce more benefit than its cost even if the forecasts of prices prove to be correct, and hence the analysis is not yet a proper means for determining how much money should be spent on the various programs. Nor is it possible to assume that projects in different fields with equal benefit-cost ratios have the same economic merit, thus restricting the technique primarily to the comparison of projects in the same field. Yet benefit-cost analysis is an extremely promising evaluation method for public expenditures, which, in the limited cases where it can be applied, could put policy judgments on a much firmer economic basis than is usually possible. While we have many reservations about specific details of procedure, this point is fundamental: with so large a share of the total investment of the country channeled through public bodies and hence subject to political decision making, it is most desirable that benefit-cost techniques, properly designed, be applied as widely as possible, and that the findings be given a heavy weight in policy formation.

273

This conclusion presupposes that the analysis is used to evaluate projects and not merely as a propaganda device.

1. *The Present Program*

Examination of the economics of the present program shows a very wide range in the quality of projects. Table 54 gives the benefit-cost ratios of projects that were included in the list of budget requests for the Corps of Engineers and the Bureau of Reclamation for the fiscal year 1957. This set of projects will constitute the bulk of the program of the two agencies for the next several years. Table 55 tabulates the projects by their benefit-cost ratios. Keeping in mind the major sources of bias in the present procedures, it can be seen that a substantial part of the projects cannot be considered to have passed the test of justification if we make an increase in the real national income of the country the criterion. Over half of all the projects have benefit-cost ratios of less than 1.6, and many have ratios barely in excess of 1.0. Because of the wide range of concepts and of quality in benefit-cost estimation, it is not possible to pick any one ratio and say that all projects that exceed it are justified. But given the magnitudes of the biases that have been listed in the preceding chapters (and our list is far from exhaustive), the economics of many of the projects must be called into question.

Table 54. Benefit-cost ratios of projects for which funds were requested in the budget for 1957

Project	Total cost (in millions)	Benefit-cost ratio
CORPS OF ENGINEERS		
Navigation		
Arkansas River and Tribs., Ark.	1,000.0	1.20
Missouri River	341.0	1.53
Delaware River Phila. to Trenton, Pa., N.J., Del.	61.3	1.69
Warrior Lock and Dam, Ala.	18.2	1.56
Mississippi R. St. Anthony's Falls	30.0	1.5
Lock 19, Keokuk, Ia.	13.0	1.5
Markland Lock and Dam, Md., Ky., Ohio	73.6	2.07
New Cumberland Locks and Dams, Ohio, W. Va.	43.1	1.69
Greenups Locks and Dams, Ky., Ohio	60.9	1.79
Hildebrand Lock and Dam, W.Va.	14.9	1.81
Illinois Waterway	79.7	2.40

Conclusion

Project	Total cost (in millions)	Benefit-cost ratio
Navigation		
Tampa, Fla., Harbor	11.0	2.52
Mobile Harbor, Ala.	5.8	2.93
New York and New Jersey Chls.	59.9	1.40
Buffalo Harbor, N.Y.	17.3	1.56
Cleveland Harbor, Ohio	19.5	2.33
Norfolk Harbor, Va.	8.4	2.24
Flood control		
Los Angeles City Drainage Area	348.0	2.9
Anacostia River Basin, Md., D.C.	5.6	2.27
Central and Southern Florida	120.0	6.0
East St. Louis and vicinity, Ill.	21.4	33.0
Little Sioux River, Ia.	17.3	1.13
Kansas Cities, Kan., Mo.	44.8	2.79
Louisville, Ky.	24.0	3.3
Maysville, Ky.	6.7	1.95
Wichita and Valley Center Kan.	13.0	1.35
N. Adams, Mass.	16.2	1.19
Cape Girardeau, Mo.	4.5	1.82
Rio Grande Floodway, N.M.	5.0	1.13
Oklahoma City Floodway, Okla.	10.0	1.21
Bradford, Pa.	8.7	1.1
Buffalo Bayou, Tex.	39.7	1.7
Dallas Floodway	9.8	2.90
Russian River Res., Cal.	12.7	2.2
San Antonio Res., Cal.	11.0	1.47
Whittier Narrows Res., Cal.	32.3	1.73
Lucky Peak Res., Id.	19.9	1.26
Coralville Res., Ia.	16.3	1.58
Rough River Res. and Channel, Ky.	9.9	2.8
Toronto Res., Kan.	19.7	1.22
Chamita Res., N.M.	12.1	1.31
Oolgah Res., Okla.	31.4	1.37
Bear Creek Res., Pa.	17.9	1.2
Canyon Res., Tex.	12.4	1.78
Ferrells Bridge Res., Tex.	17.7	1.39
Texarkana Res., Tex.	33.8	1.43
Eagle Gorge Res., Wash.	22.0	1.4
Sutton Res., W.Va.	34.2	1.84
Multipurpose		
Fort Gaines Lock and Dam, Ala. and Ga.	84.6	1.05
Folsom Res., Cal.	64.8	1.6
Jim Woodruff Lock and Dam, Fla.	46.4	1.05
Buford Dam, Ala., Fla., Ga.	38.1	1.05
Hartwell Res., Ga. and S.C.	94.3	1.11
Table Rock Res., Mo. and Kan.	68.7	1.16
Gavins Point Res., Neb. and S.D.	53.0	1.36

Project	Total cost (in millions)	Benefit-cost ratio
Multipurpose		
Garrison Res., N.D.	294.0	1.37
Cougar Res., Ore.	37.4	1.61
Hills Creek Res., Ore.	33.1	1.98
Lookout Pt. Res. and Dam, Ore. and Wash.	88.6	1.45
McNary Lock and Dam, Ore. and Wash.	286.6	1.46
Dallas Lock and Dam, Ore. and Wash.	270.0	1.63
Oahe Res., S.D.	321.0	1.08
Chatham Lock and Res., Mass.	31.7	1.30
Old Hickory Lock and Dam, Tenn.	48.8	1.14
McGee Bend Dam, Tex.	47.2	1.39
Chief Joseph Dam, Wash.	158.0	2.31
Ice Harbor Lock and Dam, Wash.	135.0	1.15
BUREAU OF RECLAMATION		
Santa Maria, Cal.	16.7	3.7
Solano, Cal.	51.0	3.8
Colorado–Big Thompson, Colo.	159.4	2.4
Michand Flats, Id.	4.7	2.55
Minidoka, Id.	10.5	3.56
Palisades, Id.	62.6	2.55
Middle Rio Grande, N.M.	29.5	2.8
Weber Basin, Id.	66.7	2.7
Columbia Basin, Wash.	759.4	4.30
Yakima–Kennewick Div., Wash.	13.3	5.7
Eden, Wyo.	7.5	1.27
Bostwick Div., Neb. and Kan.	48.6	1.51
Frenchmen–Cambridge Div., Neb.	68.2	1.33
Glendo Unit, Wyo.	42.6	1.19
Hanover Bluff, Wyo.	3.2	1.79
Helena Valley, Mont.	11.6	1.46
Kirwin, Kan.	18.5	1.02
Lower Marias, Mont.	64.9	2.08
Owl Creek, Wyo.	2.6	0.95
Rapid Valley, S.D.	9.0	1.95
Sargent Unit, Neb.	14.5	1.07
Webster Unit, Kan.	17.0	1.15
Yellow Tail, Mont. and Wyo.	93.2	1.50

Source: *Budget of the United States Government*, 1957, and *Hearings on the Appropriation Bills* before the House and Senate Committees on Public Works and on Interior and Insular Affairs, 1956. The list only contains those projects for which benefit-cost ratios were available in the Hearings. This omits certain projects which were authorized before benefit-cost ratios were required. Also, only projects with total costs greater than $2,000,000 are listed.

Conclusion

Table 55. Benefit-cost ratios of projects for which funds were requested in 1957 budget

Benefit-cost ratio	Number of projects			
	Navi-gation	Flood control	Multipurpose Corps of Engineers	Bureau of Reclamation
0 –0.99	—	—	—	1
1.0–1.29	1	8	8	5
1.3–1.59	6	8	6	4
1.6–1.99	4	6	4	2
2.0–2.99	6	6	1	6
3.0–4.99	—	1	—	4
over 5.0	—	2	—	1

Benefit-cost ratio	Ultimate total cost (in millions)			
	Navi-gation	Flood control	Multipurpose Corps of Engineers	Bureau of Reclamation
0 –0.99	—	—	—	3
1.0–1.29	1,000	115	837	100
1.3–1.59	480	157	801	122
1.6–1.99	180	130	405	12
2.0–2.99	198	431	158	388
3.0–4.99	—	24	—	838
over 5.0	—	141	—	13

Under these conditions, the improvement of benefit-cost techniques is particularly important. Once consistent concepts are applied which treat benefits and costs symmetrically and measure them fully, it will become possible to perform the economic test rigorously. A benefit-cost ratio of a project sufficiently high to warrant its inclusion in the program would, in the absence of extraordinary noneconomic circumstances, be a very strong argument for construction and should carry heavy weight with the Congress and the public. Projects with inadequate benefit-cost ratios would have to be shown to yield intangible benefits or to redistribute income in a particularly desirable pattern before they could be justified.

2. Suggested Improvements in Benefit-Cost Practice

The changes listed here would go a long way toward making benefit-cost analysis a consistent and reliable tool for the selection of projects. There would still remain questions about some of the physical assumptions underlying the benefit-cost relationships and about the degree of success in predicting prices, but the range of error would be sharply reduced. No effort will be made here to defend the recommendations, since their rationale has been presented in earlier chapters.

With regard to the general technique of benefit-cost analysis we conclude

(1) that as long as a budgetary constraint limits water-resource programs, only projects with benefit-cost ratios well in excess of 1.0 should be undertaken unless justification can be found on intangible grounds;

(2) that the interest rate on federal securities does not fully measure the social cost of capital which is raised by taxation, but that use of a substantially higher rate of interest would defeat the long-range objectives of resource policy. To prevent the construction of projects of poor quality, it is proposed that a moderate interest rate be coupled with a minimum benefit-cost ratio adequate to assure a proper rate of return for the program as a whole. An interest rate of 3 percent and a minimum benefit-cost ratio of 1.3, or an interest rate of $2\frac{1}{2}$ percent plus a benefit-cost ratio of 1.4, are combinations that serve this purpose;

(3) that an arbitrary limit to the period of analysis of fifty years is an unsatisfactory adjustment for risk because it allows no credit whatsoever for benefits accruing thereafter, but that as long as the depreciation allowances implicit in federal practice are so low, it may provide a necessary offset;

(4) that a uniform concept of cost for the criterion be adopted by all agencies; for projects for which associated cost is only a moderate share of the total, federal cost is considered most appropriate as the denominator in the benefit-cost ratio, with associated cost considered a negative benefit;

(5) that the present method of valuing the cost of land inundated by reservoirs by its market value understates the social cost and that it should be valued by a method which applies the same interest rate to the capitalization of the benefits foregone because of the project as is applied to the valuation of the benefits created; and

(6) that benefit-cost ratios for projects that are an integral part of a program not be computed by means of arbitrary rules of thumb but only on an incremental basis.

For projects in the field of-flood control we conclude

(7) that indirect benefits be limited to a moderate fraction of direct benefits, particularly for floods other than the very rare disaster-type flood, and

(8) that the method for determining the "degree of protection" be restudied and that some principles be laid down as a matter of fundamental policy to indicate how much protection should be permitted to exceed the level suggested by computations of marginal benefits and costs in different situations.

For the evaluation of navigation benefits we conclude

(9) that statistical estimates for the long-run marginal costs of the alternative means of transport be used instead of actual current rates.

In the case of irrigation we recommend

(10) that indirect, or secondary benefits be restricted to extraordinary situations, such as areas in which a supplementary water supply reverses an agricultural decline and permits more efficient utilization of existing capacity, and

(11) that most public benefits not be expressed in monetary terms but included in an intangible analysis.

In evaluating hydroelectric power projects we recommend

(12) that the cost of the federal project and of the private alternative which is used as a measure of benefit be computed at the same interest rate.

Finally (13), while we have not attempted to analyze the administrative structure of federal activities in the field of water-resource development, there is little doubt that the quality of benefit-cost analyses would be improved if there were a strengthening of the review function either through a larger staff within the Bureau of the Budget or through an independent board of review.

We have also made some study of the financial practices in this field and have found that relatively little of the cost of projects in fields other than electric power and water supply is borne by the beneficiaries. Without passing judgment on the desirability of shifting more of the cost from federal taxpayers to local interests, an ethical issue to be properly resolved by the political process, we can conclude (14), however, that pressure for projects of dubious merit would be much reduced by stiffer local charges and that the capability to collect at least some reasonable fraction of the total cost from the beneficiaries would provide a useful check on the benefit-cost calculations.

3. *Four Major Limitations of the Study*

Our analysis of evaluation standards has been carried out on certain assumptions which inevitably limit the range of applicability of our results. Four of these assumptions are so critical that we restate them here.

First, we have assumed that there are prices which reflect the true opportunity costs of resources, an assumption that is reasonable for public-works programs in a developed economy but that requires modification in underdeveloped countries. If the economy is on the verge of transformation and there is much disguised unemployment, benefit-cost analyses would have to take a different form; they would have to include implicit forecasts of the economic development in order to permit estimates of the benefits of project outputs as the structure of the economy evolves, as well as direct estimates of the social cost of the factors of production which the project absorbs. Because the United States is a developed country, the analyst is allowed the luxury of ignoring some of the relations between specific projects and the economy as a whole. In an underdeveloped economy it will usually not be possible to partition the investment problem into simple choices among independent projects; the benefit-cost analysis of any one project will depend on the outputs produced by other projects and on the general pattern of the development effort. This interdependence forces the analyst to have more recourse to centralized planning. Yet once the quantity of resources which is to be devoted to the various fields is determined, benefit-cost analysis of the type discussed in the preceding chapters will be useful in selecting the best projects of the given type.

Conclusion

Second, our entire discussion has been concerned with public investment under conditions of high employment. In times of depression, prices cease to be yardsticks of value and the creation of employment opportunities may enjoy higher social priority than expansion of the economy's capacity to produce. Benefit-cost analysis can still show the long-run economic merit of various projects, but it must be combined with criteria which reflect the needs of the day.

Third, we have assumed that intangible benefits are not so large that they outweigh the benefits that can be measured in monetary terms. We urge that an intangible analysis be a part of each project report to permit policy makers to weigh these factors; but it is implicit in our approach that, in the routine case, the intangibles will not be decisive. If we believed otherwise, there would be no point in elaborating such detailed measures of dollar benefits.

Finally, we have stressed the objective of economic efficiency, leaving judgment about matters of equity to politicians and to the voting public. If redistribution of income were the major objective of the programs, our procedure would have little to recommend it; but the concentration of benefits among groups that frequently are small, and the limited progressivity of the federal tax structure by which the programs are financed, make it difficult to justify the programs on grounds of equity.

BIBLIOGRAPHY

BOOKS

American Society of Civil Engineers. *Tentative Report of Committee on Cost Allocation for Multiple Purpose Water Projects*, and *Appendix*, July, 1948.

Arrow, K. J. *Social Choice and Individual Values.* New York: Wiley, 1951.

Barger, H. *The Transportation Industries, 1889–1946.* New York: National Bureau of Economic Research, 1951.

Barrows, H. K. *Floods, Their Hydrology and Control.* New York: McGraw-Hill, 1948.

Baumol, W. J. *Welfare Economics and the Theory of the State.* Cambridge: Harvard University Press, 1952.

Chipman, J. S. *The Theory of Intersectoral Money Flows and Income Formation.* Baltimore: Johns Hopkins University, 1951.

Ciriacy-Wantrup, S. V. *Resource Conservation Economics and Policies.* Berkeley: University of California Press, 1952.

Clark, J. M. *The Economics of Planning Public Works.* Washington: U.S. Government Printing Office, 1935.

Engineers Joint Council. *Principles of a National Water Policy.* New York: Engineers Joint Council, 1951.

Fisher, A. G. B. *Economic Progress and Social Security.* London: Macmillan, 1945.

Galbraith, J. K. *American Capitalism.* Boston: Houghton Mifflin, 1952.

Golzé, A. R. *Reclamation in the United States.* New York: McGraw-Hill, 1952.

Hicks, J. R. *Value and Capital.* Oxford: Clarendon Press, 1939.

Hoyt, W. G., and W. B. Langbein. *Floods.* Princeton: Princeton University Press, 1955.

Huffman, R. E. *Irrigation Development and Public Water Policy.* New York: Ronald Press, 1953.

Keynes, J. M. *General Theory of Employment, Interest and Money.* New York: Harcourt, Brace, 1936.

283

Bibliography

Krutilla, J. V., and O. Eckstein. *Multiple Purpose River Development, Studies in Applied Economic Analysis.* Baltimore: The Johns Hopkins University Press, 1958.

Leopold, L. B., and T. Maddox, Jr. *The Flood Control Controversy.* New York: Ronald Press, 1954.

Lerner, A. P. *The Economics of Control.* New York: Macmillan, 1944.

Lewis, A. W. *Overhead Costs.* New York: Rinehart, 1949.

Little, I. M. D. *A Critique of Welfare Economics.* Oxford: Clarendon Press, 1950.

—— *The Price of Fuel.* Oxford: Clarendon Press, 1953.

Locklin, P. D. *Economics of Transportation.* 3rd ed.; Chicago: Irwin, 1947.

Lutz, F. and V. *The Theory of Investment of the Firm.* Princeton: Princeton University Press, 1951.

Maass, A. *Muddy Waters: The Army Engineers and the Nation's Rivers.* Cambridge: Harvard University Press, 1951.

Marco, A. De Viti De. *First Principles of Public Finance.* New York: Harcourt, Brace, 1936.

McKean, R. N. *Cost-Benefit Analysis and Efficiency in Government.* The RAND Corporation, Santa Monica, California, RM–1445–RC (to be published).

McKinley, C. *Uncle Sam in the Pacific Northwest.* Berkeley: University of California Press, 1952.

Moley, R. *What Price Federal Reclamation?* New York: American Enterprise Association, 1955.

Picken, I., and I. K. Fox. *The Upstream-Downstream Flood Control Controversy in the Arkansas-White-Red River Basin Survey.* Public Administration Case Study, forthcoming.

Pigou, A. C. *The Economics of Welfare.* 8th ed.; London: Macmillan, 1952.

Ransmeier, J. S. *The Tennessee Valley Authority.* Nashville: Vanderbilt University, 1942.

Reder, M. *Studies in the Theory of Welfare Economics.* New York: Columbia University Press, 1947.

Resources for the Future, Inc. *The Nation Looks at its Resources.* Washington: Report of the Mid-Century Conference, 1954.

Schumpeter, J. A. *Capitalism, Socialism and Democracy.* 2nd ed.; New York: Harper and Brothers, 1947.

Sharfman, I. L. *The Interstate Commerce Commission.* Vol. III–B; New York: The Commonwealth Fund, 1931–37.

Bibliography

Scitovsky, T. *Welfare and Competition.* Chicago: Irwin, 1951.

Smithies, A. *The Budgetary Process in the United States.* New York: McGraw-Hill, 1955.

Twentieth Century Fund. *Electric Power and Government Policy.* New York: Twentieth Century Fund, 1948.

White, G. F. *Human Adjustment to Floods.* Chicago: University of Chicago Press, 1945.

ARTICLES

Beckett, J. A. "A Study of the Principle of Allocating Joint Costs," *Accounting Review*, 1951, pp. 327–333.

Boegli, W. E. "Economic Effects of Irrigation in a Subhumid Area," *Proceedings of the American Society of Civil Engineers*, Separate No. 398, February 1954.

Boiteux. "Sur le gestion des Monopoles Publics astreints à l'équilibre budgétaire," *Econometrica*, January 1956.

Borts, G. H. "Increasing Returns in the Railway Industry," *Journal of Political Economy*, August 1954, p. 323.

―――― "Production Relations in the Railway Industry," *Econometrica*, January 1952, pp. 71–79.

Campbell, R. W. "Accounting for Depreciation in the Soviet Economy," *Quarterly Journal of Economics*, November 1956, pp. 481–506.

Ciriacy-Wantrup, S. V. "Benefit-Cost Analysis and Public Resource Development," *Journal of Farm Economics*, November 1955, pp. 676–689.

―――― "Cost Allocation in Relation to Western Water Policies," *Journal of Farm Economics*, February 1954, pp. 108–129.

Dantzig, D. V. "Economic Decision Problems for Flood Prevention," *Econometrica*, July 1956, pp. 276–287.

Eckstein, O. "Investment Criteria for Economic Development and the Theory of Intertemporal Welfare Economics," *Quarterly Journal of Economics*, February 1957, pp. 56–85.

Fleming, M. "Optimal Production With Fixed Profits," *Economica*, August 1953, pp. 215–236.

Foster, H. A. "Flood Insurance," *Proceedings of the American Society of Civil Engineers*, Vol. 80, Separate No. 483.

Freund, R. J. "The Introduction of Risk into a Programming Model," *Econometrica*, July 1956, pp. 253–263.

285

Bibliography

Gertel, K. "Recent Suggestions for Cost-Allocation of Multiple-Purpose Projects in the Light of the Public Interest," *Journal of Farm Economics*, February 1951, pp. 130–134.

Heady, E. O. "Some Fundamentals of Conservation Economics and Policy," *Journal of Farm Economics*, November 1950, pp. 1182–1195.

Hirshleifer, J. "An Isoquant Approach to Investment Decisions," The RAND Corporation, Santa Monica, California, P–1158, 23 August, 1957.

Isard, W., and Kuenne, R. E. "The Impact of Steel Upon the Greater New York–Philadelphia Industrial Region," *Review of Economics and Statistics*, November 1953, pp. 289–301.

Jarvis, C. S. "Symposium on Flood Control," *Geophysical Union Transactions*, 1939.

Johnson, D. Gale. "Allocation of Agricultural Income," *Journal of Farm Economics*, November 1948, pp. 732–745.

Kahn, R. F. "Home Investment and Unemployment," *Economic Journal*, 1931, pp. 173–198.

Kaldor, N. "Welfare Propositions in Economics," *Economic Journal*, September 1939, pp. 549–552.

Krutilla, J. V. "Criteria for Evaluating Regional Development Programs," *Papers and Proceedings, American Economic Review*, May 1955, pp. 120–132.

Lampert, J. B. "A Study of Methods of Determining Flood Control Damages and of Evaluating Flood Control Benefits," unpublished master's thesis, Massachusetts Institute of Technology, 1939.

Maass, A. "In Accord with the Program of the President," C. J. Friedrich and J. K. Galbraith, eds., *Public Policy*, Vol. III, Cambridge: 1952, pp. 77–93.

———— "The King's River Project," H. A. Stein, ed., *Public Administration and Policy Development: A Casebook*, New York: 1952, pp. 533–572.

———— "Protecting Nature's Reservoir," C. J. Friedrich and J. K. Galbraith, eds., *Public Policy*, Vol. V, Cambridge: 1954, pp. 71–106.

Manne, A. S. "Multiple-Purpose Enterprises—Criteria for Pricing," *Economica*, August 1952, pp. 322–336.

Margolis, J. "Secondary Benefits, External Economies, and the Justification of Public Investment," *Review of Economics and Statistics*, August 1957, pp. 284–291.

———— "Welfare Criteria, Pricing and Decentralization of a Public Service," *Quarterly Journal of Economics*, August 1957, pp. 448–463.

Bibliography

Marts, M. E. "Use of Indirect Benefit Analysis in Establishing Repayment Responsibility for Irrigation Projects," *Economic Geography*, April 1956, pp. 132–138.

Patton, D. "The Traffic Pattern on American Inland Waterways," *Economic Geography*, January 1956, pp. 29–37.

Ramsey, F. P. "A Mathematical Theory of Saving," *Economic Journal*, 1928, pp. 541–552.

Regan, M. M., and E. L. Greenshields. "Benefit-Cost Analysis of Resource Development Programs," *Journal of Farm Economics*, November 1951, pp. 866–878.

Regan, M. M., and E. G. Weitzell. "Economic Evaluation of Soil and Water Conservation Measures and Programs," *Journal of Farm Economics*, November 1947, pp. 1275–1294.

Renshaw, E. F. "Measurement of Benefits from Navigation Projects," *American Economic Review*, September 1957, pp. 652–661.

Samuelson, P. A. "Evaluation of Real National Income," *Oxford Economic Papers*, January 1950, pp. 1–21.

————— "Full Employment versus Progress and Other Economic Goals," M. F. Millikan, ed., *Income Stabilization for a Developing Democracy*, New Haven: 1953, pp. 547–582.

————— "Principles and Rules in Modern Fiscal Policy: A Neoclassical Reformulation," *Money, Trade and Economic Growth* (Essays in honor of John H. Williams), pp. 157–176.

————— "The Pure Theory of Public Expenditure," *The Review of Economics and Statistics*, November 1954, pp. 387–389.

Scitovsky, T. de. "A Note on Welfare Propositions in Economics," *Review of Economic Studies*, November 1941, pp. 77–88.

Selby, H. E. "Indirect Benefits from Irrigation Development," *Journal of Land and Public Utility Economics*, February 1944, pp. 45–51.

Whipple, W., Jr. "Principles of Federal Hydro-Electric Power Development," *Proceedings of the American Society of Civil Engineers*, July 1955, Vol. 81, Paper No. 739.

UNITED STATES GOVERNMENT DOCUMENTS

Commission on Organization of the Executive Branch of the Government (1949), *Report on Department of the Interior*, March 1949.

————— *Task Force Report on Natural Resources*, Appendix L, Jan. 1949.

Commission on Organization of the Executive Branch of the Government (1955), *Task Force Report on Water Resources and Power*, 3 vols., June 1955.

287

Bibliography

Commission on Organization of the Executive Branch of the Government (1955), *Report of the Task Force on Power Generation and Distribution*, 2 vols., June 1955.

Cost Allocation, mimeographed, No. 57981-2, March 12, 1954. No issuing office given.

Federal Inter-Agency River Basin Committee, Subcommittee on Benefits and Costs, *Measurement Aspects of Benefit-Cost Analysis*, November 1948.

—— Subcommittee on Benefits and Costs, *Proposed Practices for Economic Analysis of River Basin Projects*, May 1950.

—— Subcommittee on Benefits and Costs, *Qualitative Aspects of Benefit-Cost Practice*, April 1947.

President's Advisory Committee on Water Resources Policy, The. *Water Resources Policy*, December 22, 1955.

President's Materials Policy Commission, The. *Resources for Freedom*, 1952.

President's Water Resources Policy Commission, The. 1950. Vols. I and III of the Report. Vol. I. *A Water Policy for the American People*; Vol. III. *Water Resources Law*.

Tennessee Valley Authority, *Financial Statements for the Fiscal Year Ended June 30, 1953*. A TVA pamphlet, Knoxville, Tennessee.

—— *Power Operations*, 1953. A TVA pamphlet, Knoxville, Tennessee.

U.S. Army, Corps of Engineers, *Annual Reports of the Chief of Engineers*.

—— *Engineering Manual for Civil Works*.

—— *Orders and Regulations*.

U.S. Board of Investigation and Research, *Public Aids to Transportation*, House Doc. No. 159, 79 Cong., 1 sess.

U.S. Bureau of the Budget, *Circular A-47*, December 31, 1952.

U.S. Congress, House of Representatives, *Report on the Arkansas River and Tributaries Project at Enid, Oklahoma*, House Doc. No. 81, 83 Cong., 1 sess.

—— *Report on Channel Port Royal to Beaufort, S.C.*, House Doc. No. 469, 81 Cong., 2 sess.

—— *Report on Chief Joseph Dam Project*, House Doc. No. 374, 83 Cong., 2 sess.

—— *Report on Colorado River Storage Project*, House Doc. No. 364, 83 Cong., 2 sess.

—— *Report on Columbia River and Tributaries*, House Doc. No. 531, 81 Cong., 2 sess., Vols. I–VIII.

Bibliography

U.S. Congress, House of Representatives, *Report on Columbia Slough, Oregon*, House Doc. No. 270, 81 Cong., 1 sess.

—— *Report on Frying Pan–Arkansas Project*, House Doc. No. 187, 83 Cong., 1 sess.

—— *Report on Green River Watershed, Ky. and Tenn.*, House Doc. No. 261, 82 Cong., 1 sess.

—— *Report on Lynn Harbor, Mass.*, House Doc. No. 568, 81 Cong., 2 sess.

—— *Report on the Upper Iowa River*, House Doc. No. 375, 83 Cong., 2 sess.

—— *Report on West Branch of the Susquehanna River, Pa.*, House Doc. No. 29, 84 Cong., 1 Sess.

—— Committee on Public Works, *Hearings of the Subcommittee to Study Civil Works*, 82 Cong., 2 sess.

—— Committee on Public Works, *Hearings on the Great Lakes–St. Lawrence Basin Project*, 81 Cong., 2 sess.

—— Committee on Public Works, *Report of the Subcommittee to Study Civil Works*,

(1) *The Civil Functions Program of the Corps of Engineers U.S. Army*, House Committee Print No. 21, 82 Cong., 2 sess.

(2) *The Flood Control Program of the Department of Agriculture*, House Committee Print No. 22, 82 Cong., 2 sess.

(3) *The Allocation of Costs of Federal Water Resource Development Projects*, House Committee Print No. 23, 82 Cong., 2 sess.

(4) *Economic Evaluation of Federal Water Resource Development Projects*, House Committee Print No. 24, 82 Cong., 2 sess.

U.S. Congress, Senate, *Rail Freight Service Costs in the Various Rate Territories of the U.S.*, Senate Doc. No. 63, 78 Cong., 1 sess.

—— *Report on Collbran Reclamation Project, Colorado*, Senate Report No. 1719, 82 Cong., 2 sess.

—— Committee on Foreign Relations, *Hearings on the St. Lawrence Seaway*, 83 Cong., 1 sess.

—— Senate Committee on Interstate and Foreign Commerce, *Progress Report of the Subcommittee on Domestic Land and Water Transportation*, Senate Report No. 1039, 82 Cong., 1 sess.

U.S. Department of Agriculture, *Long-Range Agricultural Policy*, 1948.

U.S. Department of Commerce, *The St. Lawrence Survey*, N. R. Danielian, Director, 1941.

U.S. Department of the Interior, *Annual Report of the Secretary of the Interior*, 1952, 1953.

Bibliography

U.S. Department of the Interior, *Supplementary Instructions to the Statement on Cost Allocation*, March 1954.

—— Bureau of Reclamation, *An Experiment in the Measurement of the Indirect Benefits of Irrigation—Payette, Idaho*, prepared by M. E. Marts for Region 1, Boise, Idaho.

—— Bureau of Reclamation, *Columbia Basin Joint Investigations*, Problem 21, *River Transportation*, 1945.

—— Bureau of Reclamation, *50 Years of Reclamation*, 1952.

—— Bureau of Reclamation, *How Reclamation Pays*, 1947.

—— Bureau of Reclamation, *Reclamation Manual*, Vol. XIII, "Benefits and Costs," March 1952; revised edition, October 1952.

—— Bureau of Reclamation, *Report of Panel of Consultants on Secondary or Indirect Benefits of Water-Use Projects to Michael W. Straus, Commissioner, Bureau of Reclamation*, June 26, 1952.

—— Bureau of Reclamation, *The Reclamation Program, 1953–59*, 1952.

—— Geological Survey, *Floods in the United States*, by Clarence S. Jarvis and others, Water-Supply Paper 771, 1936.

U.S. Federal Coördinator of Transportation, *Public Aids to Transportation*, Vol. III *Public Aids to Transportation by Water*, 1939.

U.S. Interstate Commerce Commission, Bureau of Accounts and Cost Finding, *Explanation of Rail Cost Findings Procedures and Principles Relating to the Use of Costs*, 1948.

U.S. National Resources Planning Board, *The Economic Effects of the Federal Public Works Expenditures, 1933–1938*, Washington, 1940.

U.S. Weather Bureau, *Climatological Data, National Summary, Annual*, 1950, 1953, 1955.

INDEX

Ackerman, E. A., 10n
Agriculture, and irrigation, 194–195, 196, 218
Agriculture, Department of, 104, 105, 107; and Bureau of Agricultural Economics, 104; and "Long-Range Agricultural Policy," 105; Secretary of, 11, 14, 112, 114, 115, 116
Agronomy, 116
Airlines, 170
Alaska, 192
Allais, M., 135n
Allocation of joint costs, 259–272; and alternative justifiable expenditure, 265, 266, 268; and benefit method, 264–265; and benefit-cost analysis, 262–263; as political issue, 259; principles of, 266–269; and priority of use, 264; and proportionate use of capacity, 263–264, 267; and separable costs–remaining benefits, 260, 265, 266, 269–271; and use of total or of incremental cost, 271–272
Allocation of resources, 19, 25, 62, 169; over time, 42–46, consequences, 45–46; imperfections, 44, 45; and market mechanisms, 42–46; optimum, 42–44
Alternative cost principle, 168–175, 239–245, 246, 254; and benefit-cost analysis, 52, 53; and form of constraint, 69–70

Alternative justifiable expenditures, method of, 265, 266, 268
Aluminum industry, 251–255 *passim*
Amortization, 56, 57, 91–94, 244. *See also* Depreciation, methods of
Analysis, economic, 7, 262, 267; and electric power, 239–257; and flood control, 117–151; and irrigation, 197–226; and navigation, 167–188
Analysis, financial, 7, 17, 18, 50, 262, 263; and electric power, 257–258; and flood control, 151–159; and irrigation, 226–236; and navigation, 188–191
Appropriations, Bill, 6; Committee, 4
Arkansas River Basin project, 223–226, 231, 232, 234
Arkansas–White–Red River Inter-Agency Committee, 12
Army, Secretary of the, 8, 11, 14, 150
Arrow, K. J., 38n
Atomic Energy Commission, 239

Barger, H., 165, 166
Barrows, H. K., 117n, 121n, 134n
Baumol, W. J., 38n, 100n
Beckett, J. A., 261n
Benefit, deferred, 89, 90; direct, 51, 197–202; function, 76; indirect, 41, 42, 51; induced, 205, 206–208, 209, 212, 213, 221,

291

Index

Missouri Basin, 234, 238, 244; River, 3, 110, 147, Valley Authority, 10, 12
Moley, R., 192n, 226n
Multiplier effects, 207

National defense, 162
National Resources Planning Board, 11
Natural gas, 251, 252, 254
Navigation, 1, 2, 3, 40, 52, 60, 74, 108, 112, 160–191, 226, 261, 265, 266, 274, 275, 277, 279; and alternative costs, 168–175; and Channel Port Royal to Beaufort, S.C., 187; and Columbia Slough, 176–178; and estimation of project benefits, 167–175; and harbor improvements, 186–188; and inland waterways system, 160–166, 167; and St. Lawrence Seaway, 179–186, 188; and transportation, 210, 211, 259; and user charge, 188
New York–New England Inter-Agency Commission, 12

Obsolescence, 82, 91n, 93, 94
O'Brien, J. B., Jr., 257n
Ocean harbors, 160, 167, 182, 186; and improvements, 186–188
Ohio River, 173, 191
Omnibus Bill, Rivers and Harbors, 2, 3; Flood Control, 2, 3
Opportunity cost, of federal capital, 94, 97–99, 103. *See also* Constraint
Orders and Regulations, 126 133, 150

Parity, ratios and projections, 105, 106; and naïve model, 107n, 108n

"Partnership approach," 18, 64n, 152, 157
Patton, D., 163n
Petroleum, 165, 182
Pick, General L. A., 6n, 179, 184. *See also* Corps of Engineers, Chief of
Picken, I., and I. K. Fox, 116n
Pipelines, 162, 166, 170
"Postage stamp" principle, 257, 258
Power rates, 240, 241, 257–258
President, of United States, 2, 4, 140, 222; budget, 4, 5; and flood control, 112; and first Hoover Commission, 10; and St. Lawrence Seaway, 179; and veto of Rivers and Harbors Bill of 1956, 150, 215; Eisenhower, 4, 6, 11, 14, 15, 16
Prices, 81; discrimination, 170; projections, 104–108; support, 201, 207, 208
Priority of use, method of, 264
Private Enterprise. *See* Competitive economy; Market mechanism
Profit maximization, 19, 20, 21, 22, 25, 26, 27, 73, 240
Project, evaluation, 1, 17, 25, 33, 34, 47; authorization, 47, 49, 68, 82; criteria, 16; interdependence of complex system, 31–32; justification, 47–49; justification or evaluation, 47–50; need for, 15–17; need for internal reforms, 11–15; procedures, 2–8; standards, 1, 2; and separable segments, 68–69; and "with and without" principle, 37–38
Proportionate use of capacity, method of, 263–264, 267